AMERICAN INDIAN SPORTS HERITAGE

Joseph B. Oxendine, EdD
Temple University

87-656

Human Kinetics Books
Champaign, Illinois

Developmental Editor: Sue Ingels Mauck
Copy Editor: Patrick O'Hayer
Assistant Editor: JoAnne Cline
Production Director: Ernie Noa
Projects Manager: Lezli Harris
Typesetter: Theresa Bear
Text Design: Keith Blomberg
Text Layout: Denise Peters
Cover Design: Jack Davis
Printed By: Braun-Brumfield

ISBN: 0-87322-120-6

Copyright © 1988 by Joseph B. Oxendine

Library of Congress Cataloging-in-Publication Data

Oxendine, Joseph B.
    American Indian sports heritage.

    Bibliography: p.
    Includes index.
    1. Indians of North America—Games. 2. Athletes,
Indian—United States.   I. Title
E98.G2094   1988   796'.08997   87-2860
ISBN 0-87322-120-6

Printed in the United States of America

10 9 8 7 6 5 4 3 2 1

Human Kinetics Books
A division of Human Kinetics Publishers, Inc.
Box 5076, Champaign, IL 61820
1-800-DIAL-HKP
1-800-334-3665 (in Illinois)

To Earl Hughes

His uncommon courage, goodwill, and spirit of family and community exhibit the best of the Big Bud Clan.

Acknowledgments

Throughout this project I was assisted by persons too numerous to mention. Still, there are several individuals whom I wish to recognize who assisted me in special ways.

Alan Applebee read the first six chapters at an early stage and made extensive suggestions both in substance and style. Also reading the manuscript at various stages were Vine Deloria, Jr., Kendall Blanchard, Wilcomb Washburn, Robert Wheeler, and Theodore Hetzel. Each offered helpful suggestions and encouragement. Wheeler also provided me with most of the photographs of Jim Thorpe shown in chapter 10.

I am especially indebted to Billy Mills who hosted me at a sports workshop at the Pine Ridge Reservation, an experience that stimulated my interest in pursuing the study of Indian sports.

Special thanks go to Linda Muraresku for typing the entire manuscript, ably and patiently, through the several drafts required. She was assisted by Roxanne Barardi.

Finally, I am indebted to the many individuals with whom I discussed this topic: scholars and general sports fans, Indians and non-Indians. All expressed an interest in the topic, and encouragement.

Contents

Preface

Several years ago I was invited to assist in conducting a workshop on sports and recreation at the Pine Ridge Indian Reservation in South Dakota. During that experience I was struck by the fact that a surprisingly small number of young people on the reservation aspired to continue sports participation at a level higher than their current high school teams despite evidence of substantial athletic skill. In general, these young Indians had no ambition to compete in college, professional, or more advanced amateur sports.

The depressed economic and social climate on the reservation was reflected in similarly low aspirations of most young persons, whether in sports, education, or employment. It appeared to me that the heritage of sports excellence among American Indians was not an important factor for these young people. Perhaps they were not even aware of it.

Soon after that workshop I became convinced that providing visibility to Indian sports heroes, past and present, as role models might serve to promote pride and ambition among young people on that reservation. Developing a greater awareness of the strong Indian sports tradition might also contribute to a sense of community pride. Consequently, this project was initiated to focus attention on American Indian sports persons and sports traditions as a means of contributing to these individual and group goals.

I began by focusing on prominent Indian athletes of the 20th century. These included, for example, Jim Thorpe and his colleagues at the Carlisle Indian School during the first two decades of this century, John Levi and others at Haskell Institute during the 1920s, and more recent performers such as baseball player Allie Reynolds in the 1940s and 1950s and runner Billy Mills in the 1960s.

It soon became clear to me that to understand Indian sports and to appreciate personal performances, one must first place these activities in historical perspective. The nature of Indian sports programs and the motivations that have driven individual performers are intimately related to the traditions of the various Indian groups. Cultural connections of sport, which were so prominent traditionally, have continued into modern times, although perhaps to a lesser degree.

American Indian sports have evolved through several phases in the course of history, and this book will trace the shifting emphases over the past two centuries. The first phase to be presented (chapters 1 through 6) is the traditional role of sport in Indian society (i.e., prior to serious contact with, and alteration by, non-Indian cultures). What were the games played by the various Indian communities? Which activities were most widespread? What ceremony, ritual, and significance was related to each?

The second phase includes the emergence of Indians into modern sports. Chapters 7 through 11 trace their entry into popular activities such as football, baseball, and basketball during the last decade of the 19th century and their emergence as prominent and visible participants during the first three decades of the 20th century. This period can be described as the heyday of Indian sports. Brief profiles of some of the leading Indian athletes over the past 100 years are also included. Chapter 10 is devoted exclusively to the life and athletic exploits of Jim Thorpe, the most prominent of all Indian athletes.

The third phase, discussed in chapters 12 through 14, includes the period following 1930 during which Indian sports prominence diminished. Except for a few notable examples, Indian athletes have not been visible at the national level during this period. The reasons for that decline are analyzed. In addition, chapter 14 discusses some developments during the past decade that signal a reawakening of interest in sports among Indians and promise a renewal of visibility for Indian sports.

This work focuses primarily on sports and games among Indians within the United States. Although we recognize the traditions and excellence of Native Americans in Mexico, particularly in long distance running, and of those in Canada, who have excelled in ice hockey and lacrosse, these will not be emphasized.

Prologue

In *Sports in America*, James Michener (1976) suggested that sports emphasis in this country was "about right." His estimate was based on the attitudes and observed behavior of the populace as well as on governmental support for sports programs. He categorized several countries (e.g., East Germany, Russia) as excessively preoccupied with sports, others were rated as having more than average interest, and some (e.g., Sweden, India) were viewed as emphasizing sports far less than average. Although he recognized the rapid sports growth in the United States during the previous decade, Michener argued that "we are still well within the bounds of reason" (p. 375).

Within this context, how would one describe the emphasis of sports and games in the traditional life of American Indians?[1] How prominent were their sports, what forms did they take, and what was the societal context of these activities? Further, how widespread were the games and how similar were the meanings attached to sports among different Indian communities? In more recent times, how has the Indian responded to modern sport? What caused the Indian's diminishing visibility in sports following the heyday of the early 20th century? These are some of the

[1]The terms *Indian*, *American Indian*, and *Native American* are used interchangeably in this book. The original people of North and South America had no word which resembled *Indian*. Each group (tribe) had its own name. The name Indian was provided by Columbus who in 1492 thought he had reached India. Beyond their own tribal designations many Indians today refer to themselves as Native Americans, while others prefer American Indian. Still others simply use the term Indian.

questions this book addresses. Historical literature is investigated in dealing with these issues along with some current opinion and attitudes.

Sport Emphasis

By all accounts (e.g., long-standing traditions, artifacts, ball courts, folklore, and the writings of early travelers), sports occupied an extremely prominent role in the traditional life of most Indian communities. In fact, it can be argued that the role of these activities was excessive. Michener (1976), for example, uses terms such as "addiction," "sports mad," and "the tyranny of sports" to describe situations in which sport occupies too prominent a role (pp. 375–376). James Adair (1775/1968) would certainly have so categorized the sports climate among the Choctaw Indians of Mississippi during Colonial times. In 1775 he observed *chungke* (a game in which spears are tossed at a rolling stone disk) and reported that "all the Americans are much addicted to this game...[and] the players will keep running most of the day, under the violent heat of the sun" (p. 402).

The notion that the sport of chungke was overemphasized in Choctaw culture was also expressed by Romans (1775/1921). In a separate report during the same year, he stated that the game was "plain proof of the evil consequences of a violent passion for gaming upon all kinds, classes, and orders of men; at this they play from morning to night, with an unwearied application" (p. 79). In an earlier (1698) report (cited in Culin, 1907) the officer on a French ship on the Mississippi River observed the same game and wrote that "they pass the greater part of their time in playing in this place with great sticks, which they throw after a little stone which is nearly round" (p. 485).

During the mid 19th century, J.G. Kohl described the strong sports interests among the Chippewa Indians in Wisconsin. He reported that "great ball players, who can send the ball so high that it is out of sight, attain the same renown among the Indians as celebrated runners, hunters, or warriors" (cited in Culin, 1907, p. 566). Although he acknowledged the prominence of sport, Kohl showed no appreciation for its significance. In fact, he expressed disdain at the importance accorded to the game of lacrosse when he observed that "it is to be desired that the Indians would display the same attention to more important matters" (p. 566).

These observations, reported by non-Indians, could lead one to conclude that early American Indians were indeed "sports mad." However, one must view sports and games within the context of Indian culture.

Non-Indian literature, folklore, and traditions among today's Indians show unmistakably that sports were steeped in tradition and intimately related to all phases of life, especially to ceremony, ritual, magic, and religion. Investigation reveals, furthermore, that although many of these activities began as religious rites and evolved into sports over time, they nevertheless retained their connections to customs and traditions. Consequently, sports were never viewed as addenda to more serious aspects of life but as an integral part of it.

Although sports were often used for recreational purposes and for social relaxation, they also extended deeply into the fabric of the culture. As early as 1636, Jean de Brébeuf (cited in Culin, 1907), a Jesuit missionary, provided a clue to the perceived connection between sports and supernatural powers. He described game ceremonies among the Huron Indians in which a strong relationship between sports activities and healing was assumed. Early writers also pointed out the connection between Indian sport and climatic conditions, funeral rites, fertility, celebrations, and other matters of individual or community importance. Within this cultural context, consequently, even extensive sports involvement would not be viewed as overemphasis. Rather, they were a central part of that society, reflecting the character of the tribe or the mood of the day, the season, or the era.

Even though abundant evidence indicates the prominence of sports in the life of Native Americans, the interpretation of this finding is related to one's overall perception of Indian culture. The image of early American Indians is one of extremes. On the one hand, they are pictured as stoic, unfriendly, morose, savage and in fact, constantly making war on the white settlers. Conversely, they are viewed as friendly, deeply religious, artistic, athletic and fond of ceremony and festive occasions. This second characterization seems more consistent than the first with the notion of the importance of sport and games within Indian culture. However, which of these contradictory views is true? Or is there truth in both portrayals?

Diverse Life-Styles

The great diversity among traditional Indian cultures makes it impossible to discuss Indian customs, or Indian sports, as a cohesive entity. Differences in languages, means of livelihood, social structures, and traditions inhibit attempts to generalize absolutely about sports or, for that matter, any other cultural phenomenon. For example, at the time of Columbus' arrival, Native American tribes were scattered throughout all parts of North, Central, and South America. There was no universal language. In fact, the Bureau of Indian Affairs (1970) reports that approximately 300 different languages and many more distinct dialects were in use at that time. Many different religions were practiced, though most focused on natural phenomena such as the earth, sky, sun, moon, wind, or storms.

Cultural patterns differed from one tribe[2] to another, depending upon their languages, the means by which they obtained food, tribal traditions, and geographic or climatic conditions. Some groups were essentially hunters, and others were fishermen, farmers, shepherds, or seed gatherers. Some lived in tepees of various construction; others lived in earth lodges, stone apartments, caves, and huts or shelters made of brush. Some groups lived primarily in small, single-family units. Others lived in more communal structures such as longhouses. Although commonalities existed among tribes in a geographical area, no two tribes were exactly alike. Obviously, such differences in life-style impacted both the nature and meaning of sports.

Of necessity, hunting, fishing, farming, and occasional warfare took priority in tribal life. Following these, however, sports usually occupied a prominent role. This was true particularly before the serious confrontations with non-Indians during the 19th century. Even tribes subsequently described as warlike spent much time in leisure and fun. In addition to the inherent enjoyment of athletic activities and their significance in a broad cultural context, most adult Indians encouraged young people to participate in games as a means of developing critical survival skills such as physical prowess and cunning—qualities that were essential for hunting, war, and other challenges in adult life.

The life-style of traditional Indians was most typically relaxed, happy, and relatively free from worry, fears, or animosity. Nature had provided abundant game food (buffalo, deer, turkey, fish, etc.) and fertile soil for farming. For the most part, wars were infrequent, and those that occurred were contained within limited contexts. The quality of health in this pollution-free environment was good; for example, epidemics were rare and medicinal techniques were comparatively advanced. In most tribes high priority was placed on ritual and a life pleasing to the gods.

Indian Images

Did the typical Indian culture encourage sport and games, or did it stifle such activities as frivolous? Establishing some understanding of the Indian

---

[2]Use of the term *tribe* among traditional American Indians refers to "a body of persons bound together by blood ties who were socially, politically, and religiously organized [and] who lived together, occupying a definite territory, and spoke a common language or dialect" (Bureau of Indian Affairs, 1970, p. 3).

character is crucial to the validity of claims about sports patterns. Within the non-Indian community, the Indian image has covered the full range of the positive-negative continuum. Further, these diverse views have persisted from the first contact with Indians on this continent to the present day.

One of the more thorough analyses of the American Indian personality was provided by George Catlin a century and a half ago. Catlin, the famous artist-observer of Indians, lived and traveled among numerous tribes along the Missouri Valley, the plains, and farther west for a period of eight years during the 1830s. The letters, notes and paintings in his two volumes of *North American Indians*, published in 1841, represent perhaps the most descriptive and certainly one of the most authoritative reports on Indian life prior to 1850. His pictorial and verbal illustrations of Indian culture include references to numerous ball games as well as other sports and amusements. It is important to note that Catlin's travels were mostly among Indians west of the Mississippi River, groups that had not yet encountered the harshest confrontations with non-Indians. Such conflicts were to reach a peak thirty to forty years later.

Among Catlin's descriptions of Indian life-styles during the 1830s was a strong refutation of the somber, negative characterizations that even at that time had become commonplace. After acknowledging several misconceptions and myths, Catlin (1841/1965) stated:

Amongst them all, there is none more common, nor more entirely erroneous, nor more easily refuted, than the current one, that 'the Indian is a sour, morose, reserved and taciturn man.' I have heard this opinion advanced a thousand times and I believed it; but such certainly is not uniformly nor generally the case. . . . They are a far more talkative and conversational race than can easily be seen in the civilized world. This assertation will somewhat startle the folks in the East, yet it is true. . . . Jokes and anecdotes, and laughter are excessive, to become convinced that it is natural to laugh and be merry. . . . They are fond of fun and good cheer, and can laugh easily and heartily at a slight joke of which their peculiar modes of life furnish them an inexhaustible fund. (p. 84)

Having devoted a great deal of effort toward clearing up misconceptions of the Indian personality, Catlin described the prominence of games and sports in several situations. For example, while traveling among the Mandan Indians in the upper Missouri region, he stated that "these Indians have many days which, like this, are devoted to festivities and amusements . . . [and] almost all their hours are spent in innocent amusements" (p. 141).

As an artist, Catlin gained an appreciation not only for the culture and for the games themselves but also for the skill and physiques exhibited by young men and boys. He referred to the

> beautiful models that are about me . . . models equal to those from the Grecian sculptures transferred to the marble; such inimitable grace and beauty . . . whose daily feats, with their naked limbs, might vie with those of the Grecian youths in the beautiful rivalry of the Olympic games. (p. 15)

To further illustrate the playful nature of Indian youth, as well as their swimming skill, Catlin vividly described an incident that happened to him and two companions during the 1830s. The three men found themselves in a small boat being escorted across the Knife River along the upper Missouri basin. He reported that they were ushered into the river by one of the local Minatarees women, and then a dozen or so young girls ages twelve to fifteen were to escort them to the opposite bank. Of the girls he reported that:

> They all swam in a bold and graceful manner, and as confidently as so many otters or beavers; and gathering around us, with their long black hair floating about on the water, whilst their faces were glowing with jokes and fun, which they were cracking about us, and which we could not understand . . . whilst we were amusing ourselves with the playfulness of these dear little creatures who were floating about under the clear blue water, catching their hands onto the side of our boat; occasionally raising one-half of their bodies out of the water, and sinking again, like so many mermaids. (p. 196)

He then described how the young girls teased them by spinning the tub-shaped boat around and around in the middle of the river while the occupants had no oars or other means of controlling their own predicament. For a period of time, this and other games were played for the amusement of spectators along the shore, if somewhat to the anxiety of the occupants. Then the girls

> all joined in conducting our craft to the shore, by swimming by the sides of, and behind it, pushing along in the direction where they designed to land it, until the water became so shallow, that their feet were upon the bottom, when they waded along with great coyness, dragging us towards the shore, as long as their bodies, in a crouching position, could possibly be half concealed under the water, when they gave our boat the last push for shore, and raising a loud and exulting laugh, plunged back again into the water. (p. 197)

Incidents such as this led Catlin to vehemently refute the prevailing negative stereotype of the Indian.

More recently, Indian author Vine Deloria, Jr., (1969) has refuted the somber characterization of Indian personality.

> The Indian people are exactly opposite of the popular stereotype. I sometimes wonder how anything is accomplished by Indians because of the apparent overemphasis on humor within the Indian world. Indians have found a humorous side of nearly every problem and the experiences of life have generally been so well defined through jokes and stories that they have become a thing in themselves. (p. 146–147)

A rich sense of humor is also prevalent in Indian folklore. Tales of tricksters, games of matrimony, and even spiritual matters very often involve humor as well as a moral. Humor in story-telling has been widely used as a means of instruction for children.

Baldwin (1969) has observed a laughing game in several Indian communities. Two children stare at each other without expression, and the first one to laugh or to lose composure is the loser. Teams will often select champions to compete against each other. In such a contest, group members use a multitude of gestures, comments, and antics in an effort to break up the opponent. This game, though not unique among Indian children, helps to substantiate the continuing existence of a sense of humor, as well as competition, among today's Indians.

The social climate and personal disposition of Native Americans thus encouraged sports and games. Though dampened somewhat by the events of the past one and one-half centuries, this interest in sport continues today. However, over the years it was not generally reflected in Indian–non-Indian relations.

The Contrary View

Catlin's picture of the Native American is in bold contrast to the warlike image frequently portrayed in history books, popular literature, motion pictures, and word of mouth. If the latter image were accurate, there would have been little encouragement for sport and games.

The basis of the negative portrayals of the Indian are diverse and somewhat obscure. However, such reports were most often made by soldiers, missionaries, traders, and others who frequently encountered the Indian in conflict situations. It has been speculated that this negative characterization grew out of the need for relieving guilt feelings of those who had taken unfair advantage of the Indian. Regardless of the origin or motivation for such portrayals, however, there is little reason to believe that

Indian peoples of the 10th century, the 15th century, or the 20th century have been predominantly concerned with antisocial activities. A greater proportion of the evidence indicates that most Indians, when unharrassed, assumed a pleasant, relaxed life-style, spending considerable time and energy in games, amusements, and festivals.

Given the widespread distribution of books, magazines, and films, as well as the transmission of popular stereotypes by word of mouth, it is easy to understand how the negative Indian image has been so strongly established among non-Indians during the 20th century. What is not so clear is how it got started in the first place. It is probable, however, that a range of factors, including fear, guilt, contempt, pity, and ignorance, all contributed to the creation of this image.

A series of novels written during the 17th, 18th, and 19th centuries illustrates the development of the negative Indian image. A recent (1985) exhibit at the Rosenbach Museum and Library in Philadelphia, entitled *Carried Away by Indians: Indian Captivity Narratives and the Evolution of a Stereotype*, included more than two dozen narratives and novels written by persons who were allegedly captured and held prisoner by Indians for long periods. These became popular novels and include vivid details of barbarism to which they were reportedly subjected prior to being released or escaping. Certain obvious errors and exact duplications of incidents among the novels raise doubts about the authenticity of some of these writings. In addition, several persons, when allowed to leave their captives, chose to remain with the Indians. Nevertheless, the novels made interesting reading for the early colonists and, no doubt, contributed much to the Indian stereotype that persists to the present day.

It is also probable that much of the Indian image as an unfriendly and uncommunicative people grew out of actual observations of Indians in a foreign and hostile environment. Though it should be obvious that an unnatural environment produces unnatural behavior, this fact was rarely noted by early writers who described the Indian. Consider, for example, the behavior of Indians who had been captured and held prisoner by army troops. Their behavior under these circumstances could be expected to be highly atypical, as would that of other Indians who were observed after traveling long distances to Washington, DC, to meet with high government officials. Visiting Indian leaders were uncomfortable sitting in the splendor of presidential offices and mingling with persons who were sophisticated in a language and manners foreign to them. This climate was particularly stressful when they were being forced to relinquish lands on which they and their forefathers had lived.

A reasonable comparison might be a situation in which the non-Indian, without the communicative and other skills necessary for intelligent behavior, is suddenly found among Indians. It should come as no surprise to learn that Indian opinions of white people, based on observations of ill-mannered travelers, devious traders, soldiers, and insensitive missionaries, were not as complimentary as most would like to think. The few encounters between the groups led many Indians to assume that all white people were liars or thieves, a conclusion that was not entirely true. For example, the widely respected Chief Joseph (Vanderwerth, 1971) of the Nez Perce tribe told a large congressional delegation in Washington, DC, in 1879 that his father had warned him that "the white man will cheat you out of your home" (p. 214).

American Indians and their culture were held in low esteem by many non-Indians, particularly during the 19th century. From the time of the Europeans' arrival on this continent, the term *savage* was used interchangeably with *Indian*. As recently as 1889, the Reverend E.F. Wilson, having a total lack of understanding of the important role of betting in Indian sports, wrote: "The Sarcees, like most other wild Indians, are inveterate gamblers. They will gamble everything away—ponies, teepees, blankets, leggings, moccasins—till they have nothing left but their breech-clout" (cited in Culin, 1907, p. 460). James Adair (1775/1968) in 1775 not only referred to the Choctaw games of chungke as "stupid drudgery" (p. 402) but further stated that it seemed to be "of early origin when their forefathers used diversions as simple as their manners" (p. 401). Such comments reveal ignorance of and a lack of interest in Indians and their culture. Although they acknowledge the prominence of sport among these Indian groups, Wilson and Adair described them in an unfavorable manner.

The Indian in Sport

Given the great diversity among Indian cultures throughout America, it is erroneous to imagine a unified picture of Indian sports. Although several games were nearly universal, many others were limited to one tribe or to a small number of tribes in a given locality. Moreover, even where similar games existed, they were often associated with different traditions or cultural significance. Despite these limitations, however, the most prevalent and popular sports will be presented, and common features will be noted and discussed.

Games were an integral part of the culture of all tribes. They were evident in ceremonies and festivals relating to war, hunting, harvest, birth, death, and other important community events. The characteristic of *play* was universal, although the nature and variety of games differed from tribe to tribe.

Games and sports were developed and distributed by the Indians themselves. In his voluminous work on Indian games, Stewart Culin (1907)
found

> no evidence that any of the games described were imported into
> America at any time either before or after the conquest. . . . They
> appear to be the direct and natural outgrowth of aboriginal institu-
> tions in America. They show no modifications due to white influence
> other than the decay which characterizes all Indian institutions under
> existing conditions. (p. 32)

Culin concedes, however, that during the late 19th century an interchange
of games began to occur, particularly noting the adoption of playing cards
and some board games by the Indians and the assimilation of lacrosse
into non-Indian culture.

The rapid westward movement of the non-Indian population during
the 18th and early 19th centuries resulted in some important changes in
Indian life-style. Among these changes was a serious disruption in games
and play. The threat by non-Indians to take over traditional Indian lands
became evident, and Indians became preoccupied with defending themselves and their lands from invaders. This fact, along with the natural
evolution of games, meant that certain of the traditional games diminished
or were eliminated by the end of the 19th century. Culin (1907), for
example, cites several contemporary reports (e.g., Hoffman and Mooney)
that certain games "were formerly played" (p. 73) or "are described by
the older people but are no longer played" (p. 438). Several of these games
are discussed in chapters 2 to 6.

At the same time, some non-Indian games were being incorporated into
the Indian culture. With the increased interaction with the non-Indian
culture, principally through mission schools or boarding schools, Indians
suddenly emerged during the late 19th and early 20th centuries to assume a prominent role in the popular sports of the non-Indian population. Numerous Indian athletes captured the imagination of the general
public with their tenacity and extraordinary accomplishments.

For example, teams from the Carlisle Indian School in Pennsylvania
were extremely successful in the early part of this century. John Steckbeck described their achievement in *The Fabulous Redmen* (1951): "For some
twenty-odd years the Redmen raced across the stage of big-time football,
leaving in their wake many a bewildered team. . .then vanished from the
American sporting scene forever" (p. vii). Indian prowess was particularly notable in the football and track teams of the Carlisle School and
the Haskell Indian School in Kansas. A number of Indians also excelled
in major league baseball during the first two decades of the 20th century
and in professional football after it developed during the 1920s.

At the time Steckbeck's book was published (1951), it appeared that the Indian may indeed have "vanished from the American sporting scene forever" (p. vii). Indian visibility and participation in popular sports at the national level diminished considerably after around 1930. This resulted from a combination of factors that included (a) the closing of the Carlisle School, (b) the scarcity of other Indian institutions of higher education, (c) the poor quality of reservation and local Indian schools, (d) a resistance on the part of many Indians to be assimilated into non-Indian society and non-Indian sports, (e) laws that prevented Indians from entering all-white colleges, and (f) a multitude of social conditions both on and off the reservation.

The Indian Reorganization Act of 1934, though designed as legislation friendly to the Indian cause, may have inadvertently contributed to the decline of sports emphasis. The Act, along with related sentiment, tended to emphasize activities "important" to the Indian cause. Friends of the Indian at that time did not view sports as a helpful means of promoting Indian well-being. For example, the Indian Rights Association, perhaps the foremost institutional friend among non-Indians, expressed great satisfaction with Haskell Institute's decision to de-emphasize athletics in the early 1930s. In January 1933 that organization, in its publication *Indian Truth*, referred to the "disastrous" results that athletes had inflicted at the Carlisle Indian School where athletes "were students in name only" (p. 4). The organization stated further that big time athletics "is not a good move for a government Indian school" (p. 4). Although supporting modest athletics at Haskell on a "sane basis" (p. 4), the Association discouraged participation against major universities, a course that Carlisle had followed so successfully.

Though several of the problems that have inhibited Indian sports continue today, others have diminished considerably. As a result, the Indian is beginning to regain some prominence in sports, and representatives are now participating in most professional and amateur sports.

Complexities and Distortions in Indian Sports

Several major difficulties accompany the task of presenting American Indian sports in historical perspective. Foremost among these is the lack of adequate recorded history. Of course, there is no written history of the American Indian prior to the arrival of Columbus in 1492. It was another two to three centuries before significant cultural information was recorded about the Indian. Consequently, most of the relevant literature has been produced within the past two centuries, a period during which Indian culture was being greatly influenced by non-Indians. Nevertheless, Indian oral history and mythology have contributed importantly to the body of information about sports and games. In addition, archaeologists and anthropologists have been able to establish hypotheses about traditional Indian culture, including sports, on the basis of playing implements, ball courts, eyewitness reports, and other evidence that has become available during recent years.

Over the past two centuries, reporting on Indians and Indian sports has been seriously distorted. The 19th century, for example, was a very atypical period for Indians, given the almost constant rash of "Indian wars." In addition, the non-Indian population of this country increased rapidly and constantly pushed westward into traditional Indian lands. Along with the general mistreatment of Indians, this caused Native American lifestyles to bear less and less resemblance to traditional patterns.

It became practically impossible, furthermore, for non-Indians to observe Indian games and ceremonies in the Indians' traditional form and significance. When they did enter the Indians' midst, it was usually as an oddity, either not able or not wishing to participate fully in the activities. For example, Beauchamp (1896) reported on his participation in a dice game (using beans) with the Onondagas in New York State during the late 19th century. He noted that "though the game was intensely exciting, the scientific spirit restrained my enthusiasm. I was not playing for beans, but for information" (p. 270). Surely such detached observation tended to restrain the behavior of Indians who were aware that they were being watched and studied. By the time sizable numbers of Indians had acquired a facility with the English language, their rituals, games, and ceremonies had been appreciably altered.

Several Indian games were essentially religious rites; they were more religion than *play* in today's meaning of the term. The court ball game in the southwest and in Mexico (see chapter 2), the ring and pin game, and to some extent chungke (see chapter 4) fall into this category. As such, non-Indians were not usually allowed to view these activities in their traditional form. Consequently, complete and accurate descriptions of these activities have not been reported in the literature.

Despite the many diversities among the tribes and in addition to the communications problems, there were commonalities that transcended most traditional Indian cultures. According to Culin, who was perhaps the foremost Indian sports historian, many games and practices tended to be universal and were found in most tribes. In fact, his work, published in 1907, includes a description of a large number of games and sports activities that he reported to be morphologically identical and universal for all tribes. These games and customs were transmitted through normal communication and interaction that took place among tribes during their centuries of residence in this hemisphere.

In recent years a major problem in reporting on Indian sports performers has been the lack of a systematic way of identifying persons as Indians. During the last two decades, Indians have participated in practically all sports in all parts of the country, both as amateurs and as professionals. Although some have been identified or recognized as Indians, others have not. The lack of a uniform identification system, as well as a central record-keeping mechanism, makes the task of highlighting Indian athletic performance particularly difficult. In former years it was relatively easy to identify a Native American. Today's increasing interaction among races, including assimilation and other social developments, makes such identification less clear. Some Indians, both full-blood and mixed-blood, have welcomed such identification whereas others have not.

This book seeks to tell the story of sports among American Indians through the years. First, we examine the nature and role of games and sports in traditional Indian life. Next, we discuss the emergence of Indians on the sporting scene of non-Indian America. During the early decades of the 20th century Indians assumed a status which far outshone their small numbers in this society. We then consider how the Indian diminished in sports prominence through the middle of the century, and the reasons for this decline are outlined. Finally, some encouraging signs in contemporary Indian sports are pointed out. These recent developments offer some hope of a genuine revival of Indian sports emphasis.

Part I
Sports and Games in Traditional Indian Life

Chapter 1

Indian Concepts of Sport

Games among traditional American Indians ranged from the seemingly trivial activities primarily for the amusement of children to major sporting events of significance for persons of all ages. The latter activities often commanded the interest and participation of whole communities. In this chapter, the full range of play and sports will be discussed, and their role within the culture will be explored.

This chapter will also provide a general overview of the characteristics most common to traditional Indian sports throughout this continent. Attitudes about sport and patterns of behavior have been identified not only on the basis of early observers of Indian customs but also from continuing tradition and folklore that have survived through the ages. Each of these means will be used to illustrate how Indian sport characteristics stand in stark contrast to the behaviors and attitudes most commonly reflected in today's popular sports.

Some of the more important factors characterizing traditional Indian sports include the following: (a) a strong connection between sport and other social, spiritual, and economic aspects of daily life; (b) the serious preparation of mind, body, and spirit of both participants and the community as a whole prior to major competition; (c) the assumption that rigid adherence to standardized rules and technical precision was unimportant in sport; (d) strong allegiance to high standards of sportsmanship and fair play; (e) the prominence of both males and females in sport activity, but with different expectancies; (f) a special perspective on team

3

membership and on interaction and leadership styles; (g) the role of gambling as a widespread and vital component in all sports; and (h) the importance of art as an expression of identity and aesthetics.

Culin (1907) grouped Native American games into two categories: *games of dexterity* and *games of chance*. Games of dexterity were athletic activities involving speed, strength, stamina, and strategy. They required long hours of training on the part of young people to attain the competency needed in later years. Although these athletic contests were steeped in cultural importance, it is also evident that they were enjoyed immensely.

Games of chance were played for general interest and for gambling purposes. These games, which were prevalent among tribes throughout the continent, were predominantly dice games, stick games, and the moccasin game. Goods and property were wagered on the outcome of games of chance; this was also true for athletic contests. Generally, results of games of chance were based on pure luck and did not involve the mental gymnastics or strategy required in chess, checkers, cards, or other popular table games of today. However, players attempted to deceive opponents and to call upon their psychic powers to make the correct guess. Although games of chance occupied a prominent role in the life of most Indian tribes, they are not considered central to this review of Indian sports. Nevertheless, chapter 6 will be devoted to a discussion of these games.

Meaning of Terms

Terms such as *games, sport, play,* and *athletics* as used in this text require definition and clarification. In sports literature and popular discussion, the terms are often used interchangeably, although clear distinctions are made occasionally. Moreover, we will cite authors from several centuries in this study, and terminology may have various meanings according to different authors writing during separate periods. In fact, even today the concept of sport is among the most widely discussed, and least understood, of all phenomena.

In this text, the term play is used in a broad sense to refer either to the form of an activity or to a style of behavior. Though it may involve children or adults and may be casual or intense, play is usually nonserious. It is activity engaged in for enjoyment. Among children, play frequently involves mimicry and adventure. It typically includes no ulterior motive or gain. Regardless of the purpose of an activity, one's attitude or approach can have a play-like quality. For some persons, even their work can sometimes meet this standard of play.

The term game is a subset of play. Games are organized, formal activities involving competition. Two or more players or sides are identified. Furthermore, the term sport is a subset of games and typically requires physical exertion by the participants. Sport usually includes participants and nonparticipating observers (spectators) who enjoy the activity vicariously. In this discussion, athletics is used synonymously with sports.

Distinctions between play, games, and sports cannot always be determined on the basis of the activity itself. For example, when children or adults engage in top-spinning, swimming, or the making of string figures in a casual and noncompetitive way, this is viewed as play, or the "mere amusements" described by several authors. On the other hand, when the same activities are organized on a competitive basis and a winner is determined, this is referred to as a game. When a game creates enough interest or importance to attract spectators, it becomes a sport. In traditional Indian society, this sometimes occurred with individual activities such as chungke, archery, or snow snake (a game in which a snake-like stick is cast across the ice or snow). However, team games such as lacrosse and shinny (a ball game similar to today's field hockey) more frequently attracted large audiences and are more generally referred to as sports.

Cultural Significance of Sports

In most of the traditional Indian societies, games of skill or dexterity were rarely played by adults for mere amusement or fun. Rather, they were played for some purpose that was a matter of importance to the community. To a considerable extent, sports were enjoyed in the same manner as are popular sports today; in addition, however, they were interrelated with social issues. The particular significance varied with the tribe, the sport, and the community need at the time. Although it may not be apparent in most of today's Indian communities, sports were originally meshed in tradition, ritual, and ceremony.

According to Black Elk (Brown, 1953), many athletic contests started out as rites and later evolved into essentially athletic contests of great popularity. However, they continued to have cultural importance, though the original meaning became less clear as time passed. For example, while speaking of the game "the throwing of the ball" in 1953, Black Elk stated that "there are only a few of us today who still understand why the game is sacred, or what the game originally was long ago, when it was not really a game, but one of our most important rites" (p. 128). This game is described in detail later in the chapter.

Reverend W.M. Beauchamp (1896) offered further comment on the cultural connection of sport, and the changing nature of that relationship as he reviewed it just prior to the turn of this century. Writing about the Onondaga Indians in New York state, he stated:

> As of old, almost all games are yet played for the sick, but they are regarded now more as a diversion of the patient's mind than a means of healing. The game of dish (a dice game) was once much used in divination, each piece having its own familiar spirit, but is more commonly a social game now. (p. 269)

Reports from Indian groups ranging from the northeast to the southwest and from Canada to Mississippi show that the religious significance of sport enhanced its status in the lives of Indians. This spiritual connection, along with the inherent value of sport itself, ensured that it would be more than frivolous activity. Victory in sport brought the highest favor of the gods and held evil spirits in abeyance. Adversity in the form of sickness, draught, sterility, or other misfortune would not follow in the wake of victory. Therefore, participants entered into sport with a high level of commitment.

Sometimes the game was focused toward a specific goal, such as the bringing of rain in a time of draught, celebrating success in hunting or in battle, healing the sick, or encouraging fertility for one or more persons. At other times the motivation was more general—perhaps simply to please the gods or to establish the superiority of one god over another. It is significant that many early commentators, particularly those writing prior to 1800, would include an explanation of a contest's cultural or religious significance along with the description of the game itself. In addition, the widespread practice of wagering on the outcome of games added to their significance. (The practice of betting in sports is discussed later in this chapter and in chapter 6.)

One can argue that today's sports and games among non-Indian groups are likewise more than idle amusement because they are rarely played exclusively for the physical values to be derived. For example, golf matches among friends may be played for a soda, for a dollar a hole, or for higher stakes. High school athletic contests or evening bowling matches have league championships, trophies, and recognition at stake. Certainly, professional athletes play for money and recognition. Even neighborhood pickup softball games often involve bragging rights or other benefits. In comparison, however, Indian games were more deeply rooted in ceremony and practically all contests involved betting. Preparation for Indian sports included spiritual as well as physical exercises, and the outcome was assumed to be influenced by a power beyond the control of the participants.

Early Evidence of Cultural "Purposes" for Games

As long ago as 1636, certainly prior to any substantial non-Indian influence, Jean de Brébeuf made note of the relationship between games and healing among the Hurons near Thunder Bay, Ontario (cited in Culin, 1907):

> Of three kinds of games especially in use among these peoples—namely, the games of crosse [lacrosse], dish, and straw, the first two are, they say, most healing. Is not this worthy of compassion? There is a poor sick man, fevered of body and almost dying, and a miserable sorcerer will order for him, as a cooling remedy, a game of crosse. Or the sick man himself, sometimes, will have dreamed that he must die unless the whole country shall play crosse for his health; and no matter how little may be his credit, you will see them in a beautiful field, village contending against village as to who will play crosse the better, and betting against one another beaver robes and porcelain collars, so as to excite greater interest. Sometimes, also, one of these jugglers will say that the whole country is sick, and he asks a game of crosse to heal it; no more needs to be said, it is published immediately everywhere; and all the captains of each village give orders that all the young men do their duty in this respect, otherwise some great misfortune will befall the whole country. (p. 589)

After studying the sports traditions of several tribes in the eastern part of the United States and Canada, Michael Salter (1971) identified four religiomagical connections related to games: (a) mortuary practices, (b) sickness, (c) climatic conditions, and (d) fertility. He made no attempt to distinguish between magic and religion as a factor in the games, designating each as human efforts to use games to bring about desirable changes or conditions that cannot be otherwise effected. Salter pointed out that the mortuary games were designed to honor the dead, to comfort the bereaved, to placate any spirits, to honor the successor, and to promote tribal unity. These games were not always viewed as playing in the usual sense by the participants, and the mood in which the game was played was often more important than the outcome. The favorite game of the deceased was usually selected for play. Mortuary games among the Hurons and the Delaware included a wide range of both athletic contests and games of chance.

Although rain dances have received much attention and comment among non-Indians over the years, games were also widely practiced as a means of affecting all types of climate conditions. Favorable climatic conditions were important for Indian livelihood, and rituals were employed to avoid draught, too much rain, severe cold, heat, snow, hail, or violent winds. Salter (1971) cites one incident among the Hurons in 1637 in which the tribe played a game of lacrosse to avert adverse weather conditions. Despite this effort, disastrous weather occurred. This caused the Indians to lose faith in the shaman (the individual who mediated between the natural and the supernatural) who had assumed the leadership role. Nevertheless, confidence in the games as an effective means of climate control was sustained. Moreover, a full range of athletic games have been reportedly used for this purpose.

Games associated with healing were designed to stop suffering and epidemics. They were used for preventive as well as curative purposes and for both individual and group healing. In these games the shaman played a strong role and prescribed most of the activities. A variety of games were used for healing purposes; however, lacrosse was the most widely played game.

A firsthand account of the important connection between games and healing among the Ojibway in Ontario, Canada, was given by George Copway (1851/1972):

> I remember that, some winters before the teachers from the pale faces came to the lodges of my father, my mother was very sick. Many thought she could not recover her health. At this critical juncture she told my father that it was her wish to see the Maidens' Ball Play, and gave as her reason for her request that were she to see the girls at play it would enliven her spirits with the reminiscences of early days as to tend her recovery. (p. 55)

Games were often played at Thanksgiving for a great variety of fortunate occurrences. These ranged from the birth of children to a bountiful harvest of crops. According to Salter (1971), several tribes scheduled their major annual ceremony to coincide with the maturation of corn and other crops.

Mysticism was also an integral part of athletic contests, and it was generally assumed that the outcome of games was influenced by supernatural powers. Among the Tarahumare in Mexico, for example, it was believed that

> a race is never won by natural means. The losers always say that they were influenced by some herb and became sleepy on the race-course, so that they had to lose. The help of the medicine man is needed in preparing the runner for the race. He assists the manager to wash the feet of the runner with warm water and different herbs, and he strengthens their nerves by making passages over them. He also guards them against sorcery. Before they run he performs a ceremony to "cure" them. (Lumholtz, 1895, p. 304)

Although it has become less clearly defined, the ceremonial significance of Indian sport has continued into the 20th century. However, the quality of participation in sports with no cultural connection to Indian life appears to be affected. For example, when Indians began participating in popular, non-Indian sports, it was often suggested that they did not perform to their maximum capacity. This opinion was offered especially when Indians participated on teams with non-Indians. In a situation devoid of the traditional Indian ritual, many Indians seemed to lack interest in performing beyond the obvious requirements of a particular task. Long and rigorous training schedules in preparation for subsequent events outside the total cultural context were often foreign to their concept of sport. For instance, while playing major league baseball with the New York Giants, Jim Thorpe was accused of being lazy by manager John McGraw (Wheeler, 1979, p. 157). Thorpe was never so characterized, however, when surrounded by fellow Indians at the Carlisle School. Other prominent Indian athletes were likewise viewed as slothful by contemporaries because of their lack of enthusiasm for a rigorous training regimen. Furthermore, many Indians in recent years have dropped out of sports participation altogether. Perhaps the artificiality of the sports climate contributes to this loss of interest and involvement.

Contrary Point of View

The prominence of the ritual–game connection has recently been called into question by Blanchard (1984). He acknowledges some relationship between these two elements but he argues that Culin and others influenced by his work have overemphasized the connection between ritual and games as an acceptable explanation of the importance of play among Native Americans. The work ethic has been held in high esteem in the dominant American society over the past several centuries. Given the low status of play in the minds of most non-Indians, preoccupation with such activity could be viewed as unbecoming. In fact, play has been viewed as unimportant or trivial except by anthropologists and other social scientists who consistently point out that games are a basic element of a culture and meet a general human need.

Early observers often described Native American preoccupation with games in uncomplimentary terms, such as "addictive," "idle amusement," and "wasting their time" (see Prologue). Such comments appear to reflect the assumption that play and games are unimportant, especially when compared to work. Blanchard (1984) argues that although Culin appears to have had a similar view (i.e., that games are not very important), his comments about Indians were more humanistic. Blanchard speculates that because Culin did not wish to make the Indians appear lazy, he attributed to games more legitimate qualities (e.g., a religious connection). In the life of Native Americans, Culin emphasized, perhaps unduly, the connection between ritual and sport. The effort of Culin and others to protect the Indian image by emphasizing the ritual–game connection is viewed by Blanchard as a type of benevolent racism.

There may be some truth in Blanchard's characterization of Culin (and others) as being concerned with upgrading the Indian image. Nevertheless, the abundance of evidence from as long ago as 1636 and continuing through the 19th century overwhelmingly identifies sport with ceremony and spirituality. That so many observers, reporting independently, would concur in support of a positive Indian image seems unlikely. Some of those reporting a strong cultural connection, in fact, predated Culin's work by more than two centuries.

Additional support for the traditional cultural connection of ritual and sport is the fact that the practice continues in some areas even today. For example, Oren Lyons, traditional Faithkeeper of the Iroquois and also a former All-American lacrosse player at Syracuse University, informed me in July of 1986 that the connection between games and healing continues today. According to him, it is not unusual for friends to arrange a lacrosse game for a sick person's benefit. The individual is taken in his or her sick bed to the sidelines of the field, and the game is played in that person's honor.

Blanchard (1984) also questions the assumption that sport typically evolved out of ritual. He argues that this ritual-to-sport evolution (see Black Elk's statement earlier in this chapter) could in fact go in the opposite direction. Lesser (1933/1969) has also pointed out that sports sometimes evolved into ritual. According to Blanchard, moreover, in recent times at least, sports can be unrelated to any logical or moral dogma. For example, "the actual acceptance and integration of basketball into various Indian communities has been largely a secular process" (p. 19). No doubt this is true in some instances. However, it does not refute the notion of a strong interrelationship between traditional sport and ritual.

Preparation and Ritual Related to Games

In traditional Indian cultures, major athletic contests were usually characterized by physical, psychological, and spiritual preparation. In many societies, months of physical training, along with dietary practices, took place prior to major races or ball games. In addition, short-term psychological orientation and spiritual preparation were practiced immediately before an important event. All night vigils sometimes preceded major ball games and races. Among many tribes, the ritual and ceremony surrounding these contests appear to have been as important as the contest itself.

Preparatory measures prior to major athletic contests were often symbolic, emphasizing abstinence from activities or things that signified weakness, fear, or failure. Among the most important of these was strict attention to dietary standards. For example, James Mooney (1890) reported on practices among the Cherokee in North Carolina. He stated that participants refrained from eating rabbit for several weeks prior to major athletic contests for fear that the timid and witless characteristics of that animal would be transmitted to the players during the game. This belief was so strong that players from opposing teams often made a soup of the hamstrings of rabbits and poured it along the familiar trails of opponents before major games to make them more vulnerable to timidity and confusion.

Frog's meat was also avoided because of the brittle nature of the frog's bones. According to Mooney (1896), Cherokee players were not to eat the young offspring of any bird or animal, and they were not to have contact with a human infant for seven days prior to the contest. Nabokov (1981) lists numerous dietary practices for long-distance runners in the Southwest, which have continued from antiquity to the present day.

One of the strongest taboos among the Cherokee was that the male player was not to touch a woman during the seven days before and the seven days following the game. In addition, any player whose wife was pregnant was not allowed to play because of the belief that his strength was being sapped by the developing child. Finally, if a woman touched one of the lacrosse sticks on the eve of the game, it was rendered unfit for use. In earlier times, severe punitive measures were taken against anyone violating this tradition.

Major ceremonies, somewhat resembling modern pep rallies, were established hundreds of years ago in Indian sports. The music, dancing, and speeches were strikingly similar to present day rallies at high schools or colleges prior to football or basketball games. Nearly two centuries ago, in 1791, John Bartram described one of these pregame sessions, which took place on the day prior to a major lacrosse game among the Cherokees of North Carolina (cited in Culin, 1907):

> The people being seated and assembled in order, and the musicians having taken their station, the ball opens, with a long harangue or oration, spoken by an aged chief, in commendation of the manly exercise of the ball-play, recounting the many and brilliant victories which the town of Cowe had gained over the other towns in the nation, not forgetting or neglecting to recite his own exploits, together with those of other aged men now present, coadjutors in the performance of these athletic activities in their youthful days. This oration was delivered with great spirit and eloquence, and was meant to influence

the passions of the young men present, excite them to emulation and inspire them with ambition. (p. 574)

Bartram's description is consistent in many respects with Catlin's (1841/1944) account of the ball-play dance among the Choctaws in the 1830s. Both authors describe these activities as being most colorful as well as spiritually significant. According to Catlin, ceremonies in preparation for the ball game commenced on the preceding day. The teams and their families arrived at the site at which the game was to be played and set up camp on opposite sides of the playing field. The women busied themselves arranging bets for the following day. The stakes included various assortments of household goods, clothing, jewelry, dogs, ponies, and other items of value.

Four older men who had been selected as judges for the game used this time to inspect the playing field and to establish specifications regarding goalposts, field boundaries, markers, and obstructions. In the evening these elders went to the center of the field where they spent all night praying for wisdom and fairness so that their judgments would be entirely unbiased toward both teams.

In Catlin's description of Choctaw ceremonies, the ball-play dance began soon after dark. The players along with their parties descended upon the field with lighted torches. Each group congregated around its own goal, while the officials sat in the center of the field. Players danced around their goals to the drums and chants of the women. They violently rattled the lacrosse sticks and sang vociferously. Women also danced and sang, calling upon the Great Spirit to favor their particular team, and they urged the players to do their utmost for success. The ball-play dance lasted for approximately fifteen minutes, and then the participants returned to the encampment for about half an hour. However, the players and their parties went back and forth from the playing field to the encampment throughout the night, repeating the ceremony in precisely the same manner, and everyone was awake all night long. Catlin (1841/1944) described the ceremony of lighted torches, drum beating, dancing, and singing as "one of the most picturesque scenes imaginable" (p. 141). (See Catlin's illustration of the ball-play dance in Figure 1.1.)

A century after Bartram's report of lacrosse play among the Cherokee, James Mooney (1890) visited the same tribe and reported on a game with its related pregame activity. A comparison of the two reports reveals that most of the traditions and ceremonies had been retained for the ninety-nine year period between the two reports. (See Figure 1.2 for a photograph of a less elaborate pregame ceremony among the Cherokee in 1888.)

Mooney also described a pregame ritual that had not been reported earlier. This included a *scratching* regimen in which an official used a kanuga, which is an instrument resembling a short comb with seven very

Figure 1.1. George Catlin painting of the "ball-play dance" ceremonies among the Choctaw Indians in the 1830s. The women danced and sang near the center of the field while the players danced around their respective goals, singing and rattling their rackets. Photo used by permission of the National Anthropological Archives, Smithsonian Institution.

Figure 1.2. Ceremony preceding a Cherokee lacrosse game at the Qualla Reservation in North Carolina. Photo by James Mooney in 1888. Photo used by permission of the National Anthropological Archives, Smithsonian Institution.

Figure 1.3. Ordeal of scratching prior to a Cherokee Indian ball game in North Carolina. The shaman makes 28 scratches on the upper arms, lower arms, upper legs, and lower legs. Photo by James Mooney in 1888. Photo used by permission of the National Anthropological Archives, Smithsonian Institution.

sharp teeth made from the splintered leg bones of a turkey. The official, or shaman, used this instrument to make scratches along the arms and legs of each of the players. (See Figure 1.3.) These scratches were long and pierced the skin just enough to allow the blood to ooze out. This painful ritual was continued until twenty-eight of the scratches were made on each upper arm, twenty-eight on each forearm, twenty-eight along the thigh, and twenty-eight along the lower leg. At the conclusion, blood was trickling out of almost all parts of the player's body. This ceremony was designed to provide the essential commitment and blessings to ensure success in the game.

Other techniques used by various groups to prepare themselves mentally, physically, and perhaps what is more important, spiritually was to eat rattlesnake meat, to rub themselves with slippery substances, and to pray for speed, strength, dodging ability, and good sight. They sometimes prayed for misery and misfortune for their opponents. Though differing in form and extent, most traditional Indian communities devoted serious attention to some form of precontest preparation of players.

Lack of Standardization and Quantification

Traditional Indian athletic contests were not so rigidly standardized as are contemporary sports activities. There was a lack of uniformity in field dimensions, equipment and uniform specifications, time periods, number of points required for victory, distances for races, and even the number of participants on a team. This variability reflected the different conditions and traditions among the tribes. The lack of a common language, as well as the consequent inability to develop and distribute regulations, may have perpetuated this lack of uniformity. More important, however, Indians saw little need for precise or uniform regulations. Standardization and the related quantification of sports were introduced by the colonists because of their European orientation. Indian teams from different tribes or nations simply made adjustments as necessary. Judges in charge of the contest called the teams together prior to the game and established the ground rules.

One area in which flexibility was a decided advantage was in establishing the number of players on a team. The simple solution was that everyone played, so long as the teams were relatively even. In lacrosse and in shinny, the number of participants on a team varied from a dozen to several hundred. The more important the contest, the greater the numbers on each team. Major tribal contests often involved 200 to 300 players on each side. Catlin (1841/1944) reported that among the Choctaws "it is not an uncommon occurrence for six or eight hundred or a thousand of these young men to engage in a game of ball with five or six times that number of spectators" (p. 141). Regarding time dimensions, Catlin stated that the games started at around 9:00 a.m. The game's length was extraordinary: "I have more than once balanced myself on my pony, from that time til near sundown, without more than one minute of intermission at a time, before the game has been decided" (p. 141).

Small-scale lacrosse games involving one or two dozen participants on a side were often played on a field approximately 300 yards in length. However, major contests involving greater numbers of players usually required a playing field of one-half mile or more.

The major consistency in the popular games of shinny and lacrosse was that players were uniformly forbidden to touch the ball with their hands. Only sticks or rackets were used to advance the ball. In the ball race and in double ball, likewise, the hands could not be used. Several other aspects such as the procedure for starting the contest and for scoring points were also consistent among tribes.

In American Indian culture, winning and losing were important, but no importance was placed on the magnitude of the victory. In general, quantification in sports was not emphasized. For example, no effort was made to determine an all-time record for the most goals scored in a game or which tribe had the longest winning streak. No one was concerned about identifying the individual who tossed the snow snake the greatest distance or comparing the winning time in the twenty-five-mile race with the time of the previous year's winner. Such record keeping would make little sense because conditions and dimensions differed from one location to the next and from year to year. No one sought to determine an all-star team, to establish a Hall of Fame, to identify an all-time winning record or a consecutive-game scoring record. If a field rather larger than the usual 300 by 100 meters was to be used, no one objected.

Indians had little interest in numbers or in record keeping for its own sake. The infatuation of Americans with statistics is a more recent phenomenon. One cannot read the daily newspaper without encountering the Dow-Jones averages, earned run averages, and the gross national product. During the 19th century, non-Indians began to emphasize the need for numbers and precision in games. Reports by soldiers and travelers made note of field dimensions, the sizes of equipment, and distances and times for races. Almost without exception, some sort of measurement was related to performance activity. Allen Guttmann (1978) has noted that the Romans, more than 2,000 years ago, were responsible for the numeration of achievements, keeping detailed records of chariot races and other sporting events. In contrast, the ancient Greeks, despite their creation and promotion of the original Olympic Games, were as indifferent to record keeping as were the American Indians.

Fair Play

Another common characteristic of Indian sports activity was a high standard of sportsmanship. Overwhelming evidence indicates that fair play was typically exhibited in their athletic contests. This does not mean that the games were mild or gentle. Indeed, they were hotly contested and often involved rough play. However, given the vigorous nature of the games, the great number of participants on the field (sometimes several hundred), the lack of standardization, and the small number of officials, were it not for a high sense of sportsmanship and individual responsibility, the games could have easily deteriorated into chaos.

In 1864 Nicolas Perrot, a trader and government agent, described the good graces with which the Huron Indians of Ontario accepted any injury or misfortune during a game of lacrosse. He reported that

> whatever accident the game makes is attributed to luck, and there is in consequence no hard feelings between the players. The wounded seem as well satisfied as if nothing had happened to them thus

demonstrating that they have plenty of courage and that they are men. (cited in Jette, 1975, p. 19)

He further reported that

when these accidents happen the unlucky victim quietly withdraws from the game if he is in a condition to do so; but if his injury would not permit this his relatives carry him home, and the game goes on until it is finished, as if nothing has happened. (p. 19)

George Copway (1851/1972) also observed high standards of sportsmanship. This is his description of ball playing among the Ojibway:

It is seldom, if ever, that one is seen to be angry because he has been hurt. If he should get so, they would call him a 'coward,' which proves a sufficient check to many evils which might result from many seemingly intended injuries. (p. 570)

Jonathan Carver (1796/1956) observed Chippewas playing lacrosse and reported that

they play with so much vehemence that they frequently wound each other, and sometimes a bone is broken; but notwithstanding these accidents there never appears to be any spite or wanton exertions of strength to affect them nor do any disputes even happen between the parties. (p. 237)

In defining the delicate balance between rough play, strategy, and sportsmanship, George Belden described a game of shinny among the Dakotas in 1871 (cited in Culin, 1907), reporting that

when either party cheats, foul is called by the opposite party, when the game ceases until the judges decide the matter. If it is a foul play the play is given to the other side. *No one thinks of disputing the judges' decision* [italics added], and from it there is no appeal. (p. 639)

Referees or judges were always older men who were held in high esteem by all players. Usually, one of the judges was from each of the competing tribes. However, they were viewed as impartial, and their integrity was never questioned. Prior to important contests, in fact, these judges spent a great deal of time in prayers for wisdom and fair judgment.

Several authors have reported that judges sometimes carried sticks around with them during lacrosse play, and whenever young boys lost their tempers and became involved in fights, the judges would beat them with the sticks until these unrelated and unnecessary skirmishes ceased. Most reports seem to indicate that no more than two to four judges served as officials at the contests. At these games it was fairly common for 50 or 100 participants to take part, and on some occasions several hundred played on each side. Clearly, it would have been impossible for the judges to see and fairly adjudicate all possible violations. Unlike today's amateur and professional sports, Indian participants, by all accounts, assumed major responsibility for ensuring fair play, or justice.

Individual responsibility for fair play might be contrasted with today's major sports in which just the opposite value appears to exist—that it is the responsibility of the official, but not the player, to guarantee fair play. At athletic contests today, consequently, a much larger ratio of officials to players are assigned than was ever seen in Indian contests. For example, in major league baseball games, four (and sometimes six) umpires are assigned; two or three referees are assigned to college or professional basketball games (not counting scorers and timekeepers); and at least a half dozen individuals may officiate a football game. In professional tennis the officials outnumber the players three to one. This preponderance would seem to eliminate the need for argument by players and coaches. But the present climate seems to encourage coaches and players to berate officials vociferously. Furthermore, as television replays vividly show, using many officials does not always ensure correct decisions. Among Indian tribes, however, an attitude of fair play and support for authority enabled the contest to proceed smoothly.

To be a good player and to win were important attributes in traditional Indian sports. However, to perform with grace and integrity was equally important. Losing one's composure would lead to scorn and ridicule, and behavior such as that frequently exhibited by today's professional tennis players or by baseball managers would disgrace one in the eyes of the traditional Indian community. Despite the ruggedness of the activity or the stress placed upon the performers, self-discipline with fair play and dignity were expected at all times.

Effect of Non-Indian Culture on Indian Sportsmanship

Very early writing about Indian sports rarely made reference to any dishonest behavior. However, in the late 19th century, Carl Lumholtz (1895) suggested that coming civilization may have had a contaminating effect on Indian sports ethics. He reported that in the ball race, "just as in horse racing, rascally tricks are more or less common, *especially if the Indians had become half civilized* [italics added]" (p. 307). "Uncivilized" Indians (those not yet influenced by outside civilization) were not reported to exhibit such behavioral problems. To guard against this behavior, Lumholtz reported, the chief called all runners together before the race began and made a speech "warning them against any kind of cheating" (p. 307).

Additional evidence of the negative effects of non-Indian civilization on Indian sports morality is provided by Howell and Howell (1978) in their discussion of the legendary coach Glenn "Pop" Warner. Warner coached football at the Carlisle Indian School in Pennsylvania for eleven years between 1899 and 1914. According to Howell and Howell, his standards of behavior were a contradiction of traditional Indian values of fair play in sports. These authors present an extensive review of the difficulty Warner had with Lieutenant Richard Pratt, founder of the school, and with Indian student athletes. Among the charges against Warner were allegations of corruption within the athletic program, abuse of Indian student athletes, notoriously foul language, misuse of funds, and violation of the spirit of game rules.

Lieutenant Pratt had founded the school to teach the white man's ways to the Indian. Howell and Howell (1978) cynically conclude that Warner was a perfect instrument for that task. They report that Warner was

> proclaimed by the athletes as "profane and abusive" and of "weak moral character"—his "influence and method . . . injurious to the school and detrimental to good discipline," "selfish," "dishonest," "an incompetent leader." The Indians had absorbed the teaching of the white man and in outrage cried out because it had offended their own morality, their own beliefs in right and wrong. (p. 27)

Although Warner's coaching methods were well received at several non-Indian universities, Howell and Howell found them an affront to traditional Indian values of fairness. John Steckbeck (1951) reviewed the style of football play under Warner's leadership and offered a kinder view, stating only that his teams were "masters of trickery" (p. vii). In retrospect, Warner's style became the prototype of the hard-driving, win-at-all-cost style of coaches in recent years. Even so, Warner's efforts to circumvent the spirit of the rules and his domineering style were contrary to what the Indian youth had expected in sports.

Folklore and Playing Rules

Indian folklore abounds with legends of war, work, and other matters of general human interest. Many of these stories were designed to promote fair play or high moral standards. One such popular narrative among the Menominee was described by Skinner and Satterlee (1915, pp. 217-546). In this tale the *above* things (eagles, geese, pigeons, owls, and all manner of fowl) challenged the *below* beings (snakes, fishes, otters, deer, and all beasts of the forest) to a great game of lacrosse. The game proceeded normally until the legendary Manabozho intervened unfairly on behalf of the above things. This interference incurred the wrath of all players and elicited their retaliation. The players along with their gods used flood waters to destroy Manabozho for his cheating. This legend was apparently created to encourage fair play.

The high standards of sportsmanship and fair play practiced by Indians do not refute the fact that *trickery* and deception were also an important part of Indian life, including games. Indian mythology is filled with incidents of trickery among animals, humans, and even supernatural creatures. In one such incident from mythology, Neihardt (1951) describes how the "two-leggeds" of the earth (including humans and various birds of the air) used deceptive strategy and trickery to outdistance the "four-legged" animals in a great race. The race was a long distance event that "circled the hoop of the earth." The consequence of the race was that if the four-legged creatures won, they would consume all the two-leggeds. On the other hand, if the two-leggeds won, then four-leggeds would be forever obligated to feed them and their descendants.

As the race started, a host of four-legged animals of various descriptions started running with all their might, as did the two-leggeds, including humans as well as various fowls of the air. However, one wise bird, the magpie, hitched a ride by sitting on the ear of the mighty (four-legged) bison bull. Depending upon the weather conditions, the rain, or the wind, the contesting forces took turns leading and falling behind. The magpie sat patiently upon the bison's ear and waited. Near the end of the race, a great rainstorm made the wings of the birds so heavy that they fell far behind. As the four-leggeds came within sight of the finish line, they began celebrating with great noisemaking. At this point the magpie, who was not at all tired, rose from the bison's ear and easily flew across the goal line ahead of all four-legged animals. The Voice of Thunder then proclaimed to the magpie, "By thinking, you have won the race for all your relatives, the two-leggeds. Hereafter you shall wear the rainbow in your tail, and it shall be a sign of victory." In addition, the four-leggeds were made slower and were required to feed the two-leggeds. (pp. 202–205)

Guile, or trickery, such as that used by the magpie was rather common in Indian traditions. It was accepted as appropriate behavior for gods, for superhumans, and for people. However, this was never confused with dishonesty, which was not allowed, and no one was allowed to dispute a decision rendered by someone in a position of authority.

The Nature of Games for Men and Boys

Certain games were played only by men and some were restricted exclusively to women. This separation of the sexes for certain activities was evident both for games of skill and for games of chance. In addition, some games were played by men and women together. The particular pattern of participation varied among the different tribes. However, it was a widespread, if not universal, custom that women were not to participate in lacrosse or the hoop-and-pole games. In fact, they were often not even allowed to observe the latter activity. The game of double ball was universally restricted to women and girls, and the hand-and-foot ball game was played primarily by women.

Most sports activities of a rugged nature were engaged in primarily by boys and men. Rules pertaining to body contact were generally undefined or nonexistent. Participants were expected to accept whatever physical abuse or injuries occurred without complaint and without anger. Bravery was strongly encouraged as a matter of course. Games for young boys usually reflected the rough-and-tumble nature of activities that would follow in adulthood.

Stories describing the roughness and seeming brutality of lacrosse, shinny, and certain other combative games are legendary, and several reports of the death of participants during games have been made. Despite the rugged nature of lacrosse, Copway, (1851/1972) writing about a game among the Ojibway, reported that

> no one is heard to complain, though he be bruised severely or his nose come in close communion with a club. If the last-mentioned catastrophe befall him, he is up in a trice, and sets his laugh forth as loud as the rest, though it be floated at first on a tide of blood. (p. 570)

Young boys emulated the men in adopting games of courage and challenge that provided an opportunity for them to exhibit their physical prowess. Tug-of-wars, push-of-wars, mass wrestling, boxing, and certain endurance events were typical boys' games. Sitting on the clam was a popular game among several tribes. In this game one boy buried a clam in the sand and sat on it while his teammates circled around to protect him against an equal number of invaders. The opponents who were outside the circle attempted to break through the protective line, drag the boy off the clam, and steal it. If successful, the boys changed sides and and started over. This game, of course, led to a great deal of rough play.

Some foot races were organized so that boys started the race equidistant from a line or object and ran toward each other to see who could reach the destination first. Any slowing down or veering off line as a runner approached the line would not only cause him to lose the race but would also indicate a lack of courage. These races led to many collisions and injuries.

Young boys' spirit of daring was described by Hamilton (1972) in a game in which Indian youth would attack and destroy the nest of wild bees. The invasion involved great planning and was engaged in with considerable ceremony. However, despite the boys' most discreet stalking efforts, the bees never seemed to be surprised when the nest was finally attacked.

After being stung repeatedly, the youths made great efforts to avoid screaming or crying, which would, of course, be a sign of weakness. They were also obliged to join the next army that was organized for the search and destruction of another nest.

Sports for Women and Girls

The prominent role of women in Indian culture has often been unrecognized by the general public. However, high levels of achievement and importance were commonplace for women in most tribes. Indian women on occasion assumed roles as chiefs, medicine women, peace negotiators, scouts, and members of the most important councils. Among the Iroquois nations, women selected the chiefs. Women regularly planted, tended, and harvested crops and were the dominant influence in the family. In *American Indian Women*, Gridley (1974) stated that the negative image of Indian women accepted by the non-Indian public is attributable to uninformed writers who falsely judged them to be practically slaves. Early explorers and settlers did not understand the subtleties of Indian culture and thus communicated erroneous impressions.

Active involvement of Indian women in community life extended into the field of sports. According to Cheska (1982), "North American Indian women participated in ball games as active, agile players and as avid, ardent spectators" (p. 19). Further, the "Indian women played almost all types of ball games that the men did, with modifications, however" (p. 19). Among the most popular games for women was that of double ball. Culin (1907) cited reports in which women in more than two dozen tribes primarily west of the Mississippi River played double ball. Figure 1.4 is a photograph of the women's horse race in 1899 at the Crow fair in Montana. The women used no saddles in this very popular activity. The rugged and strenuous nature of girls' play can also be noted in Figure 1.5, a reproduction of Seth Eastman's 1849 painting of Menominee women playing lacrosse. There is certainly no sense of gentility or timidity in the scene. Running games were very popular with girls and women; the ball race was prevalent in the Southwest. Lumholtz (1895) described the seriousness with which women engaged in these races and reported that they

> hold their own races, one valley against another, and the same scenes of betting and excitement are to be observed, although on a smaller scale. . . . The women get even more excited than the men, and it is a strange sight to see these stalwart Amazons racing heavily along, but with astonishing perseverance. They wear nothing but a skirt, which when creeks or water holes come in their way, they gather up, a la Diane, and make short work of the crossing. (p. 311)

Figure 1.4. Start of women's horse race at the Crow Indian fair in Montana. This bareback race was photographed by Fred Miller in 1899. Photo used by permission of the National Anthropological Archives, Smithsonian Institution.

Figure 1.5. Women's lacrosse game among the Menominee, prior to 1849. From oil painting by Seth Eastman. Photo used by permission of the National Anthropological Archives, Smithsonian Institution.

Evidence indicates that girls and young women did exceptionally well in running events. In 1868 John Cremony, an army major reporting from New Mexico, indicated that among the Apaches the women "generally manage to carry off the palm, providing the distance is not too great" (cited in Culin, 1907, p. 803). He described a major track meet sponsored by the U.S. Army at Fort Sumner, New Mexico. About 100 Apaches and Navajos entered the half-mile competition for prizes provided by the Army. Participants included men between the ages of fifteen and forty and women between fifteen and twenty-five.

Among the competitors was the Apache girl, Isha-kay-nay, a clean limbed, handsome girl of 17, who had always refused marriage, and she was the favorite among the whites. Each runner was tightly girded with a broad belt, and looked like a race horse. Ten entered for the half mile stake, which was a gaudy piece of calacoo for a dress or shirt, as the case might be. At the word they went off like rockets, Mah-kah-wen leading handsomely, and Isha-kay-nay bringing up the rear, but running as clean and easy as a greyhound. Within four hundred yards of the goal she closed the gap, went by like a steam engine, and got in an easy winner, six yards ahead of all competitors. For the quarter-mile race she again entered, but was ruled out by the other Indians, and their objections were allowed, it being decided that the victor in either race should not enter for another. (pp. 803–804)

Most reports emphasize the high status and seriousness of women's sports. Catlin (1841/1944), however, described one exceptional incident. In reporting on a double ball game among the Sioux women, he stated that

after the men enjoyed their surfeit of whiskey, and wanted a little more amusement, and felt disposed to indulge the weaker sex in a little recreation also; it was announced among them, and through the village, that the women were going to have a ball play! . . . The men are more than half drunk, when they feel liberal enough to indulge the women in such amusement; and take infinite pleasure in rolling about on the ground and laughing to excess, whilst the women are tumbling about in all attitudes and scuffling for the ball. (p. 125)

Such an incident is a rarity in reports on Indian sports, and as is suggested by Gridley (1974), the meaning could be significantly distorted by the reporter. The majority of reports clearly indicate that women participated in sports as seriously and with as much integrity as did the men.

In contrast to the Catlin report, a more traditional view of sport among the Sioux, one showing a prominent role for girls, is described by Black Elk in Brown's *The Sacred Pipe* (1953). In this account Black Elk describes *the throwing of the ball* as one of the seven sacred rites of the Oglala Sioux.

This activity has more ritual significance than a typical ball game, and it gives evidence that ball games were closely connected to ritual, that they were a serious part of tribal life, and that females were often central to the spiritual, as well as the sporting, life of the community.

Black Elk stated that Tapa Wanka Yap (the throwing of the ball) was a game that reflected the course of man's life in which the goal was to catch and control the ball. The ball itself represented the universe, and the odds against attaining that goal were great. The obstacles (representing ignorance) ensured that only a few could succeed in reaching the goal. So it was in the ball game: Only a few managed to capture it.

This ball game rite was revealed to Moses Walking in a vision many years ago. In the game a ball made of buffalo hair and covered with buffalo hide was painted red and blue to represent the earth and the heavens. Ceremonies commenced with extensive prayers. Then sacred, sweet grass was burned over coals to purify the ball and other equipment used during the game and related rituals.

When preparations were completed, the ball was handed to a girl, youthful and pure, who initiated the game in the center of a court. The girl first tossed the ball in the direction that the sun goes down, and all people scrambled for it. Next, she tossed the ball in the direction where the giant lives, then in the direction that the sun comes up, toward which we always face. Finally, the girl tossed the ball straight up into the air. At this point in Moses Walking's vision, all the people were turned into buffalo and as such were not able to catch the ball because they had no hands. It became obvious that only two-legged people can catch the ball and consequently can control the earth. Four-legged animals cannot play ball and therefore cannot control the earth.

In the real world, the game was played among the Sioux, and all the decoratively dressed players attempted to catch the ball each time the young girl threw it into the air. Anyone fortunate enough to catch it was blessed and given a horse or some other important prize. According to tradition, just as the ball descends from the heavens towards the earth, so also does God's power descend to the persons below.

According to Black Elk, all persons taking part in this ball game rite smoked the sacred pipe or touched it at the conclusion of the event. A great feast was then held to celebrate this festive occasion. The ball game, based on the vision of Moses Walking, was played among the Oglala Sioux for many generations. It was always more a sacred rite than merely a game for fun. It is significant in the traditions of the Sioux that a young girl was the focus of control.

Despite these examples of the important status of Indian women, anthropologist Ernestine Friedl (1975) has cautioned against concluding that women achieved equal status with men in Native American, or any other, society. In *Women and Men*, she reported on the relative status of the sexes among the Hopi, Iroquois, Washo, and the North Alaskan Eskimo on this continent; she also assessed sexual status among more than a dozen closely knit cultures in other parts of the world. After analyzing patterns of labor, subsistence, and rituals along with controls over such items as food, property, political power, and sexual access she concluded that

> a degree of male dominance exists in all known societies, if we define male dominance as a situation in which men have highly preferential access, although most always exclusive rights, in those activities to which the society accords the greatest value, and the exercise of which permits a measure of control over others. (p. 7)

Girls and women participated in games quite regularly and vigorously until the point of adulthood and marriage. Indications are that sport involvement diminished significantly once women began raising families. Writers have made limited references to the sport participation of Indian women during adulthood. Perhaps responsibilities for child rearing and farming, along with other chores, reduced opportunities for play. An equivalent reduction did not occur with men.

Characteristics of Team Membership

The concept of team play in sports was developed and perfected by American Indians prior to any contact with outsiders. Their most important sports were *team* games (lacrosse, shinny, double ball, and others discussed in chapter 2). However, most sports brought to this country by the Europeans were *individual* sports (wrestling, gymnastics, track, boxing, rowing, handball, etc.). Although new arrivals in this country developed team sports such as football, baseball, and basketball during the 19th century, it seems fair to assume that non-Indians learned the importance and strategy of team play from Indians.

In traditional Indian sports, teams were characterized by strong kinship ties. In addition, the whole community rallied in support of the team. According to Blanchard (1981), both of these characteristics have persisted to the present among the Choctaw community of Mississippi. In recent years he found that baseball and basketball teams were typically composed of individuals with close family ties. Furthermore, the closer those ties, the more likely was one to interact with that person (e.g., pass the basketball to him or her during team play or assist in some other way). It has been suggested by several authors that closely knit bands within tribes exhibited the same type of preferential treatment in team play. More traditional Indian teams today, particularly those in remote or isolated areas, are especially closely knit and virtually closed to outsiders.

In traditional Indian life, all community citizens were a part of the team either as player or avid supporter. For a major lacrosse game, all able-bodied, young men in the community were players, and old men, women, and children were equally interested and involved in supportive roles. Such roles included aiding the players in their preparation (physical, psychological, and spiritual), participating in all-night vigils and prayers, aiding and arranging wagers, officiating, and exhorting players during the game. All members of the community saw themselves as members of the team effort. Major athletic events provided one of the most satisfying ways to develop community or tribal unity as well as some means of interaction with an outside group. In the non-Indian community, however, involvement with the team has always been more selective. Some persons chose to be on the team and some did not. Some decided to be spectators and others did not get involved at all.

Balance and Diversity

Members of traditional Indian teams were expected to develop a broad range of skills and to perform a variety of roles as needed by their team during the course of a game. This can be contrasted with the tendency in today's non-Indian sports to *specialize* for a particular position or role. For example, in football there are placekickers who are expected to perform that role and nothing else. Similarly, there are punters, deep receivers, goal line defensemen, special team players, and even players who center the ball only in punting situations. In basketball there are point guards who are expected to initiate plays, and others are essentially rebounders or scorers. Indian teams generally avoided such rigid specialization.

Indian diversity and all-around skill was epitomized by Jim Thorpe and other members of the Carlisle athletic teams who not only played diverse roles in one sport but also took part in a wide variety of other athletic endeavors. Even though Thorpe was clearly better in some track activities than in others, he frequently entered as many as eight events during a meet in order to earn points for his team. Despite some evidence to the contrary (e.g., the Choctaw apparently specialized by position in racket-ball, a form of lacrosse), Indians typically practiced to develop diverse skills to meet the full range of eventualities arising in a given sport. It is also clear that emphasis was placed on team success rather than on individual notoriety. Special recognition was rarely given to prominent Indian athletes, and then only by non-Indians.

The Indian concept of life emphasized wholeness and balance and recognized the interrelatedness of all things. The Indian strived for well-roundedness and avoided extreme specialization. After developing adequate competence in an activity, he or she went on to other skills. When Indians knew that they could perform a certain feat, there was no need to continue practice or repetition. Such overpractice would be detrimental to other skills needing development. Emphasis on balance was reflected in all areas of life and was not restricted to sport.

The need for relatedness has been observed in many aspects of Indian life. One situation in which this attitude has caused difficulty is military service. During the past half century, the Indians have occasionally been criticized because of their lack of interest in routine military chores. After joining the service with the express purpose of fighting wars, they often saw little relevance to many of the tasks they were asked to perform. They often resisted and resented the performance of those mundane, apparently unrelated duties.

Leadership Style

In traditional Indian sports, no single individual was given full authority or responsibility for providing leadership and direction for the team. Of course, in the non-Indian community, one individual is selected to serve as the brains and the voice of the whole team. However, all members of an Indian team assumed personal responsibility for the welfare of the team, which was consistent with traditional Indian forms of government that involved the ideas and deliberations of all members of the community. Such sharing of authority and leadership seems inconceivable, for example, on a modern football team—players who attempt to share ideas with the quarterback are viewed as troublesome to the team's progress.

Indian antagonism to autocratic leadership was intense. Concerning political life among the Choctaw in 1775, Romans (1775/1921) wrote: "Their leader cannot pretend to *command* on an expedition; the most he can do is endeavor to persuade. . . . Should he pretend to order, desertion would at least be his punishment, if not death" (p. 76). Contempt or resentment for the dictatorial leader or hard-driving coach extended into the 20th century. As reported earlier in this chapter, Pop Warner, the very successful football coach at the Carlisle Indian School from 1899 to 1914, exhibited this style. He was resented and criticized by a great number of Indian athletes. In addition, the autocratic and demanding John McGraw, manager of the New York Giants during the first two decades of this century, was clearly ineffective with Jim Thorpe. The clash of personalities between the two was widely chronicled in the press. Through the years the most effective leaders both in sports and in community affairs have not been those who provided opportunities for all members to have a say in the group's welfare. A style of persuasion and rational discourse has proven most effective.

The tendency of Indians to resent excessive displays of authority by coaches, managers, or team captains has continued to the present day. Blanchard (1981) has observed that the Choctaw Indians are still not responsive to direct command. He further reported that when the coach occasionally lost his temper or exhibited forceful behavior, he always couched that behavior in humor to avoid being taken too seriously. In addition, a dramatic difference was shown between the Choctaw youths and area white youths who were asked to respond to a picture of a football coach apparently scolding his team on the sidelines. Whereas 93% of the whites viewed this as appropriate behavior (i.e., the way a coach is supposed to act), 94% of the Indians saw it as bad (i.e., excessively harsh).

Art in Sport

One of the more universal characteristics of Indian sport was the inclusion of art in all aspects of the activity. All games reflected the character and identity of the tribe in some decorative manner. Costumes, equipment, and implements for play were decoratively painted, beaded, or carved. Balls, racquets, dice, gambling sticks, snow snakes, and other articles reflecting individual artwork and tribal symbols have been collected in museums around the country. Decorative body paint was regularly used

Figure 1.6. George Catlin's 1830s painting of Tullock-chish-ko (He Who Drinks the Juice of the Stone). Catlin described this person as the most distinguished ball player of the Choctaw nation. Photo from National Archives and Records Administration.

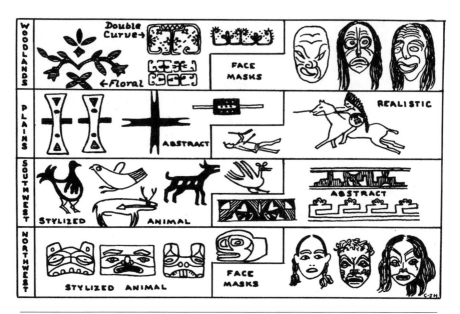

Figure 1.7. Illustrated chart by C.J. Howell showing the art styles of Indian America: Woodlands, Plains, Southwest, and Northwest. Photo used by permission of the University Museum, University of Pennsylvania.

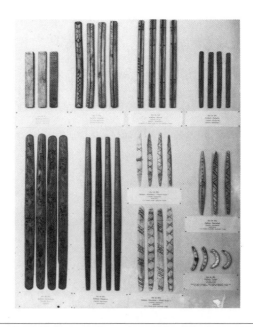

Figure 1.8. A variety of decorated gaming sticks. Photo used by permission of the University Museum, University of Pennsylvania.

by ball players and runners as well as by warriors. George Catlin and other painters and early photographers provide evidence of the universality of art in Indian sport. George Catlin's painting of the famous Choctaw lacrosse player is included in Figure 1.6 and illustrates the decorative body paint and costumes that were typical for lacrosse players within that tribe. C.J. Howell has developed a chart illustrating his version of the variety of art styles found in four different sections of the country. This drawing is shown in Figure 1.7. Almost all game implements were decorated for artistic and identification purposes. Figure 1.8 shows some gaming sticks decorated in a typical fashion. The artistic character of Indian sport is presented throughout the text in discussions of implements, costumes, facilities, and ceremony related to sports.

Betting on Games

Betting on athletic contests was a regular practice for both participants and spectators. Gambling in sports was a deeply ingrained tradition and appears to have been universal for tribes on this continent. Betting was used for both relatively minor athletic contests and for major tribal events. The major events, however, led to much heavier wagering.

Betting served several purposes in Indian culture. Sports activities provided an outlet for the strong gambling interests that were culturally established. The bets seemed to add to the importance and general legitimacy of the contests. Although the players were not professional athletes in the sense of today's salaried performers, gambling provided them with an opportunity to gain important material goals through athletic prowess. It should be noted, however, that these goods remained within the community. Sport gambling was a type of "circular economics." The winnings indirectly found their way back into the community till and thus contributed to the common good. Victors did not take the money and run. Therefore, any destructive influence on the community as a result of sport gambling was minimal.

When betting on games occurred, odds or handicaps were never established. Indians assumed that any performer having proper preparation and adequate allegiance to the Great Spirit could win over anyone else. Thus, all opponents wagered items of the same value. At the conclusion of the game, the winner took all the items wagered and the loser received nothing.

George Belden described a typical betting ceremony before a game of shinny played among the Dakota Indians in 1871 (cited in Culin, 1907). He reported that several old men who had been appointed to act as umpires seated themselves between the two organized groups of contestants. The players then proceeded one by one to advance and make their bets.

> First one warrior advanced and threw down a robe before the old men; then a warrior from the other side came forward and laid a robe upon it; and so all bet, one against the other. Presently there was a great number of piles of stakes, some having bet moccasins, headdresses, beadwork, earrings, necklaces, bows and arrows, and even ponies. All these were carefully watched over by the old men, who noted each stake and the depositor on a stick. If you did not wish to bet with any particular warrior you laid your wager on the big pile, and instantly it was matched by the judges against some article of corresponding value from the pile of the other side. (p. 639)

Another betting ceremony was described to Culin (1907) by George Starr prior to a Choctaw lacrosse game during the late 19th century. Starr was particularly impressed with the great skill of the stake holders both in correctly matching wares from the different betters and in remembering the ownership of the various goods. He reported of a particular stakeholder that ''his memory is remarkable, and he never fails to turn over the stakes correctly'' (p. 603). At the conclusion of the contest observed by Belden, he reported that ''when the judges had awarded all the winnings, among which were 14 ponies, each took up his trophies and returned to the village, where for the remainder of the day the game was fought over again and again in the teepees'' (cited in Culin, 1907, p. 640). The literature does not mention any dissatisfaction with the matching of bets or with the disposition of the winnings at the conclusion of the contest.

Early missionaries were the first to raise questions about the morality of betting on athletic contests. The practice, however, was an integral part of Indian culture and was in fact supported by the respected elders and medicine men who generally officiated at the ceremonies. Non-Indians, especially the missionaries, brought their own attitude of immorality to the practice of gambling. (The practice of gambling is dealt with more extensively in chapter 6, which is devoted entirely to games of chance.)

Summary

Indian sport was intimately related to ritual and ceremony. In addition to the pure joy involved in participation, sport was used as a means by which the Indians communicated with a higher spirit, seeking blessings on their individual or community welfare. Such communication related to healing, climate, celebration, seeking success in upcoming events, or other matters of individual or community importance.

Over the years, activities that began as religious rites often evolved into sport. Nevertheless, sport retained its important cultural significance. This was reflected in the extensive spiritual preparation for sport as well as in the attitude and manner of participating. High standards of sportsmanship and artistic expression prevailed. The placing of wagers was an important aspect of sports contests.

The Indian concept of sport came into conflict with that of the non-Indian in the late 19th and early 20th centuries. Neither the highly commercialized nature of professional sports today nor the more casual attitude prevailing in amateur activities captures the essence of Indian sport. The near deification of today's superstars, the adherences to precise and uniform standards, and the adversarial behavior of participants bear little resemblance to Indian practices in sport.

Chapter 2

Ball Games

Although a variety of games and amusements were popular among American Indians, "the most valued activity was that of ball play," according to Catlin (1841/1944, p. 140). Certain individual activities such as foot racing, swimming, and archery may have rivaled ball games in breadth of participation, but none compared in terms of group interest. In addition, ball games held cultural significance that was reflected in traditions and legends going back for thousands of years. This chapter will present a sampling of the prominent ball games played by Indians in traditional times, including style of play, implements used, and as far as possible, the social significance of those games.

A great many different types of ball games were played by Indians across the North American continent. At least twelve distinct categories of such games are described in the literature, although some were restricted to one tribe or limited to one section of the continent. This chapter will include only those ball games that were widely played by large segments of the Indian population in North America.

The balls used by Indians in games came in many shapes and forms, which included carved pieces of wood, stones, sticks, bones, rubber, animal bladders, and various other objects. The more sophisticated balls were made of animal hides filled with hair, straw, cornhusks, feathers, or some other material. These balls were sewn either in a gathered bag shape or with the seam going around the center, the general style of today's baseballs.

Rubber balls were first developed by the Indians of South America with materials from the rubber trees growing on that continent. Rubber, and rubber balls, gradually migrated to Central and North America. Rubber was not available in Europe until approximately the 17th century when explorers transported it to that continent from the New World. Although rubber balls were quite prevalent in South and Central America, they were not extensively used in North America. However, there is evidence that the rubber ball was used in the court ball games in the southwestern part of the United States during ancient times, and Wissler (1922) reported that the Aztec Indians had developed and were using hollow rubber balls prior to the arrival of Columbus. For most of North America, however, it seems that balls were most often made of stuffed animal hides, wood, stone, or other materials.

In Indian games the ball was usually propelled by being kicked, batted, or thrown with a racket or stick. Players were prevented from using the hands in most games. One well known Cherokee legend held that the moon is actually a ball that in ancient times was thrown against the sky. On that occasion two tribes were playing against each other, and one had the better team and had almost won the game. Thereupon a player on the losing side picked up the ball with his hand, which was strictly forbidden, and tried to throw it to the goal at the far end of the field. Instead, the ball struck against the solid sky and has remained fastened there to remind players never to cheat by using their hands.

Foremost among Indian ball games were lacrosse, shinny, double ball, and various forms of football. These games will be discussed in this chapter. Even though the *ancient court ball game* had great religious and ritualistic significance, it did not spread into most parts of the United States. Rather, it was restricted to Central America, Mexico, and the southwestern part of the United States. Furthermore, it had begun to deteriorate from its original form before being observed and described by non-Indians. The *ball race* made use of a ball and was very popular throughout the southwestern part of the United States. However, because its purpose was essentially a competition of running speed and endurance, it is included in chapter 3, which deals with running.

Lacrosse

By most accounts the most popular game among Indians throughout North America was lacrosse. This game has been called various names by Indians and others over the past several centuries. Perhaps the most common name among traditional Indians was the *game of ball* or *ball game*, which gives some indication of its widespread, almost universal popularity. *Indian stickball* was a casual term used by non-Indians. The game was also called *baggataway* (with various spellings) and other Indian terms descriptive of either the racket or the ball. *Racket* and *racketball* were widely used late in the 19th century, particularly in the south, and Culin (1907) included reports on this game from numerous writers who used the terms racket and lacrosse interchangeably. Use of the more general term *ball play* was diminishing in 1907, when he published his report on Indian sports. He reported that the term racket was preferred in the southern parts of the United States and that lacrosse was most frequently used in the north.

The overwhelming and almost universal popularity of lacrosse is apparent from reports by travelers throughout the 17th, 18th, and 19th centuries. It was played extensively in all parts of Canada and the United States except the southwest. Moreover, folklore supports the prominence of lacrosse in the lives of Indians in the south, the northeast, the midwest, the plains, and throughout Canada.

When the white man came to America, lacrosse was the most popular Indian game. It had a quality of intensity and integrity that was apparent even to the uninformed observer. According to Jette (1975):

> The accounts of the missionaries and travelers who had actually viewed the game also indicate that it was a most earnest game, but a generally harmless one, conducted with an unwritten code of fair play. It was depicted as the finest and greatest of all Indian games, a noble one, played with a high degree of perfection, grace, adroitness and dexterity, and under the watchful eye of the gods. (p. 18)

Origin and Development of Lacrosse

The exact origin of lacrosse is lost in antiquity. Clapin (1894) reported that the game of *soule* played in medieval times among the mountaineers of France is somewhat similar to lacrosse. Jette (1975, p. 14) concluded that the name lacrosse was given by French missionaries and voyagers because the game closely resembled "la souls," which was played with a "crosse." Most historians concede that this game was developed among the Indians of America prior to any contact with the Europeans. After reviewing extensive research on this topic, Culin (1907) decided that "there can be no doubt that, though the game of racket may have been modified in historic times, it remains an Aboriginal invention" (p. 563). Its popularity on this continent was enormous, and lacrosse was quickly adopted by the early settlers in the United States and Canada.

Wissler (1922) concluded that the Algonquin Indians invented the game of lacrosse. He theorized that the game was first played about 1,000 years ago in the southeastern part of the United States and spread to all other parts except perhaps the southwest. However, many Iroquois Indians believe that their forefathers first played the game in the region that is now upper New York state and Eastern Canada.

Beauchamp (1896) wrote that lacrosse was "the oldest remaining and the most widely spread ball game. Almost three centuries ago, at least, the Hurons and others played it, village against village, almost as it is played today" (p. 272). By all accounts lacrosse is one of the oldest American sports currently in existence and is likewise one of the few major sports of purely American origin.

Wissler (1922) speculated that one of the primary motivations for developing and promoting lacrosse was to use it as training for war. It contained many of the components necessary for early Indian warfare (e.g., courage, ruggedness, skill, speed, and endurance). It has been described as being halfway between sport and deadly combat. However, to depict this ball game primarily as overt training for war is to distort the character of the Indian people, and the contemporary accounts of these contests readily demonstrate that such was not the case. The games were played for the enjoyment and satisfaction of both the participants and spectators and for the ritual surrounding those events. The games were often used as a healing remedy, as a ritual to bring needed rain to crops, as celebrations for a multitude of events, and as omens of good fortune. Adding to the importance of the games were the stakes that were bet on the contests. The leaders were no doubt also interested in activities that would develop the physical and mental capacities of the young men for hunting, warfare, sports, and general physical well-being. However, lacrosse was primarily a game for enjoyment and for social significance, not a training regimen.

The lacrosse season seems to have varied with different tribes in various parts of the country. More groups played in the late summer and autumn than during any other period. This was true of southern farmers, who had more free time after crops had been planted and cultivated. In addition, some groups apparently wished to complete the season of lacrosse play before the weather became too cold for the naked or scantily clothed bodies. Some northern groups played in the spring after the major hunting season was over or during the summer when animals were not to be killed. During the French colonization of Canada in the 1660s, Nicholas Perrot (cited in Jette, 1975), a trader and government agent, reported that Indians west of Lake Superior in Canada began their first games after the melting of winter's ice and completed the last games just prior to seed time. Wulff (1977) quotes another French traveler during colonial times, Abbe Ferland, as stating that among the Seneca the games "begin at the melting of the ice and continue at intervals until harvest time" (p. 16). At any rate, the lacrosse season seems to have been selected on the basis of the work demands of tribal life.

The widespread popularity of lacrosse is clear. On the North American continent, it was the closest thing to a national pastime. It was established as the national sport in Canada in 1859 and remains so today. Its popularity was pointed out in 1860 by Kohl (cited in Culin, 1907): "The name of the ball play is immortalized both in the geography and history of the country. There is a prairie, and now a town, on the Mississippi known as the 'prairie de la Cross' '' (p. 566). (The town of LaCrosse is located in the state of Wisconsin.)

Kohl emphasized the place of lacrosse as a sport in the lives of Indians:

Of all the Indian social sports the finest and grandest is the ball play. I might call it a noble game, and I am surprised how these savages attain such perfection in it. Nowhere in the world, excepting, perhaps, among the English and some of the Italian races, is the graceful and manly game of ball played so passionately and on so large a scale. They often play village against village, or tribe against tribe. Hundreds of players assemble, and the wares and goods offered as prizes often reach a value of a thousand dollars or more. (p. 566)

Costumes for lacrosse play were simple indeed. Numerous reports from the early literature indicated that players were entirely naked. (It should be noted that among most tribes only men and boys played this game). However, from the 18th and 19th centuries onward, most reports described the players as wearing brief loin cloths. The costumes were loosely attached—if a player was encumbered by someone catching on to his clothes, they would be quickly removed.

Catlin (1841/1944) reported that among the Choctaw, players were not allowed to wear moccasins or anything else except a breachcloth with a belt and a tail made of horse hair that projected from the back of the belt. In addition, a mane made of horsehair dyed with various bright colors was worn around the neck. On most occasions their bodies and faces were painted in the same manner as when they were going into battle. Catlin's painting from the 1830s of Choctaw lacrosse players ready for action is shown in Figure 1.1. A late 19th century illustration of a Cherokee lacrosse player, less decoratively attired, is shown in Figure 1.3. This photograph of a *scratching* ceremony in North Carolina was taken in 1888 by James Mooney. Figure 2.1 shows Iroquois players wearing breechcloths, feathers, and painted faces.

However, in colder climates or in colder seasons, more clothing was worn. Figure 2.2 is from an illustration made in 1852 by Seth Eastman entitled *Ball Play on Ice*. This print apparently depicted Dakota Indians playing lacrosse on the St. Peters River at Fort Snelling, Minnesota.

Hoffman (1890) pointed out a rare exception to the *men only* character of lacrosse among the Santee Dakota Indians and at the same time recognized the unusual nature of that occurrence:

When the women play against the men, five of the women are matched against one of the latter. A mixed game of this kind is very amusing. The fact that among the Dakota women are allowed to participate in the game is considered excellent evidence that the game is

Figure 2.1. Iroquois lacrosse game from a painting by Langdon Kihn. Photo used by permission of the University Museum, University of Pennsylvania.

Figure 2.2. Dakota Indians playing lacrosse on a frozen lake. From a painting by Seth Eastman in 1852. Photo used by permission of the National Anthropological Archives, Smithsonian Institution.

a borrowed one. Among most other tribes, women are not even allowed to touch a ball stick. (p. 135)

In 1771 Bossu (cited in Culin, 1907) reported that among the Choctaw the women often commenced playing as soon as the men's game was completed and that the nature of their game was apparently similar to that of the men. According to him,

they are very active, and run against each other with extreme swiftness, pushing each other like the men, they having the same dress, except on those parts which modesty teaches them to cover. They only put rouge on their cheeks, and vermillion, instead of powder in their hair. (p. 598)

The Playing Field

The traditional lacrosse field was very large (compared to sports fields of today), but there appears to have been no set standard for the preferred size. Usually, the greater number of players, the larger the field. In wooded areas the dimensions and even the shape of the field depended upon the terrain and available open space. Typical sizes seemed to be in the range of 200 yards in width and one-quarter to one-half mile in length. However, numerous reports exist of lacrosse fields that extended one to two miles.

In the latter part of the 19th century, lacrosse fields became smaller and more standardized. The Cherokees in North Carolina, perhaps because of the limited number of young male players, were among the first to play on fields consistently described as approximately 100 yards long. The Iroquois of New York also report that their field dimensions have remained relatively standardized since well back into the 19th century. The gradual reduction of the field for other groups to today's regulation size was probably also influenced by colonists who wished to standardize the playing fields.

There were goalposts at each end of the playing field. These goals, sometimes referred to as *byes*, were gate-like targets approximately six feet in width with a cross bar at a height of anywhere from ten to twenty feet. Usually, the ball was heaved through the goal for a score. Catlin's painting of these tall lacrosse goals for a Choctaw game are shown in Figure 1.1.

Equipment

The origin of the lacrosse stick or *cross*, is uncertain. In 1851 Morgan (cited in Culin, 1907) reported that the Iroquois in New York believed that the stick originally used had a solid and curved head and that the bat with the leather network had been developed later. ''These substitutions were made so many years ago that they have lost the date'' (p. 294). It has been reported elsewhere that buckskin string was once used to pull or bind one end of the stick and establish the permanent curve, or bow, on the end. At some later point, a leather network was placed between the stick and the binding that held the curved end. The racket used most often in the south was small and had a netted area that was round (see Figure 2.3). In this part of the country, players typically held one stick in each hand. Figure 2.4 includes a photograph of Cherokee ball players holding two rackets. This photograph was taken by Mooney around 1888.

Rackets used by players in the north were larger and included a tapered netting constructed by curving one end of the stick. Figure 2.5 shows the Iroquois racket that was developed on the Tuscarora reservation in New York and has been widely adopted over the past several decades throughout the United States. This racket is approximately five feet in length, and the player must use both hands to manage it effectively.

The most prominent lacrosse ball in the very early days appears to have been a wooden knot obtained from a rotted tree. This wooden ball was very hard and the curved or twisted grain of the knot made it relatively durable. Some reports indicate that the ball was oval shaped, which would be the natural shape of the wooden knot. For example, in 1662 Perrot wrote that ''the ball with which they play is of wood and nearly the shape of a turkey's egg'' (cited in Jette, 1975, p. 18). However, the wooden knot

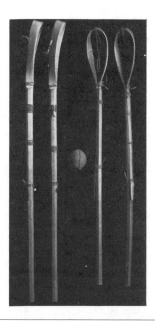

Figure 2.3. Yuchi lacrosse sticks and ball. Photo by F. Speck. Date not recorded. Photo used by permission of the University Museum, University of Pennsylvania.

Figure 2.4. The Wolftown lacrosse team, Qualla Reservation in western North Carolina. Note the two lacrosse sticks for each player. Photo by James Mooney in 1888. Photo used by permission of the National Anthropological Archives, Smithsonian Institution.

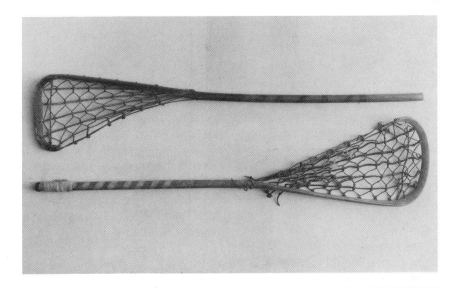

Figure 2.5. Iroquois lacrosse sticks manufactured on the Tuscarora Reservation near Niagara Falls, New York. These have been widely used throughout the United States over the past several decades. Photo used by permission of the National Anthropological Archives, Smithsonian Institution.

was usually rounded by carving and was often decorated with carvings or paint.

From around 1800 onward, the most common ball was sewn together from buckskin or other animal hide and stuffed with hair, grass, sand, or some other substance. The ball was either nearly round (sewn with a stitch around the circumference of the ball) or it was bag-shaped (gathered at one end and sewn at the point).

The home team was usually responsible for furnishing the ball, and they occasionally selected one that would be inconvenient for the sticks of the other team. The ball might be so small that it would go through the racket netting of the opposing team, or it might be too large to fit into the cradle of their lacrosse sticks. This, however, has not been reported as a widespread or general practice.

Nature of the Game

Descriptions of lacrosse itself, especially those made prior to 1850, reveal remarkable resemblances among various tribes. Lacrosse was essentially the same game whether it was being played among the Seminoles of Florida, the Mohawks of Ontario, the Seneca of New York, or the Miami of Michigan. The one major difference was that in the southern states two lacrosse sticks (one in each hand) were used whereas in most northern and western areas, only one (larger) stick was used. Otherwise, the pattern of advancing the ball, scoring, and restrictions against use of the hands were very similar.

A typical description of the game of lacrosse played by the Muskogee Indians in Georgia more than 150 years ago was provided by Colonel Willett (1831).

This day I crossed the Toloposa and went five miles to see a most superb ball play. There were about eighty players on a side. The men, women, and children, from the neighboring towns, were assembled upon this occasion. Their appearance was splendid; all the paths leading to the place were filled with people; some on foot, some on horseback. The play was conducted with as much order and decorum as the nature of things would admit of. The play is set on foot by one town sending a challenge to another; if the challenge be accepted, the time and place are fixed upon, and the whole night before the play is employed by the parties in dancing, and some other ceremonious preparations. On the morning of the play, the players on both sides paint and decorate themselves, in the same manner as when they are going to war. Thus decorated, and stripped of all such clothing as would encumber them, they set out for their appointed field. The time of their arrival is so contrived, that the parties arrive near the field at the same time; and when they get within about half a mile, in a direction opposite to each other, you hear the sound of the war song and the yell; when, presently, the parties appear in full trot, as if fiercely about to encounter in fight...each player places himself opposite to his antagonist. The rackets, which they use are then laid against each other, in the center of the ground appointed for the game . . . The play is commenced by the balls being thrown up on the air, from the center; every player then, with his rackets, of which each has two, endeavors to catch the ball, and throw it between the poles; each side laboring to throw it between the poles towards their own towns; and every time this can be accomplished, it counts 1. The game is usually from 12 to 20. This was lost by the challengers. Large bets were made upon these occasions; and great strength, agility, and dexterity are displayed. The whole of the present exhibition was grand and well conducted. It sometimes happens that the inhabitants of a town game away at these plays all their clothes, ornaments, and horses. Throughout the whole of the game the women are constantly on the alert, with bottles and gourds filled with drink, watching every opportunity to supply the players. (p. 108)

Points were scored in lacrosse by carrying or throwing the ball between the goalpost or trees. Sometimes, however, the players had to throw the ball so that it actually hit the post or goal tree. The number of points needed to win the game likewise varied greatly and usually ranged between 12 and 100. It normally took from one-half to a full day to complete a game.

The size of each team varied greatly, but the most important thing was that teams had equal numbers. The participants would line up on the field and be counted before the game to ensure that the teams were equal; any extra team members were not allowed to play. The number of players on each team typically ranged from fifty to several hundred.

The Rugged Character of Lacrosse

Lacrosse has been universally described as a very vigorous, rough, and often a hazardous game. Some writers believe that it makes today's American football look like child's play. Of course, the players did not wear protective clothing, so lacrosse games naturally resulted in many injuries. George Starr's description of a lacrosse game among the Choctaw Indians expressed sentiments that would seem appropriate to a spectator at today's prize fights or a particularly rough ice hockey game (cited in Culin, 1907).

The most exciting point in a close game is when the last goal is neared. Then the play becomes very fast and the rules are not strictly observed. A goal may be made in a few moments or the contest may last for an hour. In wrestling, the players seize each other by the belts, dropping the ball sticks. With the exception of the prohibited butting almost everything is permitted. At the present game five men were crippled, of whom two died. (p. 604)

It should be noted, however, that the occurrence of a death in a contest was unusual even for this rugged game. Also, Adair (1775/1968) wrote concerning the Choctaw Indians in Mississippi in 1775 that ball playing "is their chief and most favorite game; and is such severe exercise, as to shew it was originally calculated for a hardy and expert race of people, like themselves, and the ancient Spartans" (p. 399–400).

More than a half century later, in the 1830s, Catlin (1841/1944) confirmed the rough character of lacrosse among the Choctaw:

In these desperate struggles for the ball, when it is up where hundreds are running together and leaping, actually over each other's heads, and darting between their adversary's legs, tripping and throwing, and foiling each other in every possible manner, and every voice raised to the highest key, in a shrill, yelps, and barks! There are rapid successions of feats, and of incidents that astonish and amuse far beyond the conception of anyone who has not had the singular good luck to witness them. In these struggles, every mode is used that can be devised, to oppose the progress of the foremost, who is likely to get the ball; and these obstructions often meet desperate individual resistance, which terminates in a violent scuffle. . . . There are times when the ball gets to the ground, and such a confused mass rushing together around it, and knocking their sticks together, without the possibility of anyone getting or seeing it, for the dust that they raise that the spectator loses his strength, and everything else but his senses; when the condensed mass of ball sticks, and shins, and bloody noses, is carried around the different parts of the ground, for a quarter of an hour at a time, without anyone of the mass being able to see the ball; and which they are often thus scuffling for, several minutes after it has been thrown off, and played over another part of the ground. (p. 143)

Contrary to several other observers, Catlin (1841/1944) admitted that fist fighting occasionally took place between contesting individuals. When this occurred, no third person was allowed to interfere with the two combatants. Instead, the remainder of the players continued the game, paying no attention to the contestants. The major hazard was that players scuffling on the ground might be trampled if the ball happened to come into their vicinity. Some authors have reported that the officials had a responsibility for breaking up any skirmishes and carried large whips with them to beat the players until they separated. Starr (cited in Culin, 1907) reported that to minimize severe injuries or death, players were required to leave all weapons at the campsite, some distance from the playing field. Confrontations were settled without resorting to deadly weapons.

Despite these reports of violence, however, the preponderance of evidence suggests the good nature of the participants. Rough play was viewed as a regular part of the game and was not a reason for losing one's temper. For example, Carver (1796/1956) reported nearly two centuries ago that

> the Chippewas play with so much vehemence that they frequently wound each other, and sometimes a bone is broken; but notwithstanding these accidents there never appears to be any spite or wanton exertions of strength to affect them, nor do any disputes ever happen between the parties. (p. 237)

Even earlier, Long (1790) had reported that the Chippewa Indians play "with great good humor and even when one of them happens in the heat of the game to strike another with his stick it is not resented" (p. 52). Further, Adair (1775/1968) reported that among the Choctaw "it is a very unusual thing to see them act spitefully in any sort of game, not even in this severe and tempting exercise" (p. 399).

Given the extensive reports of rough play and injuries, one could easily gain the impression that brutality and cruelty were rampant in lacrosse as played by the Indians. This was not the case. Although lacrosse was not for the timid, overwhelming evidence shows that it was played in a climate of friendship and fairness. Although he witnessed games among the Iroquois and conceded that players were occasionally injured, Haines (1888, p. 262) concluded that the games were "conducted with the utmost fairness, during which disputes seldom arise." Beauchamp (1896, p. 273) stated that "with all its occasional rudeness it is less dangerous than baseball or football."

Had lacrosse been a game of cruelty or excessive violence, this fact would surely have been made known by the many missionaries who observed and described the game; however, none has so described it. In "Primitive Indian Lacrosse: Skill or Slaughter?" Jette (1975) concluded that

> the primitive Indian game of lacrosse was far from being the slaughter too often conceived in the history of sports classes. Rather, it was a game of great skill, which demanded a high degree of stamina and endurance, and which was played with passion. It was a noble game, although a vigorous one. (p. 18)

Recent Evolution of Lacrosse

Indians began teaching the game of lacrosse to white settlers during the late 18th and early 19th centuries, particularly among the French colonists in Canada. Before then colonists had been essentially observers. There were early contests between the Indians and the white settlers, most of which were not popular because of the Indian's clear superiority in the game. Indians were frequently reported to have used fewer players in an effort to equalize the competition. The Montreal Canada Club, founded in 1839, established the first standard rules in 1867. The National Lacrosse Association of Canada was also formed in 1867. During the 1870s, lacrosse became firmly established in the non-Indian culture, and the game and equipment were standardized. An Indian team from the Iroquois toured Scotland and England in 1867 and introduced the game in those countries. It has since become popular in other European countries and as far away as Australia.

Lacrosse is now firmly established as a significant sport in the schools and colleges of the United States, particularly in the Middle Atlantic states. The National Collegiate Athletic Association conducts national championships for both men and women. More than 120 colleges and 200 high schools have varsity lacrosse teams for men, and an even larger number have varsity teams for women. It is ironic that a sport viewed almost exclusively as a man's game is now played predominantly by women in many parts of the United States.

Writers in the 18th and 19th centuries consistently referred to the overall excellence of Indian lacrosse, and the tradition of outstanding play in large measure continues today, particularly among the Iroquois Indians of New York state. Their skill is exhibited not only in internal tribal play but also in competition with area colleges, sports clubs, and international teams. (See chapter 14 for a discussion of the revival of lacrosse among the Iroquois, including international competition against countries to whom they introduced the sport more than a century ago.)

Figure 2.6 is a 1904 photograph of an Onondaga team (of the Iroquois Confederacy). Note that the sticks are very similar to, though a bit larger than, the Iroquois sticks of the present, as shown in Figure 2.5.

The soccer shirts worn by the players are probably the result of continued international exchanges with England, which had begun some forty years earlier. Figure 2.7 is a photograph of a 1986 contest in which the Iroquois National Team is competing against the Australian National Team at Buffalo, New York.

How good were the Indian players and teams? In view of today's emphasis upon All-American, Hall of Fame, and other forms of recognition, some readers may regret that no documentation exists to recognize the particularly outstanding Indian players of earlier years. It must be emphasized, however, that traditional Indians tended not to highlight individual exploits but rather placed importance on team or tribal achievements. Moreover, no national press was available to publicize such accomplishments. Nevertheless, several observers reported that in competition against non-Indians, the Indians handicapped themselves by playing one person against two or three opponents.

Figure 2.6. Onondaga lacrosse team of 1904. Photo courtesy of Rick Hill, Iroquois National Lacrosse Team.

Figure 2.7. Iroquois National Team competing against the National Australian Team in July 1986. Photo by Steward/Gazit.

One notable exception to the anonymity of individual achievement was provided by Catlin (1841/1944), who gave lasting recognition to Tullock-chish-ko (He Who Drinks the Juice of the Stone) as "the most distinguished player of the Choctaw nation" (p. 142). Because of his fame, his excellent physique, and colorful costume (breechcloth, beaded belt, a tail made of colorful dyed horsehair, and a mane around the neck) Catlin painted his full-body portrait, including lacrosse sticks. (This painting is shown in Figure 1.6). In modern times numerous Indian lacrosse players have attained significant recognition in this sport through college, club, or community teams. Among these may be included Jay Silverheels (Harry Smith) who was given a screen test while touring through California with an all-star lacrosse team from New York state and later became the character Tonto on "The Lone Ranger" television program.

Shinny

Shinny was not as intensely popular as lacrosse, but it was a game that was "practically universal among tribes throughout the United States" (Culin, 1907, p. 616). Cheska (1982) states that shinny "was the most universally played game in the continent" (p. 21). In different localities it was called by other names such as Gugahawat, Ohonistuts, Kakwassethi, and Oomatashia. Shinny was a very old game, and it had diminished somewhat in popularity by the late 19th century. In fact, some writers of the era referred to it as a game formally played by large groups of Indians. Nevertheless, in traditional Indian life it was extremely popular.

In most tribes shinny was played predominantly by women and children. For women it served much the same role as lacrosse did for men. However, shinny was not quite as exclusive, and in some areas of the continent, both men and women participated in the game either separately or together. Among the Assiniboin Indians in Montana, Denig (cited in Culin, 1907) reported that shinny "is usually played by men 20 to 30 years of age" (p. 636). Meeker (1901) noted the general attractiveness of the game among the Oglala Sioux:

Shinny is played by women, large girls and school boys. The women of one camp will play against the women of another camp. The boys and girls of one school will play against another school; for, although not quite up to the dignity of men, the game is scarcely limited to women. (p. 31)

Walker (1905) found that the Oglala Sioux men played the game of shinny, and he described it as "their roughest and most athletic game" (p.

Figure 2.8. Dakota women preparing to play a game of shinny probably at Miller or Pierre, South Dakota. The photo is believed to have been taken by Harry A. Smith around 1910. Photo used by permission of the National Anthropological Archives, Smithsonian Institution.

283). He also acknowledged that women played the game, although not with or against the men.

In general, shinny was quite similar to modern field hockey. The object of the game was to drive the ball past the opponents and through their goal. The ball was struck with a curved stick very much like a field hockey stick. As in most other Indian ball games, the players were not allowed to touch the ball with their hands.

It was reported by Culin (1907, p. 617) that the Makah Indians along the Pacific Northwest would play shinny in order to celebrate the capture of a whale. Among that group the ball used was made from whale bone. However, in most tribes the elaborate formal ceremony that usually accompanied lacrosse was not used for shinny. Nevertheless, the formality and the numerous spectators depicted in Figure 2.8 supports the concept that this was a most important game.

Equipment

Shinny sticks ranged in length from just over two feet to nearly four feet. However, we know from historical accounts and from surviving shinny sticks on display in museums that the usual length of the sticks was from

Figure 2.9. Shinny stick and ball used at Wyoming Wind River Reservation. Photo used by permission of the University Museum, University of Pennsylvania.

thirty to thirty-six inches. The striking end of the stick was curved and usually widened and flattened—somewhat like a crude and enlarged golf club. Shinny sticks were usually carved and brightly painted with designs and symbols of particular significance to the individual or tribe. Some sticks had thongs, colored quills, or other decorative materials attached to the handle. A typical shinny stick and ball are pictured in Figure 2.9.

The shinny ball varied in size (from as small as a golf ball to somewhat larger than a baseball) and was made of stuffed buckskin, wood, or, occasionally, bone. As in lacrosse, a wood shinny ball was usually obtained from the knot of the tree, which made it very hard and long lasting. Balls constructed of buckskin were typical in the East and in most of the plains, and the wooden and bone balls were most frequent in the far West. The buckskin ball was usually sewn with a medium seam to make it as nearly spherical as possible. The bag shaped ball was used prominently by the Penobscot, Sac, Fox, and a few other tribes. A loop or hook was usually sewn into the buckskin holes so that the ball could be hung up when not in use. Shinny balls made of dry pumpkin or squash have also been reported, but they were probably mainly decorative or ceremonial.

Great pains were taken to make the shinny balls particularly attractive and personal. Sometimes they were decorated with paintings, which might depict animals, faces of people, general scenery, or simply colorful circles. In addition, many groups wove very decorative beads on part of all of the shinny ball. In general, the manner in which the shinny balls were decorated was a matter of considerable importance.

In the late 19th century, Ewing described ball making by the Mohave Indians (cited in Culin, 1907):

> They make a ball with a buckskin cover sewed on it exactly like the cover of our baseballs. Their ball is smaller and neater, their sticks trimmer and nicer, and when they play with the Walapai there is always a row about whether the Mohave ball or the Walapai ball shall be used. The Mohave usually give in, because they know that they can win anyway. (p. 646)

Playing Field

Shinny was played on a field quite similar to that used for lacrosse. It was a rectangular area, typically 200 to 300 yards long and sometimes even larger. Hudson described what may have been the longest shinny field on record, used by the Mono Indians in Modera County, California (cited in Culin, 1907). "A game was played between the Hooker Cove people and the Whiskey Creeks, in which they started at Hooker Cove, and the goal was in a field beside the road at Whiskey Creek, 7½ miles distance" (p. 635).

Goal lines were drawn at each end of a typical shinny field, and on the goal lines two goalposts were driven into the ground ten to twenty feet apart. Points were usually scored by driving the ball between the goalposts, which were sometimes brightly painted. On other occasions simple lines were drawn on the ground or blankets were placed as markers to serve as goalposts.

A recent photograph (Figure 2.10) shows an informal game among the Innu (Montagnais) Indians of northern Quebec. This photograph was

Figure 2.10 Modern-day shinny being played on a frozen lake in northern Quebec. Photo by Serge Jauvin. Used by permission.

taken in 1982 by Serge Jauvin. Note the similarity of the sticks to those shown in Figures 2.8 and 2.9. This game was played on a frozen lake, but no skates were used. The wide range of the players' ages and participation by both males and females reflect the informality of this game.

Game Description

Shinny was strikingly similar to modern field hockey and ice hockey and may have been a forerunner of both of those games. Each side in a shinny match had from 10 to more than 100 players. The game was usually started by placing the ball in a hole in the center of the field; on command, two players would attempt to dig it out with the stick and bat it to one of their teammates. Among some tribes a referee located at the center of the field would throw the ball high into the air and allow the contesting teams to attempt to recover it. The game was organized so that some players defended the goal and others played the middle of the field and were responsible for scoring points by batting the ball toward the opponent's goal. Touching the ball with the hands during play was illegal.

In a report to the governor of the Washington Territory, on the Indians of the Upper Missouri, Mr. Edwin T. Denig described a typical shinny game, along with the preliminary betting, among the Assiniboin in Montana (cited in Culin, 1907).

Each of the players stakes something against an equivalent on the part of one on the opposite side, and every bet which consists of shirts, arrows, shells, feathers, blankets, and almost every article of trade or their manufacture, is tied together separately, and as fast as the bets are taken and tied together they are laid on a pile about the center of the playground, being given in charge of three or four elderly men, who are chose as judges of the sport. After this has been concluded, two posts are set up about three-quarters of a mile apart and the game consists of knocking the ball with sticks toward these posts, they being the outcome or limit for either party in the different directions. They strip naked, except the breechcloths and moccasins, and paint their bodies in every possible variety of manner. Each is furnished with a stick about 3 ½ feet long, turned up at the lower end, and they range themselves in two lines, commencing at the middle of the ground and extending on either side distance. The ball is cast into the air in the center of the course, struck as soon as it falls by someone, and the game begins, each party endeavoring to knock the ball to the post designated as their limit. The game is played three times, and whichever party succeeds in winning two courses out of three is judged conqueror. When the players are well chosen it is often an interesting game, some splendid specimens of foot racing can be seen; but when one of them, either intentionally or by accident, hurts another by a stroke with the play stick, a general shindy takes place. . . . Supposing, however, the game proceeds in its proper spirit and humor, each bet being tied separately, the parcels are handed out to the successful parties by the judges. (pp. 636-637)

It appears that the predominant strategy of play was hitting the ball a long distance in the air, over everyone's head, as opposed to the conservative, ball-control style which is characteristic of many of today's ball games. Some of the players developed a high level of skill in striking the ball. In 1891 Robinson observed a game in California and reported that "they played with a small ball with hard wood which, when hit, would bound with tremendous force without striking the ground for two or three hundred yards" (cited in Culin, 1907, p. 628). Even if the 300-yard claim was an exaggeration, the statement nevertheless suggests that a great deal of skill had been developed in striking the ball.

Although several authors observed shinny being played on snow or ice, they never mentioned the use of ice skates, and there was no indication that the ball was hit along the ice instead of in the air. Nevertheless, the similarity of implements and the descriptions of play suggest that shinny was a forerunner to both ice hockey and the game of field hockey.

Double Ball

Among different tribes the game most commonly called double ball was also referred to as the women's ball game, the maiden's ball play, twin ball, and several other names in different localities. Although played by men in a few northern California tribes, double ball was almost exclusively a women's game throughout the continent. In 1851 Copway (1851/1972) reported that "the most interesting of all games [among the Missisauga] is the Maiden's Ball Play. . . . The majority of those who take part in this play are young damsels, although married women are not excluded" (p. 55).

The game of double ball could be played with as few as six on each side, but teams numbering up to 100 were not unusual. The double ball itself consisted of two balls or sticks attached by a thong or string, and it was advanced toward the opponent's goal by being thrown and caught with a stick. In the literature of the 18th and 19th centuries, many references are made to the double ball game. In mythology, women were able to escape from a variety of dangers by using the double ball. For example, in the Wichita tale "The Seven Brothers and the Woman," cited by Culin (1907, p. 658), the woman was able to escape from the seven men by use of the double ball. She tossed the ball and then followed it up into the air. Culin mentioned five other tales in which women, being pursued by either men or animals, used the double ball as a means of escape or as an implement to aid them in traveling.

Catlin (1841/1944) described the ball play of Indian women along the Mississippi in the 1830s as follows:

> They have two balls attached to the ends of the strings, each about a foot and a half long; and each woman has a short stick in each hand on which she catches the string with the two balls and throws them, endeavoring to force them over the goals of her own party. (p. 165)

According to Catlin, even though the men view this as a rather hilarious event, women are most serious in their pursuit of this game.

Equipment

Catlin's report of the use of two sticks by a player is exceptional. In almost every other case, only one stick is used. The double ball stick was normally three to four feet long although some reports describe sticks as short as two feet and as long as six feet. It was most frequently made of a thin, flexible willow branch, and it was normally curved on one end, enabling the player to control the ball with some degree of accuracy (see Figure 2.11). The stick for beginners very often had a little notch near the end to make it easier to control the ball. Like most other implements involved in Indian sports play, double ball sticks were often brightly decorated with carvings, paintings, and various symbols. In some cases these markings were burned into the wood.

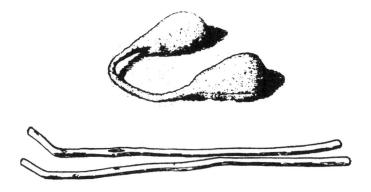

Figure 2.11. Double ball sticks with notch for easier control. Used by the Cree Indians, Wind River Reservation, Wyoming. Photo used by permission of Smithsonian Institution Press from *Twenty-fourth Annual Report of the Bureau of American Ethnology, 1902-1903*. Smithsonian Institution, Washington, DC, 1907.

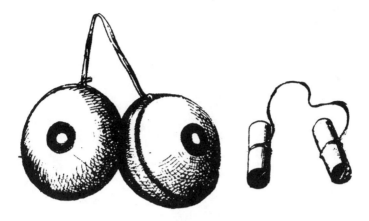

Figure 2.12. Double balls used by the Cheyenne (left) and Chippewa (right). The diameter of the balls is three inches and the billets (on right) are approximately four inches long. Photo used by permission of Smithsonian Institution Press from *Twenty-fourth Annnual Report of the Bureau of American Ethnology, 1902–1903*. Smithsonian Institution, Washington, DC, 1907.

The ball used in the double ball game was peculiar. It was constructed to be caught on one end of the stick with the two balls falling on different sides of the stick. Although the balls varied greatly in shape and construction, two basic types of buckskin balls were used. One type consisted of two separate balls made of buckskin and attached by a thong or heavy string. The second version was a buckskin ball shaped like a dumbbell: a single piece of leather enlarged and heavy at each end and thin in the center. These weighted ends were filled with sand, hair, or some other substance.

Another type of double ball was made of two billets (or sticks of wood) fastened together by heavy string. These billets were typically six to ten inches long and one to three inches in diameter, and they were fastened together by cords around six inches to one foot in length. Samples of double balls are shown in Figure 2.12. Regardless of the construction, double balls were frequently painted in bright colors and were often decorated with glass beads.

The Playing Field

Field dimensions for double ball were not standardized to any great extent. Most playing areas were described as 300 to 400 yards long, although some, particularly among the Cree, were a mile or more in length. Poles, trees, and even piles of dirt were used as goal markers on the end of the playing field. These markers, usually twelve to fifteen feet apart, served as the *goal*, *home*, or *base*, as it was variously called.

Game Description

Despite the fact that double ball was played almost exclusively by women, it was nevertheless a very vigorous activity. In a report to Culin (1907) of a double ball game among the Cree Indians, Mitchell described the game as

> played by women only, any number, but not by the old women, as great powers of endurance are required. It is in many respects similar to lacrosse. The players are given various stations in the field and carry sticks. The goals are usually 1 mile or thereabout apart. . . .The game is a very interesting one and develops much skill. It is, from a hygienic point of view, highly beneficial, as it develops a fine, robust class of women. As with all other Indian games, this game is invariably played for stakes of some kind. (p. 652)

Double ball play by women was not without social interest among the young girls and men. In describing the game and related activities among the Missisauga in Ontario, Copway (1851/1972) reported that

> young women of the village decorate themselves for the day by painting their cheeks with vermillion and disrobe themselves of as much unnecessary clothing as possible, braiding their hair with colored feathers, which hang profusely down to the feet.

> At the same time the whole village assemble, and the young men, whose loved ones are seen in the crowd, twist and turn to send shy glances to them, and receive their bright smiles in return.

> The same confusion exists as the game of ball played by men. Crowds rush at a given point as the ball is sent flying through the air. None stop to narrate the accidents that befall them, though they tumble about to their not little discomfiture, they rise, making a loud noise between a laugh and a cry, some limping behind the others. (p. 55)

Accounts of double ball play make it clear that women, like men, took sport participation seriously. They played with a high level of enthusiasm and physical abandon.

Other Ball Games

Many other ball games have been described by various travelers and writers. Most of these games, however, were either limited to a few tribes or were so vaguely described that the general procedure of the game is hard to determine. Several of these games are described in the following sections.

Ancient Court Ball Game (Pok-Ta-Pok)

One of the more prominent ball games throughout the southwestern United States, Mexico, and Central America was the court ball game. It was especially prevalent in the Mayan civilization located in the Yucatan Peninsula (where it was called Pok-Ta-Pok) and among the Aztecs (where it was known as Tlachtli). It was certainly not a casual or unimportant game. In fact, Pok-Ta-Pok was so ritualistic in style and significance that it could hardly be considered a game as the term is used today. Nevertheless, a ball was used, and contesting sides played to determine a winner.

Goellner (1953) concluded that Pok-Ta-Pok was first developed by the Maya Indians in and around the Yucatan peninsula. There is evidence that the game was widely played among the Maya as early as A.D. 700. The existence of ancient ball courts indicates that the game spread throughout Mexico, into several Central American countries, and to the southwestern part of the United States. There are indications that the game had begun to decline by the time the white man arrived on this continent. According to Goellner, the game was banned by the Spanish soon after their conquest of Central America, apparently at the insistence of the clergy who wished to discourage religious ceremonies surrounding the games. Consequently, very limited descriptions of the game in its traditional form are available.

According to Guttmann (1978), the court games were played primarily by the Mayans and Aztecs, but various other Indian groups played as well, from Arizona through Mexico, to Guatemala and Honduras. He reports that this has been the most intensively studied and thoroughly documented of all religious sports. More than forty ball courts, all within a temple complex, have been discovered. Guttmann concluded that in their original form the games were played for life or death. Apparently the games involved human sacrifices, but it is not certain whether the losers or winners were sacrificed.

The ball games were played on an elaborate and formal court that varied little in size from one place to the next. The playing areas were usually around 100 feet by 50 feet, only slightly larger than today's basketball court. Goellner (1953) described the "largest and best preserved of these courts" (p. 153), which is in Yucatan, as measuring 274 feet long and 120 feet wide. The playing surface was enclosed within parallel stone walls that formed an *I* shape if viewed from above. Religious temples were usually a part of the court structure. Figure 2.13 shows a restored ball court, with temple, at Chichén Itzá on the Yucatán Peninsula of Mexico.

Ball courts usually provided bleacher arrangements for large numbers of spectators. A special feature of these facilities was the existence of two stone rings at midcourt, one on each side of the court, elevated fifteen feet or more. These rings, which served as goals through which the ball was aimed, had center holes measuring one to two feet in diameter. Hard rubber balls, sometimes dimpled like golf balls, were used in this game.

Figure 2.13. Restored ball court temple. Chichén Itzá, Yucatán, Mexico. Photo used by permission of the University Museum, University of Pennsylvania.

The court ball game included some features of modern soccer and basketball. Teams were usually composed of five players. The game was started when an elder threw the ball into the air at midcourt. As soon as the ball touched the ground, the game began. Players were not allowed to use their hands or feet but were permitted to propel the ball toward the ring with the knees, thighs, buttocks, elbows, or other body parts. The rubber balls were so hard that they caused injury to any unprotected body part, and deerskin or other protective material may have been used to protect the players. In the game, points were sometimes scored by keeping the ball moving in the air, similar to the kicking drill used in soccer practice. According to some reports, the game was automatically won when one team knocked the ball through the elevated ring. When the rings were set lower and goals were more easily scored, several goals were required to determine a winner.

As with other games, betting ceremonies preceded the commencement of the court ball game. However, in this game religious ceremony and ritual were more significant than in any other games played in the region.

Football

Indian football has been reported among more than a dozen tribes in the eastern part of the United States and in the eastern province of Canada, and it was similar to the modern game of soccer. Early writers contrasted

Figure 2.14. Alaskan football, Norton Sound, 1905. Photo used by permission of the University Museum, University of Pennsylvania.

it to English football (soccer). The ball was normally constructed of buckskin two to four inches in diameter. However, a somewhat larger, well-decorated ball used by the Eskimo is shown in Figure 2.14. This ball was collected by G.B. Gordon in the Norton Sound of Alaska in 1905.

Figure 2.15 shows a Papago football player in 1894. In this game the ball was kicked from one team member to another in an effort to put it through the opponent's goal, which was usually two crossed poles.

The origin of the game of football among the Indians is uncertain. However, as early as 1634, William Wood (1634) described football among the Indians in Massachusetts. The caliber of play did not greatly impress Wood; he said that the Massachusetts Indians have "no cunning at all in that kind, one English being able to beat ten Indians at football" (p. 73). In the same era Roger Williams (1643) reported that the Narraganset in Rhode Island "have great meetings of foot-ball playing, only in summer, town against town, upon some broad sandy shore . . . but seldom quarrel" (p. 73). In 1792 William Bartram (cited in Dewey, 1930) reported on his travels among the Cherokee and Choctaw in the Southern United States and found that "the football is likewise a favorite, manly diversion with them. Feasting and dancing in the square at evenings, aids in their games" (p. 740).

Football play among the different tribes was so diverse that generalizations are impossible. Whereas most eastern groups played a game resembling soccer, Indians in other parts of the continent played games

Figure 2.15. Papago Indian holding wooden football, with legs painted for a game. Photo in 1894 by William Dinwiddie at the San Xavier Reservation, Arizona. Photo used by permission of the National Anthropological Archives, Smithsonian Institution.

similar to American football. In a report to Culin (1907) in the late 19th century, Hudson reported on a game among the Nishinam Indians in California in which the ball was twelve inches in diameter and "rough play was the rule, as a player is allowed to run with the ball in his hands, and interference is permissible" (p. 703).

Hand-and-Football

The game of hand-and-football was played almost exclusively by women and only in northern regions. Among some tribes it was referred to as women's football. The idea was to control the ball and to keep it in the air by using the feet and, under certain conditions, the hands. It somewhat resembled the soccer drill in which the ball is kept in the air by use of the feet, knees, and head. However, in hand-and-football the palms of the hand were sometimes used to strike the ball downward to the foot, which was then used to return it to the air. The game was normally played by two or four people; the person with the fewest misses was the winner. The ball was six to eight inches in diameter, was normally covered with buckskin, and often had a thong attached.

Meeker (1901) described the hand-and-football game among the Winnebago Indians as follows:

> They take a light soft ball, such as a stuffed stocking foot, place it on the toe, and standing on one foot, kick it up a few inches. Then as it falls they kick it back again, so as to send it up as often as possible without letting it fall to the ground, keeping count of the number of times. When it falls to the ground or when the foot is placed on the ground the ball is passed to another player. The first to count 100, or any number agreed upon, wins. (p. 43)

Nelson (1899) described a different style of "women's football" among the Eskimos. In that game four players stood opposite each other and alternately passed the ball back and forth across the square.

> The ball is thrown upon the ground midway between the players, so that it shall bound toward the opposite one. She strikes the ball down and back toward her partners with the palm of her open hand. Sometimes the ball is caught on the toe or hand and tossed up and struck or kicked back toward the other side. The person who misses least or has fewer "dead" balls on her side wins. (p. 366)

Tossed Ball

Culin (1907, p. 708) classified a variety of ball games as "tossed ball" because throwing and catching were involved. These games were played mainly by young persons and varied from formal games with precise rules to simple throw-and-catch games for amusement. George Cartwright (1792) observed that the Indians in Labrador were "very bad catchers" but they did enjoy "tossing the ball at pleasure from one to another, each striving who should get it" (p. 237). Usually a six- to eight-inch ball of soft construction was used.

Some of the tossed ball games seem similar to today's keep-away games in which teammates throw and catch the ball while opponents try to intercept. Some tribes played a game that resembles present-day dodge ball, and other games are reported in which the ball is kept in the air constantly by throwing or striking it with the hands.

It should be noted that games in which the hands were allowed to touch the ball were rare among Indians, and this is presumably why they could be described by Cartwright (1792) as "very bad catchers."

Fireball

The game of fireball was observed in July 1986 on the Tuscaroro Indian Reservation near Niagara Falls, New York. The game was described by local elders as traditional, having been played as far back as anyone could remember. Further, it has been played frequently on other reservations throughout the Iroquois confederacy.

This game is appropriately named because the playing implement is a ball of fire, that is, burning material that takes approximately twenty minutes to be completely consumed. Although it is roughly the same as soccer, fireball is a nighttime game played in total darkness except for small torches to mark the perimeters of the goals, and the ball itself is burning.

Prior to the game the ball was prepared by wrapping it in an extensive amount of cloth, tying it with cords, and binding it with soft, wire mesh to hold it together. After all of this wrapping, the ball, which was approximately the size of a soccer ball, was placed in flammable fluid until thoroughly soaked.

After the goal markers had been lighted, the players were taken to the center of the field where the ball was set aflame, and the game commenced. The fiery ball was advanced by kicking, in the same manner as in soccer, and players were permitted to bat the ball or throw it without penalty. However, the burning ball itself tended to discourage extensive use of this privilege. Most players wore shoes during the game, and the goalkeepers were allowed to wear gloves. Each time the ball was kicked, it would blaze even brighter with the stimulation of additional oxygen to the burning material. The game lasted approximately twenty minutes before the ball was totally consumed, and the team leading at that time was declared the winner. Though less serious than some other ball games, fireball appeared to be a favorite for both players and spectators.

Summary

Ball games among traditional American Indians created a level of enthusiasm that was not prevalent in individual sports. Kinship ties within the team and among team and community members ensured that these games would be major community enterprises. The team itself, often reaching 100 or more, comprised a large proportion of the young men or women in the community. The enjoyment of playing was supplemented by concurrent festivities, wagers placed on the outcome of the game, colorful displays of decorated bodies and playing implements, and the cultural connection including the purpose for which it was being played.

Ball games came in many forms and varieties for both men and women. Lacrosse was the most widely played; it was closely followed by shinny and double ball. Many other ball games were played, but none reached the universal popularity of these games. Traditional ball games were observed and described from the early 16th century into the 20th century and in all parts of North and Central America. Perhaps the least understood is the ancient court ball game (or Pok-Ta-Pok), which was also the most sacred of all known ball games. This game was played for at least 1,000 years in Central America, Mexico and the southwestern United States before being curtailed by the Spanish invaders soon after their arrival in that region.

Ball games served as a sporting, spiritual, economic, and overall cohesive force in traditional life. More than any other activity, these games reflected the positive and holistic character of the Indian population.

Chapter 3
Footracing

Footraces have been among the most universal and popular of all Indian sports. From the times of the earliest contact with outsiders, Indians have continually astonished observers with extraordinary running feats, especially in long-distance performances, and this long-standing tradition of running excellence still serves as a source of motivation and pride to Indian youth.

In traditional times running activities ranged from the informal play of children to the highly organized and ceremonial races of adults, often involving whole communities. Tribes throughout the continent placed great importance on running for both enjoyment and utilitarian values. Indian groups located in the southwest and in Mexico especially emphasized long-distance races of twenty-five miles or more. Not surprisingly, extraordinary running exploits are legendary among Indians. Oral tradition and written accounts from the 18th and 19th centuries provide evidence for many of these feats.

Running was important among Indians for several reasons quite unrelated to sports. War, trade, pursuit of game animals, delivery of messages, and a multitude of social concerns demanded that Indians travel great distances on foot under considerable time pressure. Blasiz (1933-1934) reported that the Indians in Peru had well-organized cross-country relay teams to deliver fresh seafood to the capital at Inka. Obviously, they did not have modern means of transportation, and apparently did not have horses prior to the arrival of the white man on this continent.[1]

William Myers (1928) reported that Indians "had covered the entire continent with a network of trails, over which they ran long distances with phenomenal speed and endurance" (p. 735). For example, he stated that "the Tarahumare mail carrier from Chilhouhua to Batopilas, Mexico, runs regularly more than 500 miles a week; a Hopi messenger has been known to run 120 miles in 15 hours" (p. 735). Based on reports such as these, Indian distance running certainly must rank among the most phenomenal performance feats ever recorded.

A Running Tradition

With the possible exception of lacrosse, running, especially long-distance running, has been the sport most closely identified with the American Indian. Strong interest and a high level of skill were characteristic of Indian runners in pre-Columbian times. These traits persisted through more recent centuries and continue today. The popularity of distance running has been universal among all Indian groups, especially so among those in the southwestern United States and in Mexico.

Some evidence of the general practice of running is provided by Catlin (1841/1944). He described the excellent musculature of the legs of the Indian youth in the 1830s and stated that "he who would get a perfect study for a Hercules or an Atlas, should take a stone mason for the upper part of his figure and a Comanche or a Blackfeet Indian from the waist downwards to the feet" (p. 140).

Indians of the Southwest were perhaps the most famous of all runners. The Hopi and the Zuni were recognized by numerous writers as outstanding distance runners. Stevenson (1904) reported that she "has never known the Zunis to lose a footrace with other Indians or with the champion runners of the troops at Fort Wingate, who sometimes enter into races with them" (p. 328). She emphasized that young Zuni boys began training at an early age and developed into excellent runners. Some of the most astonishing reports of long-distance running for sport and for

---

[1]Though it is generally assumed that there were no horses in this hemisphere prior to the arrival of the Spanish in Central America, there are some doubters. In a 1983 visit to the Mayan ruins in Tulun, Mexico, I was told by a Mayan guide that there were indeed horses in that area prior to the arrival of the white man. This guide pointed out two wall drawings dating back to around the 13th century that depicted reasonable likenesses of horses, one with a rider and one without. This guide believed that the Spanish systematically destroyed evidences of the Mayan Civilization, including the existence of horses, and had rewritten history following the conquest.

more utilitarian purposes came out of the Southwest and Mexico. However, ample evidence of running prominence is also available from other regions. For example, Edwin Denig reported concerning the Crows in North Dakota that "the name of being a fast and long runner is highly prized among them all; indeed after that of being a hunter and warrior that of being a good runner is next to be desired" (cited in Culin, 1907, p. 807). The Senecas of New York had runners who represented each clan and provided a major contribution to any festival or entertainment. Baldwin (1969) reported that Arapahoe Indian boys ran races nearly every morning as part of their physical training.

The widespread acclaim received by outstanding runners is suggested by Hayden (1862). He reported that "those who have shown great fleetness and powers of endurance [among the Mandan Indians] received additional reward in the form of praise by the public crier, who harangues their names through the village for many days afterwards" (p. 430). In earlier times of large population, men of the Thompson Indians in British Columbia were in constant training for running, and there were "some excellent long and short distance runners among them" (Teit, 1900, p. 280). He particularly cited two men of the Spence Bridge band who were legendary in their running exploits; one of them raced against horses and against canoes being paddled downstream.

Runners, particularly those in the Southwest, painted their bodies prior to races for identification and for artistic and spiritual purposes. This practice was almost universal during earlier times and continued to be widely

Figure 3.1. Zuni runners, painted and prepared for a ball race in 1890. Note the sticks atop the right foot of the first and third racer (from left to right). Photo by Ben Wittick, courtesy School of American Research Collections in the Museum of New Mexico (Negative No. 16234).

Figure 3.2. Group of Taos Pueblo racers who have just completed a relay run during the San Geronimo Day Festival at Taos, New Mexico in 1906. Photo by M.C. Stevenson. Photo used by permission of the National Anthropological Archives, Smithsonian Institution.

used during the early part of the 20th century. In ball races among the Zuni, Stevenson (1903) reported that "the clan symbol is painted on the breast of each runner, and that of the paternal clan is painted on the back" (p. 691). Figures 3.1 and 3.2 reveal painted runners in 1890 and 1906 respectively.

Artistic expression and identification are achieved in popular sports today by the color and design of playing jerseys and by including the team name and the player's name and number.

Some Outstanding Running Feats

Most Indians concentrated on and excelled in distance running rather than short races. For example, Adair (1775/1968) reported that he and other non-Indians could compete favorably with the Indians in short races. In long races, however, he stated that "without any seeming toil, they would stretch on, leave us out of sight, and out-wind any horse" (p. 318). He also recounted the story of a devious French peddler. After being caught cheating by the Choctaw Indians, the Frenchman was able to saddle "a fine strong sprightly horse, and long winded, like wolves"; neverthe-less, Red Shoes, the Choctaw Chief, "ran him down in about the space of fifteen miles, and had scalped the unfortunate rider some time before the rest appeared" (p. 318).

Reports from the late 19th century routinely refer to Indians who ran 100 miles or more in a single day. One such runner was described in some detail by W.J. Hoffman (1896):

A Mohavi courier, well known to the writer, has been known to make the journey between Camp Mohavi and a temporary camp 90 miles southward between sunrise and sunset. He would eat but little during the day preceding the journey, and on the morning of his departure, shortly before the summer's early sunrise, would tuck the dispatches or letters in his huge coil of hair, and being clad only in breechcloth and moccasins, was unimpeded in his progress. The trail lay along the hard, sandy banks of the river terrace, and as the temperature rose during the day he would go down into the water to wet his body and then resume his steady, easy, jogging gait, with both arms brought up beside the chest, the fists being clenched and held almost in front of the breastbone. (p. 246)

Hoffman also reported that Apache renegades in the mountainous Arizona territory frequently got off their horses and took to the trails for greater distance and speed in attempting to escape army troops.

Authors of the 19th century who traveled among the western Indians frequently referred to their great running accomplishments, particularly in the ball race. In the ball race, also called the stick kick race, the runner was required to continually kick a ball or other object in front of him. Lumholtz (1895) wrote that "Filipe, who is now dead, could run from mid-day to sunrise. He was from Marrarachic, and was the greatest runner known in the northeastern part of Tarahumare" (p. 311). In describing ball races among the Zuni in New Mexico, Owens (1891) indicated that spectators frequently accompanied the runners on horseback. He reported that the runners ran with such endurance and speed that "it is not un-usual to see a pony drop over dead from exhaustion as they near the village" (p. 42).

Despite the fact that the precision of measurements was perhaps not what we have today, the running feats reported during the 19th century are nonetheless impressive. For example, Hoffman (1896) stated that

it is well known that the Tarahumare Indians of Mexico are so named from their custom of racing while driving before them a wooden ball by means of the feet alone. It is said that frequently 70 or 80 miles are thus covered in a single race. (p. 247)

Hoffman was describing the ball race, which is discussed later in this chapter. Blasiz (1933-1934) reported that among the Tarahumare "endurance races of various lengths were promoted, some of which reached a distance of 145 miles" (p. 218).

According to Bennett and Zingg (1935), the name Tarahumare may be translated as "footrunners" (p. 3). The most important of all games of this group is the kick-ball race, which often lasted for two days and a night. When night races were run, the course was lighted with torches. It was the dream of every Tarahumare boy to be a great runner. Although training began soon after birth, it was said that practice in running was not necessary because they were always racing.

One indication of the excellence of Indian running is that they were very casual about performances that would be considered extraordinary, even today, among non-Indians. Consider Ernest Thompson Seton's observation in "Gospel of the Red Man" (1979):

> In 1882 at Ft. Ellice, I saw a Cree, who on foot, had just brought dispatches from Ft. Qu'Appelle (125 miles away) in 25 hours. I heard very little from the traders but cool remarks like "A good run" and "Pretty good run." It was obviously a very usual exploit, among Indians. . . . The Arizona Indians are known to run down deer by sheer endurance, and every student of Southwest history will remember that Coronado's mounted men were unable to overtake the natives when in the hill country, such was their speed and activity on foot. (p. 24)

The times recorded for completing ball races were indeed astonishing in view of the fact that runners had to slow down somewhat to kick the ball periodically. Lumholtz (cited in Culin, 1907) stated that he observed a twenty-one-mile race in 1892 and that the time required was 2 hours and 21 seconds. This speed was faster than that required to win prominent marathon races many years later. In the first Boston marathon (26 miles, 285 yards), which was run in 1897, the winner's time was 2 hours and 55 minutes, a pace considerably slower than that reported by Lumholtz.

An even more impressive performance was recorded by Owens (1891) and Hodge (1890), reporting independently on a ball race among the Zuni. Owens wrote that "the distance traversed is nearly twenty-five miles and they pass over it in about two hours" (p. 42). Hodge observed the same ball race and also reported that the course was 25 miles long. He further stated that "curiosity prompted me to note the time occupied in performing this feat, which was found to be exactly two hours" (p. 227). If the distance and time were accurately reported by these two writers, this performance would remain a world record even today.

However, not all outstanding running accomplishments were in endurance events; many Indians exhibited excellent sprinting speed. Hoffman (1896) described an incident that occurred at the White Earth agency in Minnesota: "One of the champion Ojibwa runners walked 23 miles after dinner, and the next morning ran 100 yards in ten and one quarter seconds, easily beating his professional opponents" (p. 246). The time recorded for that race was comparable to the official world record of twenty years later.

During the 1860s the world's best runner was Louis "Deerfoot" Bennett, a Seneca Indian from the Cattaraugus reservation in New York. As a professional runner in this country and in England during the 1850s and early 1860s, he won almost all of his races, from four miles to more than twelve miles. He established a distance standard in a one-hour run of 11 miles and 970 yards. This standard, which was established in 1863, stood until 1897 when it was broken by an Englishman. According to Lucas (1983), who described approximately two dozen of Bennett's races, "For a brief glory-filled period of three years he stood alone as the world's greatest long-distance foot racer" (p. 13). (The career of Bennett is discussed more fully in chapter 11.)

Running Societies

According to Nabokov (1981), pre-Columbian running societies were developed throughout the Americas for the purpose of promoting communication and trade. He reported that the most sophisticated of these organizations was the Chasqui, which means "to exchange" among the Inca Indians (p. 20).

The Chasqui was founded in the mid-15th century and developed a road system extending more than 2,500 miles from northern Equador to southern Chile. This system consisted of a road network through the mountains and along the western coast of South America, and the Spanish found that the Chasqui running system of communication was far superior to the horse-mail system. Nabokov also refers to earlier systems of runners and road networks through much of Central and South America. Despite a general air of secrecy surrounding the running societies, or Courier Corps, Nabokov has identified other organized groups across the North American continent including the Chemehueu in California, the Masquakie in Iowa, and the Iroquois Confederacy in New York state.

Early in the 20th century, Michelson (1927) provided an account of the ceremonial runners of the Mesquakie in Iowa. According to Michelson, these messengers lived the life of monks, vowing celibacy, adhering to strict dietary regulations, and dedicating their lives to this role. He gave a detailed account of the last ceremonial runner's investiture into the brotherhood. Michelson's report included references to similar running systems among the Sauk, Kickapoo, Nensminee, Creek, Omaha, Kansa, and Osage.

Spanish writers were impressed by the running feats of the Aztecs of Mexico. According to Nabokov (1981) Cortez reported that within twenty-four hours of his landing in Chianiztlan in May, 1519, runners had described his ship, men, horses, and guns to Montezuma, 260 miles away. Nabokov quoted William Prescott as reporting that the Aztec runners were trained from childhood and were able to run "one to two hundred miles a day" (p. 19).

Role of Indian Couriers During the Revolt of 1680

A dramatic recitation of the use of couriers in a matter of crucial importance was provided by Nabokov (1981) in *Indian Running*. He described the 1980 reenactment of a 1680 run through Indian territory extending from Taos, New Mexico, to Hopi territory at Second Mesa, Arizona, a distance of 375 miles. The early (1680) courier mission triggered the most successful Indian revolt in American history.

According to Nabokov, the 1680 revolt stemmed from the Spanish conquest and persecution of Indians, which had gone on for nearly a century. This persecution was concentrated on the destruction of the Indian religion and included the public flogging of religious leaders and the burning of sacred Kachina masks. Po pay (meaning "ripe squash") and other Indian leaders, many of whom had been flogged, gathered with a group of couriers at Taos and outlined plans for the revolt against the Spanish. Deerskins with pictographs were presented to the runners who were to go and present the plan to all Pueblo and Hopi throughout the nearly 400-square-mile territory.

Later, as the date drew near, the runners were again brought together to deliver the specific date for the uprising. The timing was based on a traditional countdown system making use of Yucca fibercords that were tied into knots. One cord was to be untied each day until the cords were all clear, which would signal the day they were to destroy the Spanish temples and rid themselves of the invaders. Runners delivered a set of identical cord arrangements to all villages.

Unfortunately, the information leaked out to the Spanish prior to the prearranged date. Therefore, a last-minute plan was established to advance the date of the revolt. The runners were sent on a third, and somewhat more desperate, mission to inform villagers of the need to attack earlier. The success of the revolt obviously depended upon the ability of the runners to get to the villagers quickly while evading the Spanish.

Although the success of the revolt is not well documented, Nabokov (1981) stated that

> the charred shells of Catholic churches were enough, the twenty-one dead priests, the ashes of church documents, and the 380 Spaniards and Mexican Indians also killed. . . . Over the next dozen years no Spaniards were to be found in this land. (p. 13)

The area was later reconquered by the Spanish, but according to Nabokov, "Spanish control of the Indians was crippled forever. The church and the Kiva have coexisted to this day. The revolt remains a victory" (p. 13).

Running for Profit

Louis "Deerfoot" Bennett and a handful of other professional runners during the 19th century ran foot races for prize money. This was unusual, however, because traditionally Indians did not run for pay, although betting was as much a part of races as it was with other sport events. However, non-Indians were so impressed with the long distance running abilities of the Indians that they not only hired them for long distance deliveries but paid them or offered prizes for sponsored races. Nabokov (1981) quotes a 1903 report by George James. He stated that he had

> several times engaged a young man to take a message from Oraibi to Keam's Canyon, a distance of seventy-two miles, and he has run on foot the entire distance, delivered his message, and brought me an answer within thirty-six hours. (p. 21)

Nabokov reported that John Bourke paid a Mohave Indian $2 to run a twenty-one-mile errand through heavy sand, a task that was completed in three and a half hours. Bourke also related that another Mohave took less than twenty-four hours to run the 200 miles from Fort Mohave to the Reservation and back. This astounding feat is roughly equivalent to running eight consecutive marathons, non-stop, at a three-hour pace!

It is likely that persons in running societies received regular remuneration for their services. For many this was their primary role in the tribe. Nabokov (1981) cites one early Spaniard, Loma de Ayala, who argued that the services of runners were so great that they should be paid the same salary as town mayors.

As recently as 1979, Bernard Fontana (1979, May) staged a traditional style race among some Tarahumare girls in the Sierra area. Two girls from a Mexican settlement were matched against two girls from a remote rural area. Each girl carried a three-foot long stick with two hoops, in a fashion consistent with their traditional races. This race was staged to be photographed and to observe the tradition, which was true with many of the sponsored races of the late 19th and early 20th centuries.

Running Folklore

In the oral history of most tribes, folklore surrounding running activities proved valuable both for general interest and for instruction. Before man's existence, according to these legends, the gods and animals had settled many questions by racing. Mythical races had, in effect, shaped the world much as we know it. Such races were used to explain the character and behavior differences between people and animals and the distinctions within the animal kingdom. They also provided an explanation for the arrangement of constellations and for earthly topology.

Fables were also used for the purpose of developing appropriate character traits among young people. Variations of the "Tortoise and the Hare" story were used in several tribes to encourage children to persevere and to keep their attention on the task at hand. Such stories emphasized that success in races is as much a matter of the mind as of the body. The intention was that these lessons of mental control, or discipline, be carried over to other behaviors in life.

Reports of gamesmanship and trickery in foot racing are widespread in Indian folklore. There were many pretenses of injury or sickness before and during the race. For example, Culin (1907) cited a report by Denig on racing behavior among the Crows in the upper Missouri. Denig noted that some performers initiated several false starts before the race actually began. He reported that such trickery was prevalent in both foot races and horse racing among Indians. This practice of false starts is occasionally used by modern sprinters in an effort to distract opponents.

An illustration of faking injury is provided in the popular "tricksters race" legend among the Blackfeet Indians. In this story, cited by Thompson (1941), Old Man challenges Coyote to a foot race. On the day of the scheduled race, Coyote appears with one leg tied up and begs to be excused from the race, indicating that he is crippled and cannot run. Old Man insists on going through with the race as planned, and Coyote finally agrees to a short race. Old Man demands that the longer race be held, and Coyote reluctantly agrees. After the race begins, Coyote continues to plead with Old Man to wait for him because of the great pain in his leg. However, as they arrive at the half-way point, Coyote suddenly takes off all bandages and runs the remaining distance without encumbrances or injury, leaving Old Man far behind. With stories such as this, young people were encouraged to guard against being distracted or deceived by their opponents.

Children's Running Games

Excellence in running was a prestigious quality in the lives and legends of most tribes. Indian folklore is filled with episodes of superhuman running feats. Not surprisingly, children placed high priority on developing and exhibiting their running speed and endurance.

Indian children were free of most limitations on movement that often inhibit the 20th century child. Play pens, high chairs, cribs, and other such restrictions were not as prevalent in traditional Indian life. Even though the Hopi women transported infants in a restrictive apparatus on their backs, such constraints were normally used only for travel. Outdoor activity was not restricted by automobile-congested streets, fences, and block-long buildings as it is in today's urban society. Only the natural terrain limited movement. Consequently, running games abounded among Indian children, including many games of follow-the-leader, crack-the-whip, tag, and formal running and jumping events.

Among the many Indians games described by MacFarlan (1958), one was called the *Kiwi trail*, or twisted trail, race in which children ran to a designated point and returned but enroute had to swing around several trees both going and coming. This tended to make the participants dizzy, and the activity became hazardous as the children tried to avoid running into trees while moving rapidly through the woods. It also provided entertainment for spectators. Another game was called *fish* and involved several children joining hands to form a net into which they attempted to capture a child (fish) as he or she ran around the designated play area. In addition, there were many *it* games similar to those played by children today. In another popular children's running game (mentioned in chapter 1), boys stood in two ranks on either side of the finish line, which was equal distance between them. At the starting signal, they would run toward each other to see who could cross the line first. The judges stood at the finish line to determine which boy arrived (from opposite directions) first. The boys ran straight toward each other, and it was a test of courage to see which one would veer to the side before crossing the finish line.

Formal Races

Formal races were viewed as most important and elicited careful mental and physical preparation by the participants. Throughout most of the continent, major footraces were surpassed only by lacrosse as a sporting event of community interest and involvement, and in the southwestern United States and in Mexico, races were more important even than ball games.

Hoffman (1896) reported an ingenious and scientific means of preparing for races. Ojibway runners tied bags weighted with shot around their ankles and wore them for several weeks, which was done to strengthen the muscles of the legs. At the time of the race, when the weight was removed, the wearer was not only stronger but felt especially light-footed. Nabokov (1981) reported that the same technique was used by the Chippewa.

Tribes used various techniques for starting short races that prevented an unfair advantage to any participant. A popular method of the Mohave Indians was described by Hoffman (1896). After the racing area has been agreed upon, a line is scratched on the ground to mark the starting point. Two runners then go to a point well behind the line and hold between them a stick approximately one foot in length.

> In starting, both racers step off briskly, at once beginning a gentle trot which increases in speed as they approach the scratch, though both endeavor to keep abreast and glance at the stick held by the two. When the true starting point is reached, the stick is dropped and both start forward, endeavoring to impede the progress of the other by every conceivable trick. (p. 246)

A more familiar method of starting the race is presented in the 1910 photograph shown in Figure 3.3. Four Crow Indians are ready to begin a race at the Crow agency in Montana. Figure 3.4 shows Hopi runners lined up for a three-mile race. It can be noted in each of these photographs that distance races were not restricted to boys and young men.

Several writers during the 19th century described formal races and the related ceremonies throughout the continent. In a report cited by Culin (1907), Frank Russell indicated that among the Pimas in Arizona,

> when a village wished to race with a neighboring one, they sent a messenger to convey the information that in four or five days, according to the decision of their council, they wished to test their fortunes

Figure 3.3. Four Crow Indians lined up to begin a race in 1910. Photograph by Richard Throssel. Photo used by permission of the National Anthropological Archives, Smithsonian Institution.

Figure 3.4. Eighteen Hopi runners line up for a three-mile race. Photo taken in 1902 by J.H. Bratley. Photo used by permission of the National Anthropological Archives, Smithsonian Institution.

in a relay race. . . . Both had the same time to practice, and the time was short. In this preparation the young men ran in groups of four or five. There were forty or fifty runners in each village, and he who proved the swiftest was recognized as the leader who should run first in the final contest. It was not necessary that each village should enter the same number of men in the race; a man might run any number of times that his endurance permitted. When the final race began each village stationed half its runners at each side of the track, then a crier called three times for the leaders, and as the last call (which was long drawn out) closed the starter shouted "Ta Wai!" and they were off on the first relay. Markers stood at the side of the track and held willow sticks and with rags attached as marks of the position of the opposing sides. Sometimes the race was ended by one party admitting it was tired out, but it usually was decided when the winners were so far ahead that their runner met the other at the center, where the markers also met. The women encouraged their friends with shouts in concert, which were emitted from the throat and ended in a trill from the tongue. At the close of the race the winning village shouted continuously for some time, after which the visitors would go home, as there was no accompanying feast. (p. 806)

Major John C. Cremony, an officer in the U.S. Army, described a track meet that was sponsored by the Army for the Apache and Navajo Indians at Fort Sumner, New Mexico, in 1868 (cited in Culin, 1907). The Army posted several prizes that were to be awarded to the winners in this event. The races ranged from 100 yards to one-half mile; the largest awards were given for the longest distances. (These events represented what Army personnel considered appropriate distances. The Indians in that region were accustomed to much longer races.) Both men and women competed, and the age requirements were fifteen to forty for men and fifteen to twenty-five for women. Cremony reported that "about a hundred Apaches and Navahoes entered for the prizes, and practiced every day for a week" (p. 803).

A more elaborate track meet was held by the Mandan Indians of North Dakota in 1862 (Hayden, 1862). The feature attraction was a three-mile race in which several heats were run in order to narrow the field for the final race. The heats were managed by having one small group of runners start around the three-mile track. After they had run a sufficient distance from the starting line, succeeding groups were started until eventually "the entire track [was] covered with runners at distances corresponding with their different times in starting" (p. 430). A second heat was then run in much the same manner with fewer runners.

The first and second heats are seldom strongly contested, but on the third, every nerve is strained, and great is the excitement of the spectators, who with yells and gestures, encourage their several friends and relations. The whole scene is highly interesting, and often continued for two or three days in succession, to give everyone an opportunity to display his abilities. . . . They also immediately on finishing the race, in a profuse state of perspiration, throw themselves into the Missouri, and no instance is known where this apparent rashness resulted in any illness. (p. 430)

According to Hayden (1862), except for moccasins, runners were naked. Their bodies were painted in various ways from heads to foot (see Figures 3.1 and 3.2).

Running Tracks

Formal race tracks were apparently developed and used by Indians many centuries ago. Culin (1907) cited a report by Russell, an archaeologist, stating that "at various points in Arizona I have found what appear to have been ancient race tracks situated near the ruins of buildings" (p. 806). He reported that one of these tracks was "five meters wide and 275 meters long" (p. 806). It had been leveled by clearing away boulders of the mesa and by cutting down obstacles. In another location he discovered what he assumed to be a running track that was 6 meters wide and 180 meters long. According to Russell,

> these will serve as examples of the tracks used by the Sobaipuris, a tribe belonging to the Piman stock. The dimensions are about the same as those of the tracks that I have seen the Jicarilla Apaches using in New Mexico. The tracks prepared by the Pimas opposite Sacaton Flats and at Casa Blanca are much longer. (p. 806)

Culin (1907) cited Hayden's description of a three-mile race course that he observed in use by the Mandan Indians in 1892. He reported that it was on the level prairie and was cleared of every obstruction and kept in condition for racing purposes only. The design of the track was an arc, which formed an almost complete circle. Posts marked the starting and terminating points and were only a few hundred yards apart. Spectators were able to observe the beginning and the end of the race from a single point. Denig (cited in Culin, 1907) reported that the Crows along the upper Missouri River had a "regular race course 3 miles in length" (p. 87) that was heavily used. Races typically required three laps around the track.

Wagering on Footraces

Betting on most footraces was consistent with practices used in other sports. Almost all formal racing events involved betting, and the more important the event, the heavier the wagering. Hayden (1862) described a typical betting procedure for a Mandan racing event.

> Each of the runners brought the amount of his wager, consisting of blankets, guns, and other property, and sometimes several judges or elderly men were appointed by the chief of the village, whose duty it was to arrange the bets, regulate the starting, and determine the results of the race. As the wagers are handed in, each is tied to or matched with one of equal value, laid aside, and when all have entered, the judges separate, some remaining with the property staked at the beginning of the race-course, and others taking their station at the terminus. (p. 430)

As with other sporting events, there were no consolation prizes—the winners collected all the goods at the conclusion of the meet.

In those track meets sponsored and conducted by the U.S. Army, valuable prizes were provided; however, traditional betting among the participants did not occur. Provision of prizes and awards by sponsors of major sporting events may have contributed to a reduction in the betting practices among Indians. It is more likely that the artificiality of these activities (i.e., their removal from a traditional climate and their control by an external group) was the primary reason for the reduction in the Indian practice of wagering.

Whereas most track meets in traditional Indian culture involved betting as a matter of course, there were other occasions when betting was not involved. Races planned and run for religious or mystical significance did not include betting or prizes. According to Stevenson (1904), "No thought of betting is in the Zuni mind when these races for rain occur" (p. 322). She pointed out, however, that a much higher level of excitement existed for betting races than for religious races.

The Ball Race

One of the most unusual of all Indian sports in the minds of modern non-Indians was the ball race (also called the kick-ball race). This activity was more a racing event than a ball game and was extremely popular in the Southwest, particularly among the Zuni, Pima, and Papago tribes. In Mexico the ball race was the foremost sporting event among the Tarahumare.

In this race a small wooden ball or stick was repeatedly kicked forward by the runner, who ran along a prescribed racing course. After kicking the ball, the runner ran after it and kicked it again. This was repeated

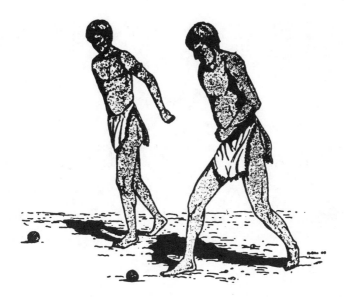

Figure 3.5. Papago kick-ball race, Arizona; from photo by William Dinwiddie. Photo used by permission of Smithsonian Institution Press from *Twenty-fourth Annual Report of the Bureau of American Ethnology, 1902–1903.* Smithsonian Institution, Washington, DC, 1907.

continuously as he moved steadily along the course. The kick was actually a throw, or flip, of the object with the top of the foot. While running at a steady pace, the runner approached the ball and positioned the foot immediately behind it (see Figure 3.5). Then he swung the leg vigorously forward, without breaking stride, and propelled the ball fifty yards or so into the distance. This sequence continued for the whole race, which typically covered a distance of twenty-five miles.

The race course was generally laid out on a circuit that went to some distant point and returned to the starting place. Ball races were sometimes held with two individuals competing against each other, but more often it was with a team of four to six who competed against another team of equal size. In such races the team members alternated kicking the ball as they all ran along in a group. The ball race was run by both men and women. However, the game was modified for women; instead of kicking the ball, they used a stick to toss a hoop or ring ahead as they ran. In another variation, women used a two- or three-pronged stick to propel a ball forward. In either case they were not allowed to touch the ball or the ring with their hands.

Several types of balls were used for the ball race. The most common appears to have been a cylindrical piece of wood approximately three inches in length and one inch in diameter. These kicking *billets* were also

Figure 3.6. Top and side view of a kick ball used by Mandan runners. Ball was collected about 1912 by Frances Densmore. Photo used by permission of the National Anthropological Archives, Smithsonian Institution.

made of bone. Also popular with some tribes were spherical balls made of stone or wood, and these were usually around 2½ inches in diameter. Occasionally, such objects as bladders, buckskin balls, and hoops (for women) were used in these races. Figure 3.6 shows a stitched kick ball used by Mandan runners.

Training for the ball race began early in childhood (Hodge, 1890):

> At almost any time a naked youngster of four or five years may be seen playing at kicking-the-stick outside the door of his home, or, if a year or two older, coming from the corn field—where he has been dutifully engaged in frightening off the crows—tossing the stick as far as his little feet will allow him. (p. 227)

The popularity of the ball race began to decline during the late 19th century. According to Fontana (1979, May) an observer of the Pima Indians reported in 1902 that "the custom of using these (kick) balls is rapidly disappearing, as, it is to be regretted, are the other athletic games of the Pimas" (p. 7). He reported further that by 1920 the ball race had been entirely discontinued among the Pimas, the Papagos, and most other Arizona Indians—except as it was played as a game in schools. However, the ball race and other traditional games continue among the Tarahumare in Mexico, who have changed the least during the past 300 years.

Significance of the Ball Race

As traditionally run, the ball race was a particularly significant and sacred custom of the tribes in the Southwest. It was accepted by many as a religious exercise. According to Culin (1907),

> the game of kicked stick was one of the games sacred to the war god in Zuni, and the implements are sacrificial upon his alter. . . .Objects similar to the kicking billets are used by the Hopi in ceremonials, and may be regarded as having a similar origin. (p. 666)

According to tradition the ball used in these races held magic or supernatural significance and tended to pull or draw the runners along with it. In fact, the Pimas believed that they could run faster while kicking a ball in front of them than they could without engaging in the ball kicking. Lumholtz (cited in Culin, 1907) reported that in the Tarahumare tradition

> a race is never won by natural means. The losers always say that they were influenced by some herb and became sleepy on the race-course, so that they had to lose. The help of the medicine man is needed in preparing the runner for the race. He assists the manager to wash the feet of the runners with warm water and different herbs, and he strengthens their nerves by making passes over them. He also guards them against sorcery. Before they run he performs a ceremony to "cure" them (p 673).

The ceremony preceding a major ball race was in some ways similar to that preceding other major sporting events. These festivities began on the evening before the day of the race and engaged the participants in meditation and ritual through most of the night and the following morning. During these ceremonies, which are normally subdued and prayerful, certain occurrences are viewed as omens either for success or for failure. Lightning bolts or shooting stars were viewed as virtual guarantees of success in the race whereas the hoot of an owl was seen as a bad omen and often encouraged the group to postpone the race.

Conduct of the Ball Race

According to Hodge (1890), the favorite time for participating in the ball race was the spring time during the height of interest immediately following the planting season. Short and rather unimportant races were held in the early spring but were "by no means so exciting as those which follow later in the season when the planting is finished" (p. 227). Apparently, this season was selected not only because of the better weather conditions but because of the greater leisure following the completion of planting chores.

The runners usually shed all clothes with the exception of the breech-cloths and sandals. Their faces and bodies were often brightly painted for the race. The hair was neatly arranged and tied on top of the head to prevent it from interfering with their performance.

The ball race itself was one of the most exciting activities among Indian sports. At the beginning of the race, the two competitors or teams were arranged appropriately near the starting line. When a team was competing, the leader was precisely at the starting line, his toe resting under or just behind the ball, ready to kick (note Figure 3.5). Other members of the team were dispersed a few yards away in the direction that the ball was to be kicked.

At the starting signal the player kicked the ball as far as possible down the prescribed trail, and then the member of his team who was nearest to where the ball landed ran to it and kicked it farther along the route. This procedure of alternately kicking and running continued through the race. While one player prepared to kick the ball, others sped past him to be near where it would land to be able to propel it even farther. In this way the players passed each other repeatedly during the race. The race was not entirely dependent upon fast running and endurance, although these were major ingredients for success, and long kicks made while running full speed were advantageous in the race. However, accuracy in the direction of the kick was equally important. Balls that landed in heavy grass or rough terrain away from the main running track were more difficult to retrieve and to kick effectively. Balls that landed in holes or among boulders slowed the whole team. According to some authors, runners were allowed to carry sticks in their hands, which could be used to dislodge balls from difficult places. They were able to dig the ball out with the sticks, but they were not allowed to touch it with the hands.

Most authors, including Hodge (1890) and Owens (1891), reported that a typical kick was lofted into the air approximately 30 feet and traveled a distance of about 100 feet. However, some reported much longer kicks, approaching 100 yards.

Lumholtz (cited in Culin, 1907) stated that during the race the runner who happened to be ahead was supposed to toss the ball with his toes, ''and at each toss it may be thrown a 100 yards or more in advance'' (p. 676). This accomplishment is difficult to perceive in view of the lightness of the small wooden balls. He reported that the players normally wore sandals on their feet. The top of the foot was unprotected, and several authors reported that the top of the foot was frequently badly bruised following a long race. Markers were placed along the trail to indicate the path to be run. There were also crosses on trees, piled stones, or other visible signs. In addition, several judges were stationed along the route to ensure that the race was being run properly.

Inasmuch as these were usually straight-away runs or runs to and from a distant object, spectators frequently accompanied the participants on horseback. Hodge (1890) reported that there could be seen

> two or three hundred equestrians—those who, more than any others, are interested in the outcome of the race by reason of the extent of their prospective gains or losses. When one side follows closely in the track of its opponents, the horsemen all ride together; but when, by reason of accident or inferiority in speed, a party falls considerably in the rear, the horsemen separate to accompany their prospective favorites. If the season is dry, the dust made by galloping horses is blinding; but the racers continue, apparently as unmindful of the mud-coating that accumulates on their almost nude, perspiring bodies as if they were within but a few steps of victory. (p. 227)

Observers reported that participants who fell far behind did not become discouraged because ill fate could befall the leading team in the ball race. Sometimes the ball would fall into a hole or some other obstruction that caused difficulty in retrieving it and gave the opposing team an opportunity to catch up. Consequently, a team was never really out of the race until the other team had actually crossed the finish line.

Some "Modern" Running Performances

One of the most astonishing running performances took place in 1876 and was later reported in *Ripley's Giant Book of Believe It or Not* (Ripley, 1976). According to this report, a Pawnee Indian, Koo-tah-we-Coots-oo-lel-r-hoo-La-Shar (Big Hawk Chief), ran the mile in 3 minutes and 58 seconds. This one-mile race was timed by U.S. Army officers using stop watches. Although this was the first sub-four-minute mile reported, "official" records credit England's Roger Bannister with first breaking that barrier more than three-quarters of a century later in 1954.

Extraordinary running feats by American Indians continued into the 20th century; however, precise measurements were often not available for performances taking place within the traditional setting. Among those occurring within a non-Indian setting, and having been verified by external observers, are the performances of Tom Longboat of the Onondaga tribe. He won the Boston Marathon in 1907, breaking the previous record by five minutes. No less outstanding were the accomplishments of Louis Tewanima, the Hopi Indian who attended the Carlisle School along with Jim Thorpe. In addition to numerous record-breaking performances in

Figure 3.7. Ellison "Tarzan" Brown winning the Boston Marathon in 1939. Photo used by permission of AP/Wide World.

Figure 3.8. Billy Mills winning the Olympic 10,000-meter race in 1964. Photo courtesy of the Harris Agency.

college meets, he finished second in the 5,000- and 10,000-meter runs in the 1912 Olympic Games in Stockholm and won the New York half-marathon in 1911. Nabokov (1981) reported that Tewanima once missed the train from Carlisle to Harrisburg and ran the eighteen-mile distance in time to enter and win the two-mile event.

Jim Thorpe was known not for his long-distance running but for his speed and versatility in track-and-field events as well as in other sports. However, the fact that he excelled in a great many events within one meet, including the decathlon, attests to his stamina. Ellison "Tarzan" Brown, of the Narraganset tribe, won the Boston Marathon in 1936 and 1939 and in so doing was one of the first men in history to run a marathon in less than two and a half hours (see Figure 3.7). As recently as 1964, Billy Mills, an Oglala Sioux, won the 10,000-meter run at the Tokyo Olympic Games and became the first American ever to win an Olympic race at that long a distance. Figure 3.8 shows Mills completing that race. (A more thorough discussion of the outstanding accomplishments of 20th century athletes is to be presented in chapter 13.)

Summary

All Indian tribes placed importance on races and on running in general. Running was important not only for races but for personal and group survival. Skill in running was necessary for success in hunting, warfare, and in the delivery of messages and materials. Running also served as a means of conditioning and preparing for other sports. In addition, many races, particularly the ball race, carried important religious significance.

Without question, Indians excelled at running even by today's standards. Indeed, it would be surprising had they not, given the devotion of all groups to running. However, as was consistent in Indian culture, attention was not devoted to quantifying times or distances of running performances. It is noteworthy that when travelers began to cite particulars of some of those running feats, they were not generally believed. Nevertheless, the consistency of reports on Indian running excellence is convincing.

Chapter 4

Additional Sports of Major Interest

Games and sports among American Indians were diverse. In addition to activities like ball games and footracing that were practically universal, others were peculiar to one tribe or several tribes in a general section of the continent. These regional games reflected the special interest or cultural background of particular groups, and some practices, such as winter sports, were influenced by the climatic conditions and terrain of the region.

Although not presuming to be all-inclusive, this chapter will present two activities (archery and water sports) that were practiced throughout the continent and two others (snow snake and hoop-and-pole) that were very popular in large regions. It should be understood that countless additional games were extremely popular in restricted localities.

Unlike ball games and footracing, archery and swimming (and other water sports) were not always viewed as sports. Archery was a skill of great utilitarian value in securing food (hunting and fishing) and in warfare, and it was used by young people primarily as a sport and for training purposes. In addition, adults participated in a great many archery games both for enjoyment and for skill development.

Swimming, too, was practiced both for fun and for its utilitarian value. Safety, travel (including the necessity for crossing bodies of water), and fishing activities demanded skills in swimming as well as boating. However, swimming races and contests utilizing canoes, kayaks, and various types of sailing vessels attained widespread popularity as recreational activities.

The games of snow snake and hoop-and-pole, or chungke, were intensely popular and were viewed as sports for their own sake. Unlike archery and swimming, they had no utilitarian value and did not facilitate acquisition of any other skill. The hoop-and-pole game, however, was viewed as a religious sport, particularly in the early days of the white man's contact with the Indian. Unlike ball games, footraces, archery, and swimming, neither snow snake nor hoop-and-pole covered the whole continent. Snow snake was restricted to those areas where snow and ice were prevalent, such as Canada and the northern half of the United States. Hoop-and-pole was played more widely, but it was most popular in the southern regions of the United States.

Archery and swimming were not uniquely Indian sports, and they have been established and retained as a popular part of the non-Indian culture. They have been promoted in schools and in amateur competition throughout this country and around the world. On the other hand, snow snake and hoop-and-pole were clearly Indian sports, and they were not adopted by the non-Indian community or included as part of the school programs for Indians, particularly at government schools. Given the aggressiveness of civilization against Indian institutions in general, both snow snake and hoop-and-pole have faded in popularity and have nearly passed from existence. Among the Iroquois nations, however, snow snake continues to be played with some frequency.

Archery

Archery is often thought of by the non-Indian population as the most typical of all Indian activities. Though widely recognized today as a sport, many persons assume that Indian use of archery was restricted to warfare and hunting. However, Culin (1907) cites at least two dozen independent reports of archery being practiced as a sport prior to 1900.

At the time the white man came to this continent, archery was used by all tribes throughout North, Central, and South America. However, Indians were neither the first nor the only civilization to develop the bow and arrow. In fact, before white settlers arrived on this continent, the bow and arrow had been used widely on other continents and apparently had been developed independently within several cultures. In *American Indian Archery*, Laubin and Laubin (1980) propose the theory that the bow and arrow originated in Asia; they believe that the bow was perfected in ancient times in Asia Minor, probably in Turkey.

Laubin and Laubin (1980) also assert that the quality of archery equipment ranged from excellent to very poor during colonial times on this continent. They report that the most advanced bows were found in the northwest, the plains, and the Rocky Mountain area. (A variety of traditional Indian bows is shown in Figure 4.1.) These bows varied widely in style and apparent sophistication, and the arrows (shown in Figure 4.2) displayed evidence of extensive workmanship and artistic expression. However, the particular purpose of these arrows and their effectiveness cannot be determined.

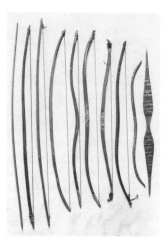

Figure 4.1. A sampling of traditional Indian bows. Photo used by permission of the University Museum, University of Pennsylvania.

Figure 4.2. Decorated Indian arrows. Photo used by permission of the National Anthropological Archives, Smithsonian Institution.

Indian Archery Skills

Early settlers marveled at the skill of the Indians in archery, and "legends grew into feats hardly possible for even Robin Hood or William Tell to rival" (Laubin & Laubin, 1980, p. 2). By the time of colonization in this country, the bow and arrow had begun to decline in popularity in Europe and had given way to newly developing firearms. Of course, not having developed firearms, Indians made heavy use of bows for hunting, warfare, ceremony, and sport.

Indians emphasized an informal, less standardized style of shooting with their handmade bows and arrows. Non-Indians developed sophisticated bows, including sights, stabilizers, and other aids, and the traditional Indian archery equipment has been viewed as primitive in comparison. Unlike today's standardized system of stationary target shooting, Indians more often engaged in *field* events—either shooting at moving targets or shooting at realistic targets while the archer moves through the fields or forest.

Although traditionally viewed as expert in archery, the Indian has not achieved particular prominence in national competitions during recent years. One notable exception was Joe Thornton of Stilwell, Oklahoma, who won the world championship in archery in 1961. He won many additional honors and was a member of the United States archery team that won the world team championship several times in the 1960s.

In general, Indian adherence to traditional (simpler) equipment and emphasis on a more practical approach to archery has caused reluctance in entering competition where equipment and rules seem far removed from reality. Releasing the arrow itself, or shooting, was but the culmination of the sport for Indians, and they chose to keep archery in a form that related to symbolic usefulness. For example, in writing about the Cherokee, McCaskill (1936) reported that

> the style of shooting of these Indians is quite different from that usually employed by white archers. They give the impression of shooting quickly, with a forward striding motion, as though a deer or rabbit, or other animal had suddenly jumped from the bushes. (p. 30)

He also reported that it was their custom to shoot at moving targets.

In the 1830s, although he was impressed with the Indian's speed, flexibility, and impromptu responses in archery, Catlin (1841/1965) surmised that the distant target shooting of the Indians was perhaps not superior to that of the non-Indian archers. He noted that most Indian hunting (he described in detail the buffalo hunts) required one to shoot only short distances. In fact, the Indians shot buffalo from horseback as they rode alongside the fleeing animals. He also reported that deer, elk, and other game were stalked so successfully that shots were usually at short range.

Nevertheless, other authors have reported archery games in which targets were placed at long distances. In a report to Culin (1907), Sawyer stated that the Thompson Indians of British Columbia typically shot at small objects at distances from 40 to 100 yards and that the Potawatomi in Kansas shot arrows at four-inch targets from 200 feet.

Archery Games

Indian archery games take several forms, including traditional target shooting for accuracy, shooting at moving targets, and speed shooting. Speed shooting was practiced in the *game of arrows*, described by Catlin (1841/1965) and several other writers. Catlin observed the game among the Mandan Indians; the object of the game was to have as many arrows in flight at the same time as possible. The archer would shoot an arrow high into the air, immediately notch a second arrow and shoot it into the air, then a third, and so on. Catlin was not amazed by the distance the arrows traveled but by the rapidity with which the Indians could reload and fire subsequent arrows. He reported that

> the number of eight or ten arrows are clenched in the left hand with the bow, and the first one which is thrown is elevated to such a degree as will enable it to remain the longest time possible in the air, and while it is flying, the others are discharged as rapidly as possible; and he who succeeds in getting the greatest number up at once is best and takes the goods staked. (p. 141)

Evidence of the Indian's great skill in the game of arrows is substantiated by Laubin and Laubin (1980). They quote a Captain Bounke as stating that "the Apaches have trials of skill with arrows and will often keep ten in the air at one time" and that "their aim is excellent, and the range attained was perhaps as much as 150 yards" (p. 122).

Archery games were associated with betting. In these games competitors usually bet their arrows, and the winners collected all or part of the arrows of the losers.

A fairly standard type of target shooting was described by Cartwright (1792). In 1792 he observed archery shooting by the Montagnais Indians on the coast of Labrador and reported that they set up

> two targets of 4 foot square, made of sticks and covered with deerskins. These they fix on poles about 8 feet high, and at 50 yards distant from each other. The men dividing themselves into two parties, each party shoots 21 arrows at one of the targets, standing by the other. That party which puts the most arrows into the target, gains the honor. . . . The victors immediately set up shouts of mockery and derision at the conquered party; these they continue for some time, when the wives and daughters of the conquerors join in the triumph and walking in procession round the targets, sing a song upon the

occasion, priding themselves not a little with the defeat of their opponents, who at length join in the laugh against themselves, and are all friends again, without any offense (seemingly) being either given or taken. (p. 238)

In other games stationary targets included bundles of hay, pieces of bark, or arrows sticking in the ground or in a tree.

In several archery games, an arrow was shot to a designated area, and that arrow served as the target for subsequent arrows. In 1900 James Teit (1900) described such a game of shooting accuracy among the Thompson Indians in British Columbia. A lead arrow to be used as a target was shot into a steep, sandy bank by one of the contestants. All contestants then fired arrows at the target. According to Teit, "The person who struck the notched end of the arrow-shaft or target, thereby splitting it in two, won the greatest number of points," and the next highest score was for those whose arrows struck alongside "the arrow target, touching the latter all along the shaft" (p. 279). Because the distances were generally from 40 to 100 yards and each player had only two arrows at a time, the participants' expectation of accuracy was very high.

An almost identical game among the Pawnee in Nebraska was described by Dunbar (1882). One player shot an arrow into the ground at a distance of forty to sixty paces, and then each player attempted to shoot so that their arrows would fall directly across the target arrow. The first one to achieve this won all the arrows that had been bet. Reports concerning numerous tribes reveal that this game was extremely widespread.

Several archery games utilizing *moving targets* have been reported. Culin (1907) cited a report by Russell describing a game among the Pima in Arizona. Several players would stand in a close circle looking outward while one player ran around the outside dragging a bundle of rags at the end of a string. The player who first shot an arrow into the moving target won all the arrows wagered. After a series of such plays, the best marksman had nearly all the arrows. According to Russell, "The same runner continues throughout the game, and receives a few arrows as compensation for his services" (p. 389).

Late in the 19th century, Reverend Dorsey (1891) described a similar, if somewhat more hazardous, game among the Dakota Indians.

A swift runner takes a cactus root into which he thrusts a stick to serve as a handle. Grasping the cactus by this handle, he holds it aloft as he runs, and the other shoot at it. . . . When one of the boys hits the cactus they say that it enrages the boy-cactus, who thereupon chases the others. Whenever the boy-cactus overtakes a player he sticks his cactus into him, turns around and returns to his former place. Again the cactus is held aloft and they shoot at it as before. (p. 337)

In another game among the Pima, the player tossed up a target (a small bundle of grass) with his left hand while holding the bow with his right. As soon as the bundle was released, he attempted to shoot an arrow into it before it landed. In still another game requiring skill and quick judgment, one of several young men would shoot an arrow in the air. Before it could land, several others would attempt to shoot to the precise landing spot of that arrow. This game required good judgment about direction, speed, and distance. The individual whose arrow came closest to the lead arrow was declared the winner.

Blasiz (1933-1934) described a very hazardous archery game played by the Uracare Indians in which a participant used a knife to strike down an arrow that was shot toward him.

> It was common practice to shoot at a human target. The arrow was aimed at shoulder level and slightly to one side of the one representing the target. As the arrow came toward the one representing the target it was his business to strike it down or deflect it from its path with a knife as it passed by him. (p. 217)

Catlin (1841/1965) provided a vivid written description along with paintings of the use of bows and arrows in buffalo hunting among the Blackfeet Indians in the 1830s. He was very much impressed with the ability of all Indian men to shoot arrows with great accuracy and effectiveness while riding full-speed on a horse. He reported that

> one of these little bows in the hands of an Indian on a fleet and well-trained horse, with a quiver of arrows swung on his back, is an effective and most powerful weapon in the open plains. No one can easily credit the force with which these missiles are thrown, and the Sanguinary effects produced by their wounds, until he has rode by the side of a party of Indians in chase of a herd of buffalo, and witnessed the apparent ease and grace in which their supple arms have drawn the bow, and seen these huge animals tumbling down. (p. 33)

He reported that the mounted Indian hunter had a quiver holding a hundred arrows, "of which he can throw 15 or 20 in a minute" (p. 33).

Of course, Indians never viewed the hunting of buffalo, deer, turkeys, or any other game as sport; rather, it was a means of securing food. Indian boys started training with bows and arrows for the skills needed in adult life when they were barely able to walk. At first they used harmless toys; however, they were given real bows and arrows at around the age of five or six and began realistic play and fairly serious training. At first the arrows were blunted to avoid being a serious safety hazard. The children were gradually given sharper arrows as they developed greater skill and appreciation for the activity. Older children began shooting at birds,

Figure 4.3. Kiowa boys with bows and arrows. Photo used by permission of the National Anthropological Archives, Smithsonian Institution.

rabbits, and turkeys and engaging in archery games. Figure 4.3 shows two Kiowa Indian boys preparing to hunt with their bows and arrows.

Swimming and Other Aquatic Activities

Indians throughout the North American continent engaged in swimming, boating, fishing, and other aquatic activities both for enjoyment and for more practical reasons. Indian settlements were typically located along streams, rivers, lakes, or bays. Daily life required regular contact with bodies of water for food, transportation, and bathing. Indians had to learn to maneuver on or in the water to overcome these natural boundaries, and swimming and boating were important elements of traditional Indian culture.

Swimming

The swimming skill of Indians has been confirmed by several early writers, and their love for swimming and other aquatic activities has been well documented. For example, Catlin (1841/1965) asserted that

> the art of swimming is known to all the American Indians; and perhaps no people on earth have taken more pains to learn it, nor any who turn it to better account. There certainly are no people whose avocations of life more often call for the use of their limbs in this way; as many of the tribes spend their lives on the shores of our vast lakes and rivers, paddling about from their childhood in their fragile bark canoes, which are liable to continual accidents, which often throw the Indians upon his natural resources for the preservation of his life. (p. 96)

The general style and quality of Indian swimming were suggested by Catlin's (1841/1965) description of swimming among the Mandan Indians. According to his report, the Indians were not only excellent swimmers but apparently originated the crawl stroke, which is prominently used for freestyle competition today. According to Catlin, non-Indians in this country during the early 19th century were unfamiliar with the crawl stroke and used the more leisurely breast stroke; however, Indians typically used the speedier and more powerful crawl stroke. Because the Indian style of swimming was so unfamiliar to the non-Indian world, Catlin took great pains to describe the stroke. The following is an excellent, and possibly the first, description of the arm phase of the crawl stroke.

The mode of swimming amongst the Mandans, as well as amongst most of the other tribes, is quite different from that practiced in those parts of the civilized world, which I have had the pleasure yet to visit. The Indian, instead of parting his hands simultaneously under the chin and making the stroke outward, in a horizontal direction, causing thereby a serious strain upon the chest, throws his body alternating upon the left and right side, raising one arm entirely above the water and reaching as far forward as he can, to dip it, whilst his whole weight and force are spent upon the one that is passing under him, and like a paddle propelling him along; whilst the arm is making a half circle, and is being raised out of the water behind him, the opposite arm is describing a similar arc in the air over his head, to be dipped into the water as far as he can reach before him, with the hand turned under, forming a sort of bucket, to act most effectively as it passes in its turn underneath him.

By this bold and powerful mode of swimming, which may want the grace that many would want or wish to see, I am quite sure, from the experience I have had, that much of the fatigue and strain upon the breast and spine are avoided, and that a man will preserve his strength and his breath much longer in this alternate and rolling motion, than he can in the usual mode of swimming in the polished world. (p. 97)

Although it has not been documented that American Indians were the first to use the crawl stroke as a general practice, it does seem clear that they developed this technique without the help of outsiders. Unfortunately, Catlin did not describe the leg kick or how the breathing is synchronized with the arm stroke, so we cannot be certain how closely the swimming technique of the Mandans resembled the modern competitive crawl stroke.

Two centuries earlier the distinctiveness of the Indian crawl was reported in Massachusetts and Rhode Island (Hallett, 1955). Of course, this was far removed from the Mandan Indians of the upper Missouri Valley. Roger Williams and William Wood in the early 1600s noted the Indians' "natural stroke was a dog paddle rather than a spreading of the arms," and Williams reported that "they could easily swim over a mile, and could float lying as still as a log. Their children were taught to swim when very young" (cited in Hallett, 1955, p. 28).

The importance of swimming well was valued by both men and women as well as boys and girls. Catlin (1841/1965) reported that all women "learn to swim well, and the poorest swimmer amongst them will dash fearlessly into the boiling and eddying current of the Missouri, and cross it with perfect ease" (p. 96). He further reported that "every morning in the summer months girls and women went for a swim in the river" (p. 96). They selected a place which was secluded and some distance from where the boys and men typically swim, and sentinels were usually posted to guard against male intruders. Nevertheless, Catlin observed that "they can be seen running and glistening in the sun, whilst they are playing their innocent gambols and leaping into the stream" (p. 96).

As mentioned earlier in this text (see prologue), Catlin's detailed account of the swimming skill of young Minataree girls along the Knife River revealed that the girls possessed a high level of skill, enjoyment, confidence, and a level of good spirits that would be admired by today's sportsmen.

Great pains were taken to develop swimming competency at an early age for all Indian children. Charles Hamilton (1972) quoted a report by Ohiyesa, a Sioux:

> We loved to play in the water. When we had no ponies, we often had swimming matches of our own and sometimes made rafts with which we crossed lakes and rivers. It was a common thing to "duck" a young or timid boy or to carry him into deep water to struggle as best he might. (Hamilton, 1972, p. 59)

Ohiyesa also described games in which young boys attempted to ride a floating log down a river. He concluded: "I would rather ride on a swift bronco any day then try to stay on and steady a short log in a river" (Hamilton, 1972, p. 59). Hamilton noted several other games played by young people in the water, including one in which young children held onto the tails of horses while they swam across the river. This gave them a feel for the buoyancy of the water as well as some security in the deep water.

Fishing

Indians also excelled at fishing, and in addition to the ordinary techniques involving hooks and lines, they were especially skilled in the use of underwater nets, spearing, and shooting with bows and arrows. Whaling along the Canadian and Alaskan coasts was an important enterprise long before the white man moved into that region. Salmon fishing has been and continues to be an important industry for the Indians, especially along the northwest coast. Among traditional American Indians, however, fishing was never considered a sport; instead, it was a necessary pursuit for obtaining food and other essentials (fertilizer, oil, bones, etc.).

Water Craft

Few artifacts are more closely associated with the American Indian than the *canoe*. Although the kayak and other types of water craft (including catamarans, sailing vessels, and crude tub-like boats) were also constructed and used, the canoe was the most popular, and the Indian was particularly expert in the construction and use of a variety of canoes.

Canoe shape and construction materials varied from tribe to tribe. Two basic types of construction were practiced: either birch bark, animal hides, or some other light material was shaped to form the hull or canoes were made by hollowing out large tree trunks. Catlin (1841/1944) thought that the Chippewa made the most beautiful and efficient canoes—made of birch rind and ingeniously sewn to be water-tight, they would ride along the water "as light as a cork" (p. 158). Construction of the birch bark canoe is shown in Figure 4.4, and Figure 4.5 shows Chippewa women canoeing to gather wild rice. The bark canoe was especially popular across the northern United States and in Canada where birch trees were plentiful. Moose hide canoes were prevalent in western Canada and in Alaska.

Standing was the typical position for canoeing among the plains Indians. Of course, to manage a canoe in this position took great skill and experience. Catlin (1841/1944) noted that experienced Indian men and women had little difficulty handling the canoes, but of the white man he stated that "if he be not an experienced equilibrist, he is sure to get two or three times soused, in his first endeavours" (p. 159).

The second type of canoe construction involved the hollowing out of tree trunks. The size of the tree depended upon the use to be made of the canoe. The soft wood and straight grain of cedar trees made them most useful. Canoe makers used axes and fire to dig out the inside and to shape the hull, and steam was used to spread the beam. The craft of shaping, balancing, and polishing the canoe was highly developed among many tribes (see Figure 4.6). The size of canoes varied from the small

Figure 4.4. Menominee Indians setting up a birchbark canoe. The bark covering has been folded around the canoe framework. Stakes hold the bark in place while it is being stitched. Photo by Walter Hoffman around 1892. Photo used by permission of the National Anthropological Archives, Smithsonian Institution.

Figure 4.5. Chippewa women using a birchbark canoe to gather wild rice. Photo used by permission of the University Museum, University of Pennsylvania.

Figure 4.6. Massachusetts Indians shaping a dugout canoe. Photo used by permission of the University Museum, University of Pennsylvania.

two-man craft to the giant eight-man canoes, or even larger. In the Pacific Northwest, giant canoes made of hollowed out Sequoia trees were ocean-going and could carry up to fifty persons. For some purposes, such as whaling, the larger canoes were attached to make a catamaran.

Circular, tub-like *bull-boats* were popular among the Mandans and other Plains Indians in the early 19th century. They were made by stretching buffalo hides over a light wood frame. The very speedy kayak was first developed by the North American Indians and was used extensively in Alaska, Canada, and the northern part of the United States. Three models of Eskimo kayaks are shown in Figure 4.7, and kayaking can be seen in Figure 4.8.

In addition to their value as a means of tribal support (fishing, transportation, etc.), water craft were also used for sport. Catlin (1841/1944) reported that one of the favorite amusements among the Chippewa Indians was a canoe regatta, and he described in great detail the excitement among the large crowds that attended the canoe races. According to his paintings, spectators lined the banks of the river and sat in boats out in the river. It is noteworthy that the Chippewa racers stood in the canoes while paddling for greater speed.

Reports of Indian activity with water craft reveal that they engaged in most of the types of sports that have been common in more recent times. In addition to rowing and sailing races, single and group tug-of-war contests with canoes were popular as a means of testing rowing strength. In tug-of-war contests, canoes were tied together with a rope approximately five feet long, and contestants attempted to row in opposite directions. The winner was the canoe pulling the other one past a given marker. In another activity contestants paddled to a distant marker, overturned the canoe, and swam back while towing the canoe. In still other games, contestants stood in canoes and jousted with those in other canoes, attempting to knock each other into the water.

Snow Snake

The game of snow snake was traditionally one of the more popular activities among American Indians living in the northern part of the United States and in Canada. Snow snake consisted of sliding or tossing a pole, or "snake," a great distance along a frozen path. The path was covered with crusty snow or ice, which facilitated sliding the snake as far as possible. This game was limited to the colder seasons of the year and to the northern part of the continent. However, a similar game involving the tossing of a bone or horn projectile along hard, dry ground was played in the plains and in the Southwest.

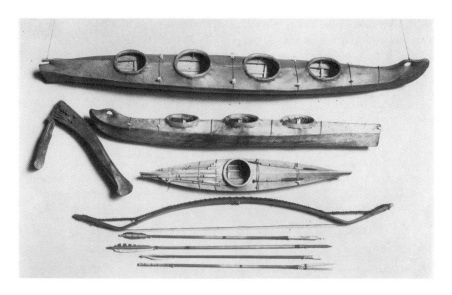

Figure 4.7. Models of three Eskimo kayaks with bow, arrows, and razer. Collected by G.B. Gordon in 1905 in Cape Nome, Alaska. Photo used by permission of the University Museum, University of Pennsylvania.

Figure 4.8. Eskimo in kayak. Photo used by permission of the University Museum, University of Pennsylvania.

Snow snake was being played at the time the white man arrived on this continent and was still popular at the end of the 19th century. Writing from New York's Seneca reservation, Hough (1888) stated that snow snake (called kow-a-sa) was "the national game" (p. 134) of the Iroquois and was still widely played.

In 1861, Reverend Jones (1861) commented on the Missisauga in Ontario:

> Their principle play during the winter session is the snow-snake, which is made of hard smooth timber, about six feet long, having eyes and mouth like a snake. The manner of play is to take the snake by the tail, and throw it along the snow or ice with all their strength. Whoever sent the snake the furthest a certain number of times gains the prize. (p. 134)

In snow snake, success depended upon the distance one could propel the snake on a given throw. This was not a team game in the sense of requiring players to interact with each other during performance. However, players were usually organized into teams of two to six, and, as in bowling, track or gymnastics, scoring was cumulative. Snow snake was usually a game for men and boys, but in some areas women also played. Women and girls often used a shorter stick.

Though snow snake did not generate the intense mass appeal of lacrosse or have the religious connotation of the ball race in the southwest, it nevertheless stimulated betting on all sides, and the typical bets were the snakes themselves, of which each player had several.

The Snake

The game of snow snake derives its name from the specially shaped pole which was referred to as the snake. This implement was usually made of hardwood and measured from two to ten feet long, although most snakes were from six to eight feet long. One end of the snake was enlarged and curved, giving the appearance of a snake's head. It was held and thrown so that the "head" curved upward and this shape enabled it to easily pass over irregularities on the icy path. The shaft of the snake often tapered down to less than one inch in diameter from the bull-like head to the tail end.

The snake was highly polished and sometimes oiled to enable it to glide easily. It was elegantly carved and decorated with eyes and other distinguishing characteristics, and was often decoratively or symbolically painted. (Snow snakes of various shapes and designs are shown in Figure 4.9.) Because of the effort required to make a snake, the loss of one or more of these on a bet proved substantial. Nevertheless, Hallett (1955) noted that tribes in New England throw away the snow snakes in the spring "lest they turn into real snakes" (p. 27).

A somewhat similar game played in warmer climates required a different type of implement. The *dart* or *slider*, made of a hard substance such as rib or leg bone, was painted and had two long feathers protruding to form the "tail." The total length of this implement was two or three feet, and darts and sliders were often found in the Dakotas and the surrounding plains. (See Figure 4.10.)

Trails

Snow snake trails were carefully constructed to ensure a long straight, unobstructed run in a predictable direction. Any level icy or snowy area was adequate for a snow snake trail. A grooved path similar to a straight toboggan trail was constructed by dragging a log or some other item through the snow. In a report to Culin (1907) Willoughby stated that on occasion "one or more of the players would take a boy by the feet and drag him down some incline, thus making a track, or path, in the snow" (p. 407).

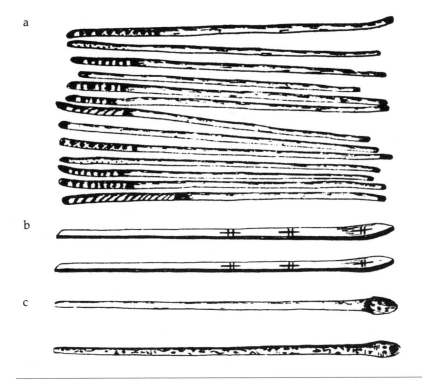

Figure 4.9 (a-c). Snow snakes of various shapes and designs, as used by (a) the Sac and Fox, (b) the Teton Dakota, and (c) the Pomo Indians of California. Photo used by permission of the Smithsonian Institution Press from *Twenty-fourth Annual Report of the Bureau of American Ethnology, 1902-1903.* Smithsonian Institution, Washington, DC, 1907.

Figure 4.10. Feathered horn dart (top) and bone dart (bottom) used by the Mandan and Yankton Dakota Indians respectively. These implements are approximately two feet long. Photo used by permission of the Smithsonian Institution Press from *Twenty-fourth Annual Report of the Bureau of American Ethnology, 1902–1903.* Smithsonian Institution, Washington, DC, 1907.

Hallett (1955) noted the same practice and observed that ''this is probably the reason the boys favored playing on the ice'' (p. 27).

Trails were sometimes constructed by piling a long mound or ridge of snow and then dragging a pole down the middle so that the snake could follow that groove rather than running off in some unpredictable direction. Sometimes water was poured into this groove; when frozen, it would create even less friction and, therefore, a faster track for the snakes. On lakes, a path was established on the icy surface by packing banks of snow on each side of a narrow trail.

Playing Snow Snake

In throwing the snow snake, the forefinger (and/or middle finger) of the throwing hand was placed across the end or tail of the snake. The thumb gripped the top side of the snake and the rest of the fingers held the bottom side. The other hand was used to balance the front end. An underhand delivery was normally used, and the snake was thrown down the path with maximum force.

Hough (1888) watched a game played by the Seneca Indians in New York and described it as follows:

Holding it thus, the player runs three or four rods [approximately 20 yards], and, just before he throws he jumps. The stick skips over the snow like an arrow, or perhaps one could better say like a snake. The skill of the game is in delivering the snake at the best slant, so that none of the original impetus given by the powerful right arm is lost.

The game is usually of four snakes—that is, the best three throws in four.

When skillful players contend, the excitement is very great among the Indians, and there is much betting, sometimes for high stakes. (p. 134)

Among the Menominees in Wisconsin, Hoffman (1896) observed that

the player would grasp the end, or tail, of the snake by putting the index finger against the end and the thumb on one side, opposite to which would be the remaining three fingers; then stooping toward the ground the snake was held horizontally from right to left and forced forward in the direction of the head, skimming along rapidly for a considerable distance. (p. 244)

Precise distances or speeds of these throws are impossible to establish. According to Morgan (1851), however, the snake could be made to "run upon the snow crust with the speed of an arrow, and to a much greater distance, sometimes running 60 to 80 rods. The success of the player depended upon his dexterity and muscular strength" (p. 303). Morgan's estimate of 300 yards to a quarter mile roughly coincides with Baldwin's (1969) observation of around 300 yards. However, other persons have reported even greater distances. For example, Hoffsinde (1957) stated that Indians have been known to hurl snow snakes faster than 120 miles per hour and for distances greater than a mile. This is astonishing and perhaps unbelievable in view of the fact that today's major league baseball pitchers cannot usually throw the ball faster than 100 miles per hour.

Furthermore, reports of throws of one mile may not be very meaningful because the trail might have been on a downhill slant. The question of these long-distance snow snake throws was raised with Oren Lyons (personal communication, July, 1986), Faithkeeper for the Iroquois Confederacy in New York state. The game is still played on a regular basis by the Iroquois. Mr. Lyons reported that the game is most often played on ice covered lakes, which are obviously flat, and he was confident that throws frequently reach a distance of between one and two miles! At any rate, because of the widespread popularity of this game, it is reasonable to assume that a high level of skill would be exhibited in the delivery of the snake as well as in preparing and constructing the trail. See Figure 4.11 for a 1961 photograph of snow-snake activity on a Seneca Reservation in New York state.

The nature of competition in snow snake varied from tribe to tribe. Two persons might compete with each other, or several individuals might make up a team. In either case the individual usually had several snow snakes that he delivered in succession. The individual or the team that hurled the snake the greatest distance won a point. Additional points were awarded for each snake that traveled farther than any snake of the

Figure 4.11. Young men participating in a game of snow snake on the Cattaraugus (Seneca) Reservation in New York. Photo taken in 1961 by Theodore B. Hetzel.

opponents. The game would be over when one person or team achieved a total score of 10 or 20 or whatever the predetermined number was.

In describing the game among the Seneca in 1851, Morgan (1851) stated:

> This game, like that of ball, was divided into a number of separate contests; and was determined when either party had gained the number of points agreed upon, which was generally 7 to 10. . . . After they [the snakes] had all been thrown by the players on both sides, the next question was to determine the count. The snake which ran the greatest distance was a point for the side to which it belonged. Other points might be won on the same side, if a second or third snake was found to be ahead of all the snakes upon the adverse side. These contests were repeated until one of the parties had made the requisite number of points to determine the game. (p. 303)

In various forms the game of snow snake was played from Maine to California, as far south as Oklahoma, and north through much of Canada. Eastern and northern groups consistently used the longer snakes that were skidded along the ice or snow.

Western and plains Indians frequently used the shorter darts made of stag's horn or ribs with a couple of feathers inserted. Whereas this dart game seemed to differ considerably from snow snakes, the manner of throwing the feathered bone darts was much the same. Dorsey (1904) reported that the Omaha in Nebraska played the game with or without snow. He stated, however, that the feathered dart glides much further on snow or ice. After being tossed the dart ''rebounds and goes into the air, then alights and glides still further'' (p. 15).

Hoop-and-Pole

One of the more widespread games reported by writers and travelers during the period from 1650 to 1900 was hoop-and-pole. It was originally a game of great religious significance. In the hoop-and-pole game, a pole, spear, or dart was thrown at a rolling hoop or wheel so that the two objects came to rest close to each other, preferably with the hoop lying on top of the pole. Several variations of this game were played among different tribes, but the most popular version was for competitors to toss long poles at a rolling hoop or wheel. In addition to hoop-and-pole, this game has been referred to as wheel-and-pole, spear-and-ring, and when a stone ring is used, chungke.

Apparently, the hoop-and-pole game was developed in the southwestern part of the United States and Mexico but spread through most parts of the continent. According to Culin (1907), the game ''was played throughout the entire continent north of Mexico'' (p. 450). He also reported that there was no record of women ever playing this game. In fact, Culin cites Cremony's 1868 report that women were barred from the site of the game among the Apache. Several other writers have supported the observation that women and girls were not even allowed to watch this activity.

Cultural Significance of Hoop-and-Pole

The hoop-and-pole game had special religious importance among many traditional Indian groups. In a report to Culin (1907), Mayerford stated that no festivity among the Apache would be complete without a hoop-and-pole game. He added to the mystery of this game when he reported that ''only those medicine men (called Dee-Yin) deeply versed in their folklore and traditions can give a minute explanation of the original meaning and symbolism of this game, and they are very reluctant to part with their knowledge'' (p. 453). Tradition has it that one of the minor gods taught the Indian forefathers the game with all its religious symbolism. Many tribes attributed healing importance to this game. Baldwin (1969) stated that the Pueblo Indians of Arizona believed that the game was connected with their war gods and that women would consequently have no part of it. He further indicated that the hoop-and-pole game is one activity in which men get away from the women and children.

There is not a great deal of consistency in the way the game of hoop-and-pole is described by different writers. Neither do they explain its significance with clarity and uniformity. Some of those persons reporting on this game obviously did not understand the playing rules or the significance of the game. In fact, the Indians were reluctant to play this game in the presence of outsiders. Moreover, the game had begun to decline by the time great numbers of travelers started observing Indian activities. In addition, the game differed somewhat from tribe to tribe. These factors resulted in an unclear picture of the precise nature of this very prominent game.

Like most other Indian sports, the hoop-and-pole game was used as a basis for gambling. Cremony's 1868 report (cited in Culin, 1907) provided a peculiar insight regarding the meaning of the hoop-and-pole game. He asked an Apache medicine man why women were excluded and was told that such a restriction was

> required by tradition; but the shrewd old Sons-in-jah gave me another, and, I believe, the true version. When people gamble, said he, they become half crazy, and are very apt to quarrel. This is the most exciting game we have, and those who play it will wager all they possess. The loser is apt to get angry, and fights have issued which resulted in the loss of many warriors. To prevent this, it was long ago determined that no warrior should be present with arms upon his person or within near reach and this game is always played at some distance from camp. Three prominent warriers are named as judges, and from their decision there is no appeal. They are not suffered to bet while acting in this capacity. The reason why women are forbidden to be present is because they always foment troubles between the players, and create confusion by taking sides and provoking dissention. (p. 302)

This view of the Indian personality is so different from most other observations of Indian sports or betting behavior that it almost incredible. It is surprising that even this serious game would evoke the kind of motivation and behavior described by Cremony. It is possible that Cremony did not understand the subtleties of the game. It is also possible that as a non-Indian he was adding a non-Indian interpretation to the activities. Perhaps "shrewd old Sons-in-jah" provided this story as a source of amusement. In any event, the suggestion that the presence of women, weapons, or betting would present a serious threat of trouble is contrary to general customs. All of these ingredients were present at other major sporting events, such as lacrosse and shinny.

Game Implements

Considerable significance was attached to the equipment used in hoop-and-pole. George Dorsey (1903) explained the meaning of the hoop among the Arapahoe:

> The disk itself represents the sun, while the actual band of wood represents a tiny water-snake, called henige, and which is said to be found in rivers, in lakes, near ponds, and in buffalo wallows. . . . This serpent is said to be the most harmless of all snakes. The wheel thus, representing the snake has a derived meaning and represents the water which surrounds the earth. The additional idea was also put forth that while the wheel represents a harmless snake, all snakes are powerful to charm, and hence the wheel is a sign of gentleness and meekness. (p. 12)

The construction of the hoop, or target, varied from tribe to tribe. In general, a sapling was bent into a circular shape six to twelve inches in diameter and bound with a network of rawhide. The rawhide formed a spiderweb design that had a particular meaning for certain tribes. According to Baldwin (1969), the Novaks believed that the game of hoop-and-pole was taught to them by the ancient spider people. Most of the hoops were completely filled in (see Figure 4.12). However, other hoops were less elaborate, either utilizing rawhide to divide the hoop into quarters or halves or else having no internal network. These hoops were often decorated with varied colors, and feathers and beads were sometimes attached.

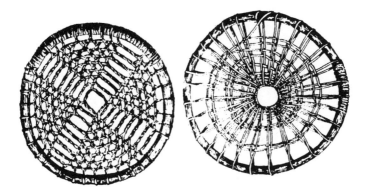

Figure 4.12. Netted hoops for hoop-and-pole game. The one on left is ten inches in diameter and was used by the Gros Ventre Indians in Montana. The one on the right is sixteen inches in diameter and was used by the Piegan Indians in Alberta. Photo used by permission of the Smithsonian Institution Press from *Twenty-fourth Annual Report of the Bureau of American Ethnology, 1902–1903.* Smithsonian Institution, Washington, DC, 1907.

Figure 4.13. Stone ring used in chungke by the Cheyenne Indians in Oklahoma. The ring is only four and a half inches in diameter. Photo used by permission of the Smithsonian Institution Press from *Twenty-fourth Annual Report of the Bureau of American Ethnology, 1902–1903.* Smithsonian Institution, Washington, DC, 1907.

Figure 4.14. Poles and game rings used by the Omaha Indians in Nebraska. The poles are only four feet two inches long and the ring is six inches in diameter. Photo used by permission of the Smithsonian Institution Press from *Twenty-fourth Annual Report of the Bureau of American Ethnology, 1902–1903.* Smithsonian Institution, Washington, DC, 1907.

Chungke was a variation of the hoop-and-hole game played mainly by tribes in the southeast. Target hoops for this game were made of stone, and these stone rings were typically smaller, usually measuring around four to five inches in diameter and had a small hole in the center. Figure 4.13 shows a stone used by Indians in Oklahoma. Slightly different stone rings were used by other tribes throughout the south.

The pole used in the hoop-and-pole game was frequently decorated with bright colors and often had buckskin strings, feathers, and claws of various animals attached. The length of the pole varied greatly, from as short as two feet to twelve feet or more. Most poles, however, measured from eight to ten feet. Figure 4.14 illustrates poles used by the Omaha Indians in Nebraska. These were fifty inches in length and had a bar on one end similar to that found on poles in other parts of the country.

In a variation of this game, shorter sticks or darts made of corn cobs and feathers were used. Sometimes the longer poles were made of single pieces of wood that were peeled and carved, but on other occasions poles were constructed of two or three parts that were either jointed in an interlocking fashion or tied together.

The Playing Court

The field or court used for the hoop-and-pole game was usually a flat area that had been carefully prepared. The playing area was made as level as possible, and sometimes it was covered with a light layer of sand. Every effort was made to allow the hoop to roll smoothly and straight. All reports make it clear that meticulous attention was devoted to the preparation of hoop and pole courts.

Culin (1907) reported on a variety of the fields and courts used for hoop-and-pole. Timber floors approximately 150 feet long were constructed for the game among the Mandan, and the Apache played on level ground approximately 100 feet in length. In addition, "the Creeks had large enclosed courts with sloping sides on which the spectators were seated. Among the Apache and Navahoe the direction of the track is from north to south" (p. 421–422).

Writing more than a half century earlier than Culin, Catlin (1841/1944) also observed a game among the Mandan and reported that it was played "on a pavement of clay, which has been used for that purpose until it has become as smooth and hard as a floor" (p. 132). The wooden floors referred to by Culin were apparently added in the late 19th century. Earlier in the century, Bradbury (cited in Culin, 1907) observed a game in Arikara, South Dakota, and described the area as a place "neatly formed, resembling a skittle alley, about nine feet in breadth and 90 feet long" (p. 861).

In 1775 Bernard Romans (1775/1921) reported that the chungke court used by the Florida Indians was longer than that typically described in other areas: "They make an alley of about 200 feet in length, where a very smooth clay ground is laid, which when dry, is very hard" (p. 79). A description of very elaborate "chunk yards" was given by William Bartram in 1849 in a report on the Creek Indians (cited in Culin, 1907, p. 486). The area for chungke play was in the rotunda or public square of the village. The yards were sometimes 600 to 900 feet in length and were "exactly level." Furthermore, the playing surface was two to three feet below the banks surrounding them. The terraces around the perimeter of the court served as seats for the spectators. Bartram speculated that the elaborate nature of these areas meant that they had also been used in earlier days as a place of public exhibitions, shows, or other games.

Playing the Game

According to most accounts, the game of hoop-and-pole began when the hoop was thrown so that it rolled down the center of the court. The

Figure 4.15. Mollhausen's 1854 lithograph of Mohave men engaged in the hoop-and-pole game. Photo used by permission of the National Anthropological Archives, Smithsonian Institution.

Figure 4.16. Apache hoop-and-pole game. Photo used by permission of the National Anthropological Archives, Smithsonian Institution.

individual tossing the hoop was not usually one of the contestants but rather a third party who controlled the play. As the hoop began rolling down the court, the two contesting players ran alongside, but at a prescribed distance from, the hoop. Shown in Figure 4.15 is Baldwin Moll-hausen's 1854 lithograph of a Mohave hoop-and-pole game. This illustration indicates the players' position in relation to the hoop and to each other. Most illustrations of hoop-and-pole are drawings or sketches based on the memory of persons who observed the game. However, Figure 4.16 is a photograph of a group of Apaches playing the game. The date of this photograph is unknown. This is one of the rare photographs that show a game in progress.

As the hoop began slowing down, the players tossed their poles so that the hoop would fall across a particular portion of the pole. Points were awarded according to how close the special markings on the pole were to the corresponding markings on the hoop. In variations of the game, contestants were awarded points for actually spearing the hoop with the pole or with an arrow. Points were accumulated by the individual performer or by the team each time the hoop was rolled. The number of points required for the game was preestablished.

In describing the pattern of play among the Arikara in South Dakota, Brackenridge (1814) reported that the game is played by two persons, each one armed with a long pole. He stated that

> one of them rolls a hoop, which, after having reached about two-thirds of the distance, is followed at half speed, and as they perceive it about to fall, they cast their poles under it; the pole on which the hoop falls, so as to be nearest to certain corresponding marks on the hoop and pole, gains for that time. (p. 255)

Among the Arapaho and Cheyenne in Oklahoma, James Mooney (1896) reported that

> it is a man's game, and there are three players, one rolling the wheel, while the other two, each armed with a pair of throwing sticks, run after it and throw the sticks so as to cross the wheel in a certain position. The two throwers are the contestants, the one who rolls the wheel merely being an assistant. Like most Indian games, it is a means of gambling, and high stakes are sometimes wagered on the results. (p. 994)

The game of chungke (also called chunkey, chunky, and tchung-kee, among others) is a variation of the hoop-and-pole game. Whether chungke originated before hoop-and-pole is unknown; however, most descriptions of chungke are from the 17th and 18th centuries. Chapter 1 cites reports of well-established traditions of chungke among the Choctaw in those early centuries. Most reports of the hoop-and-pole game are from the early- to mid-19th century.

The essential difference between the two games was that chungke was played with a round stone in the form of a disk (with hole) instead of the hoop. Adair (1775/1968) reported that the Choctaw men in Mississippi had a

> favourite game called *chungke*; which, with propriety of language, may be called "Running hard labor." They have near their statehouse, a square piece of ground well cleaned, and fine sand is carefully strewed over it, when requisite, to promote a swifter motion to what they throw along the surface. Only one, or two on a side, play at this ancient game. They have a stone about two fingers broad at the edge, and two spands round; each party has a pole of about eight feet long, smooth, and tapering at each end, the points flat. They set off a-breast of each other at six yards from the end of the playground; then one of them hurls the stone on its edge, in as direct a line as he can, a considerable distance toward the middle of the other end of the square: when they have ran a few yards, each darts his pole anointed with bear's oil, with a proper force, as near as he can guess in proportion to the motion of the stone, that the end may lie close to the stone—when this is the case, the person counts two of the game, and, in proportion of the nearness of the poles to the mark, one is counted, unless by measuring, both are found to be at equal distance from the stone. In this manner, the players will keep running most part of the day, at half speed, under the violent heat of the sun. (p. 401)

The game of hoop-and-pole continued to have symbolic importance even after it was no longer played. Writing in 1896, James Mooney reported that the game was practically obsolete among the Cheyenne and Apache, although it had been "a favorite in the older times" (p. 994). Many Indians, nevertheless, continued to carry a hoop for symbolic purposes because carrying the hoop symbolized traditional activities and "a revival of the old time games" (p. 994).

Summary

Numerous games could be presented as having importance for various Indian groups. Those discussed in this chapter (archery, aquatic activities, snow snake, and hoop-and-pole) were widely representative. The first two were universal among Indians on this continent, and the others were important for very large groups.

Archery and swimming were neither exclusively Indian nor were they exclusively sports. Despite the utilitarian nature of those activities, however, they clearly evolved into sports that were important in the everyday lives of Indians. Consequently, over the past two centuries archery has been viewed by non-Indians as a typical "Indian" sport. Boating activities, particularly canoeing and kayaking, have also been closely identified with the American Indians. The Indians developed these water crafts for speed and ease of control.

As with certain other utilitarian skills, aquatic activities and archery came to be used as sports. Practice of these activities as sports not only provided enjoyment, as with other games, but also served as a means for improving skills used in everyday activities.

The hoop-and-pole game, and the similar game of chungke, were being played prominently at the time non-Indians arrived on this continent. Because of the sacred nature of this game, and because it was sharply declining in popularity more than a century ago, its meaning was not fully revealed to outsiders. On the other hand, snow snake was purely a game of skill and enjoyment, though the "snake" itself sometimes took on certain mystical qualities. This is one of the few original Native American games that continues today as a popular outdoor winter activity among the Iroquois.

Chapter 5

Children's Play

An analysis of children's play provides an additional clue to the traditional mode of life among American Indians. Some children's games, of course, were similar to those found among children of non-Indian populations. Further, the general characteristics of play are quite similar regardless of ethnic identity, historical period, or social class. Nevertheless, a consideration of the play behavior of Indian children reveals both the mood and cultural characteristics of early Indian society.

Traditional Indian children had a great deal of time for play, and that time was filled with energetic and creative activity. However, as with Indian adult sports and general life-style, children's play in recent years has been greatly influenced by the broad range of societal changes during the 19th and 20th centuries. Restrictions in environment and space, as well as diminishing flexibility in life-style, have curtailed the extent and spontaneity of children's outdoor activities. Materials for traditional play implements have been less available. The roles of adult Indians, which traditionally served as the basis for much of children's play, have changed significantly. In addition to changes in children's play habits, Indian youth and teenagers have also altered their attitudes and aspirations toward sport performance. (This issue is dealt with in chapter 12.)

In this chapter the traditional play of Indian children is arbitrarily organized into the following categories: (a) games which were viewed essentially as preparation for adulthood, (b) games in which toys or other play implements were the focus of attention, and (c) formal games or self-testing activities that were played by both older children and adults. A representative sample from each of these groups will be presented.

Games as Preparation for Adulthood

Indian adults viewed childhood as a time for shaping the physical, cultural, and spiritual characteristics of the individual. Play was encouraged and guided as an important part of this process. Physical contests, self-testing activities, role-playing, and telling stories were central in the life of Indian youth. As in other cultures, Indian children frequently selected and created games that imitated the serious activities of adults and were viewed as practice for adult roles. Role-playing blended into play so that they became one and the same.

Boys usually selected games that enabled them to engage in their father's role as hunter, warrior, or athlete. Older men were frequently available to teach young boys the appropriate skills and the proper attitudes related to these activities. Girls played games that closely paralleled child rearing, household chores, farming, or pastimes of their mothers. Play and work became indistinguishable for both girls and boys.

The play of small children was usually imitative and dramatic, reflecting the activities and social customs of their cultures. They played warfare games that involved group role-playing. Activities such as organized hide-and-seek games, stalking, and mass combat were also popular, and individual combat games such as wrestling were widely practiced. Beauchamp (1896) pointed out the relationship between games of children and adult roles: "As the Iroquois children were to become warriors, many of their sports were of a savage and warlike nature" (p. 269).

The *mud and willow stick fight*, which has been reported from several tribes was typical of the games of war. Children would gather a large pile of wet mud and prepare an arsenal of mud balls; after battle lines had been drawn, the competitors would place a mud ball on the forked end of a flexible willow stick and throw it at the opponents. The flexible stick enabled them to sling the mud ball with great velocity over a long distance. Although some pain was inflicted when the mud balls struck their target, children were discouraged from crying or cowering.

As an activity of skill and cunning, the game of hide-and-seek was as popular with Indian children as it is today among non-Indians, and it was often played with serious intentions. This game, which was played principally by boys, developed skills in evasion, diversion, and searching—all valuable skills in both warfare and hunting. One child was blindfolded and challenged to catch the other children, who would remain nearby mocking and teasing. Played at night without the blindfold, it was called the *witch* game. Children often used tom-toms to give clues to their whereabouts. Skills in stalking as well as in avoiding capture were to be useful during later years in hunting and in warfare.

Mimicry among Indian youth extended even into religious ceremonies, including ghost games, medicine rites, and even mortuary activities. In an extensive discussion of his play patterns as a youth, Ohiyesa (cited in Hamilton, 1972), a Sioux, reported that children dared to engage in some games with religious implication but that they did so with a degree of anxiety. They played a game called *medicine dance* but sensed that

> the adults think it an act of irreverence to imitate these dances, therefore performances of this kind were always enjoyed in secret. We used to observe all the important ceremonies and it required something of an actor to reproduce the dramatic features of the dance. (p. 58)

Ohiyesa compared this to white children "playing church" (p. 58) with somewhat less serious intentions.

Ohiyesa asserted that play among the Sioux was

> molded by the life and customs of our people; indeed, we practiced only what we expected to do when grown. Our games were feats with the bow and arrow, and foot and pony races, wrestling, swimming and imitation of the customs and habits of our fathers. We had sham fights with mud balls and willow wands; we played lacrosse, made war upon bees, and coasted upon the ribs of animals and buffalo robes. (p. 55)[1]

The imitative characteristics of children's play was emphasized by Stevenson (1903) in her observation of the activities of Zuni children.

> While the youngsters have a variety of sports exclusively their own, they may be found any pleasant day enjoying some of the games of their elders, and, like their elders, they indulge in betting, for this habit is developed in the North American Indian while he is still in his infancy. The younger Zuni children play the ceremonial games, however, with but little or no understanding of the occultism associated with them (p. 468).

Boys in all tribes typically played rough games or others that offered significant challenge. Such games showed how brave and strong they were, and their behavior in these activities signaled to both adults and the young men themselves when they were ready for the full responsibilities of adulthood.

Play With Toys

Although store-bought toys were unavailable, children engaged in a wide variety of games with homemade toys. Obviously, Indian children did not have battery powered toys or video games, but they created many

---

[1]From *Cry of the Thunderbird: The American Indian's Own Story*, edited by Charles Hamilton. New edition copyright © 1972 by the University of Oklahoma Press.

toys remarkably similar to ones that attained great popularity in later years. These toys were built from sticks, stones, bamboo, feathers, corn cobs, husks, and a variety of other materials. They also had what we now call educational toys, requiring creativity in both construction and play. For example, Dorsey reported that the Teton Dakota children exhibited a high level of skill in building animal models from clay (cited in Culin, 1907).

Toys used by Indians can be broadly categorized:

1. Toys for soothing or amusing infants. These included rattles, feathers, mobiles suspended over beds, and a variety of other colorful and noisy items. They used many types of rattles made from dried gourds, pebbles, or shells. However, rattles were viewed as sacred and were consequently restricted to religious ceremonies in some groups.
2. Toys developed by children themselves. There appears to have been no limit to the forms and uses of these toys.
3. Toys made by parents for children. Dolls, which have been the most popular toys among all children are perhaps the best examples. In some cultures they were used in rituals as idols before the children received them. However, the use of ritual dolls as toys was forbidden in some groups.

Some of the most popular games using toys are discussed on the following pages. This is not to suggest, however, that all of these games were created and used exclusively by American Indians.

Tops

Tops were extremely popular among Indian youth, particularly those groups located in northern regions. Baldwin (1969) speculated that tops may have come to this country from China, noting that the Chinese were traditionally the champion makers and spinners of tops. However, Culin (1907) believed that tops existed on this continent prior to contacts with non-Indians.

Indian tops were of two basic types, but all were made from bone, horns, wood, and other hard materials. A spine, or axle, protruded from the main body of one kind of top, and long strips of buckskin were wrapped around this spine and pulled vigorously to start it spinning. Many games were played with these tops. For instance, the child would spin the top to see if he or she could run out the door, around the house, and back into the room before the top stopped spinning. Tops could be spun on any flat, reasonably hard surface, including ice, frozen ground, a wooden floor, or packed dirt.

A second type of top, perhaps the most popular, was the whip top. The individual would spin the top with the hand and then lash it in a glancing fashion with buckskin strips to make it spin even faster. Some tops had a hole cut into the side so that they made a humming noise when spun around rapidly. Skillful use of the whips enabled the children to move the top in any direction they wished, and speed races with whip tops were popular. Another popular game was to whip the top so that it struck that of an opponent and knocked it out of the contest. In whip top races, boys or girls were able to move the tops over very rough terrain without losing control. Other games included keeping the spinning top within the most restricted area, spinning the top for the longest time, or jumping it over the highest hurdle.

Many tops were elaborately decorated with carving and painting. Various tops and whips are shown in Figures 5.1 and 5.2.

Figure 5.1. Whip top (in center) and two finger tops used by the Hopi and Bannock Indians, Arizona and Idaho. Photo used by permission of Smithsonian Institute Press from *Twenty-fourth Annual Report of the Bureau of American Ethnology, 1902–1903*. Smithsonian Institution, Washington, DC, 1907.

Figure 5.2. Whip tops used by the Oglala Sioux, Pine Ridge, South Dakota. Photo used by permission of the Smithsonian Institution Press from *Twenty-fourth Annual Report of the Bureau of American Ethnology, 1902–1903*. Smithsonian Institution, Washington, DC, 1907.

Noisemakers

Noisemaking was a popular activity for Indian children, and several creative instruments were developed for this purpose. Among the more popular were *bull-roarers, whistles, buzzes, popguns, drums,* and *rattles.*

The *bull-roarer* (also called a *whizzing stick, wind whirler,* or *moaning stick*) was made of a thin, flat, rectangular slat of wood tied to the end of a string. According to Walker (1905), Sioux children played this game "from ancient times" (p. 277). He stated that the board was usually made of red cedar, about one-eighth inch thick, two inches wide, and twelve inches long. A pliable thong of twelve to eighteen inches long was attached to the board, and a wooden handle was tied to the other end of the thong. When a child took the handle in one hand and whirled the board rapidly around his or her head, the bull-roarer (the flat board) gave a whirling or whizzing sound. A bull-roarer used by Dakota Indians is shown in figure 5.3.

Apparently, the bull-roarer was first developed by the Sioux Indians who used it during funerals to ward off evil spirits. It was widely used for religious purposes by many tribes in the Southwest and in the Plains. It was sacred to many groups because it represented thunder. Bull-roarers were often employed during dry seasons to serve as thunder in rituals for bringing rain, and they were frequently painted with lightning symbols to increase their potency.

Because of its interesting noise and the ease of construction and use, children began using the bull-roarer as a toy. Despite its serious use by adults, parents had a difficult time preventing children from playing with them for the noise effect.

Another whirling toy, called a *buzz,* was popular among Indian children throughout the continent. The instrument was typically made of

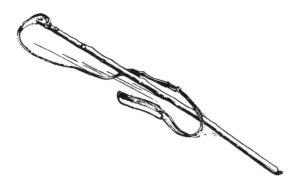

Figure 5.3. Bull-roarer used by the Oglala Sioux Indians, Pine Ridge, South Dakota. Photo used by permission of the Smithsonian Institution Press from *Twenty-fourth Annual Report of the Bureau of American Ethnology, 1902–1903.* Smithsonian Institution, Washington, DC, 1907.

a flattened piece of bone, shell, or some form of pottery. Two holes were made near the center through which cords were inserted. The cords extended eight to ten inches to each side. The strings where held at each end with the buzz in the middle. The buzz was then whirled around and around in one direction until the string was twisted tightly. When the cords were pulled outward, the buzz spun rapidly, making a buzzing sound on each pull. The buzzer retwisted the string in the opposite direction so that the pulling and relaxing continued along with the whirling or humming sound. According to Walker (1905), "buffalo fighting" (p. 277) occurred when several boys used their spinning buzzes to strike and attempt to stop those of other boys. Sample buzzes are illustrated in Figures 5.4 and 5.5. As with practically all Indian implements and equipment, art was prominently displayed.

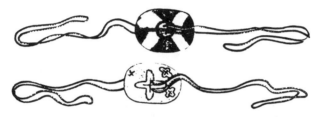

Figure 5.4. Buzzes used by the Maricopa Indians in Arizona. Photo used by permission of the Smithsonian Institution Press from *Twenty-fourth Annual Report of the Bureau of American Ethnology, 1902–1903*. Smithsonian Institution, Washington, DC, 1907.

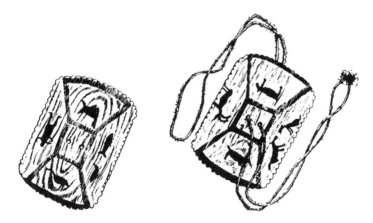

Figure 5.5. Buzzes used by the Western Eskimo, Alaska. Photo used by permission of the Smithsonian Institution Press from *Twenty-fourth Annual Report of the Bureau of American Ethnology, 1902–1903*. Smithsonian Institution, Washington, DC, 1907.

Whistles of many descriptions were used by Indians throughout the continent. Although initially used as musical instruments, war signals, hunting calls or other purposes, many whistles would end up as toys for children. Early whistles were typically made of bone, bamboo shoots, or hollowed out stems of other plants. Catlin (1841/1965) described several types of whistles and flutes that were used as musical instruments. He referred to one as a "war" whistle (p. 242), and another one with which he was particularly fascinated was called a "mystery" whistle. This was so called because the Indian boys could play harmonic sounds of "peculiar sweetness" (p. 243) with the whistles, but he and other white men were not able to make any sound at all come out of it. He reported that an Indian boy blew notes repeatedly "for hundreds of white men who might be lookers-on, not one of whom could make the least noise on it, even by practicing for hours" (p. 242). Despite the original purpose of the whistles, children soon converted them to play instruments for their own uses and, no doubt, to the distraction of their parents.

Culin (1907) reported having acquired *popguns* from seven different tribes spreading from Iowa and Oklahoma through the plains states.

Figure 5.6. Wooden popguns used by the Cheyenne, Sac and Fox, and Arikara Indians. Photo used by permission of the Smithsonian Institution Press from *Twenty-fourth Annual Report of the Bureau of American Ethnology, 1902–1903.* Smithsonian Institution, Washington, DC, 1907.

Though evidence does not firmly establish the existence of popguns prior to contact with the white man, Culin does report that excavated popguns make it "probable" (p. 758) that they were original in character. The popguns discovered were usually around a foot in length and were made by carving a tubular hole through the length of the gun into which a stick, or plunger, was forced. The popguns were usually loaded with wads of material that was made flexible by chewing or soaking in water. Reverend J. Owen Dorsey (1891) reported that the play of the Teton Dakota boys involved their shooting one another, and the one who was hit "suffered much pain" (p. 337). Sample popguns from several tribes are shown in Figure 5.6.

Drums were common in almost all tribes across the continent. There were great varieties of drums: singleheaded drums (a single skin stretched over a hoop), log drums, pottery drums, and other more elaborate drums. The war drums were sacred and were used only on ceremonial occasions. Ordinarily, drums were not toys for children. Adults tried to keep these for ceremonial use only, but children did construct their own crude drums to mimic the adults.

Rattles were popular with children throughout most of the continent. The pure joy of listening to noise, whether rhythmic or otherwise, has apparently been a general human characteristic of young people over the years. Rattles come in many forms and were made from a variety of substances. Figure 5.7 shows a rattle made of deer hooves that was used by Apache children.

Dolls

A great many dolls were used by Indian children. These were constructed of buckskin, cattails, corncobs and husks, and a variety of other materials. Some tribes did not want dolls to be too realistic because it gave the

Figure 5.7. Apache rattle made of deer hooves. Photo used by permission of the University Museum, University of Pennsylvania.

impression of a miniature dead person in the house. Parents gave dolls to very small children, but larger girls made their own. Small boys were interested in dolls but later turned to carving animals and other figures. Although dolls were prevalent throughout the continent, they took on tribal as well as geographical characteristics. They were constructed of corn materials, pine cones, seashells, buffalo hide, or other substances, depending on its availability in that region. In appearance they reflected the kinds of animals prevalent in that part of the country. The Kachina dolls of the Southwest have continued to be objects of great artistic interest in both the Indian and non-Indian communities. Two Apache dolls are shown in Figure 5.8.

Figure 5.8 Apache Kachina dolls. Photo used by permission of the University Museum, University of Pennsylvania.

Games and Amusements for Older Children and Adults

The transition from childhood to adulthood was not clear and distinct, though it usually occurred in the early to middle teenage years. Similarly, there was not always an absolute demarcation between children's games and adult's games. Some of the games described in the pages that follow were played primarily by children and others primarily by adults. When played by adults, however, they were viewed as relatively minor sports. There is ample evidence that all were played in traditional Indian societies.

Tobogganing

Coasting on the snow or ice atop a sliding apparatus was a favorite activity of children in the northern parts of the United States and in Canada. They frequently coasted on buffalo ribs, hides, or tree bark. John Ewers (1944) reported that the Blackfeet Indians of Montana and Alberta made runners for sleds from the horny rib bones of a buffalo cow. They separated five to ten ribs from the backbone and reassembled them in the same order and tied them together with rawhide. A seat made of buffalo hide was fastened in place. A buffalo tail was usually attached to the back of the sled. According to Ewers, certain men had developed a high level of skill in making sleds so that "wealthy men are said to have paid one of them a good horse to fashion a sled for one of their sons" (p. 183).

Coasting games were many and varied, but most often they involved coasting for speed, distance, or maneuverability. Boys who were most confident about their sleds would wager those sleds against those of other contestants. Sometimes riderless sleds were sent down the hillsides in a race for distance. Boys and girls who owned no sleds used buffalo hides or tree bark for the ride downhill.

Indians are credited with having developed the toboggan as well as the snowshoe. In addition to their general usefulness, these items proved to be a major source of enjoyment for Indian children of the northern tribes during the long winter months.

Cat's Cradle and Other String Games

The Navajo Indians believed that string games were taught to their ancestors by ancient spider people (Baldwin, 1969). Thus, weblike patterns were reflected in these games. String games using the fingers are very old and were a part of the culture of most ancient tribes. The general idea is to make a recognizable figure or form with a network of strings around the fingers. These activities proved fascinating to young children, who worked very hard to create new designs. In fact, Indian adults spent many hours developing designs that were difficult to re-create. There was, in fact, an infinite variety of string games, or cat's cradles.

Haddon (1903) outlined a long list of string designs, which were called "string figures," "cat's cradles," or "tricks" (p. 213). These he had learned from numerous tribes across the continent, including the Eskimo, the Thompson Indians in Canada, the Cherokee in Oklahoma, the Omaha in the Plains, and the Navajo in the Southwest. He explained the name of the figure (usually an animal, a man-made object, or natural phenomena such as lightning, stars, etc.) and how to construct it. Verbal descriptions, line illustrations, and photographs of string designs accompanied his report.

Stilt Walking

Walking on stilts was a popular activity among Indians long before the arrival of non-Indians on this continent. Stilts were usually constructed from thin saplings with a forked branch that was cut off. The individual grasped a pole in each hand and stood on the branched notch, which was perhaps a foot or two above the ground. With practice one learned to balance oneself and walk quite effectively.

McCaskill (1936) reported that stilt walking was popular throughout the continent and particularly so among the Hopi, Shoshoni, and the Mexican Indians. Although recognizing that foreign cultures may have engaged in stilt walking, McCaskill said that it was widely used by Indians prior to the coming of the white man. Culin (1907) also presented evidence of the use of stilts for walking and dancing among ancient tribes in the Southwest and Mexico.

In addition to their use for innocent amusement, Bishop Landa in 1864 (cited in Culin, 1907) referred to their use by the Maya Indians to honor a bird deity. The Zuni used stilt walking sticks for planting. Illustrations of stilts used by the Hopi, Shoshoni, and Zuni are shown in Figure 5.9. As can be noted, bindings of buckskin or other material were sometimes used to stabilize the footing. Because of their usefulness in self-testing activities and amusements, stilts have assumed widespread popularity among non-Indians over the past century. Elongated and modified stilts are frequently used by circus performers of today.

Battledoor

The game of battledoor, sometimes called shuttlecock, gained wide popularity throughout the western part of the United States and Canada. This game was played by striking a shuttlecock (usually made of corn husks and feathers) with a wooden battledoor (a flattened, paddle-type

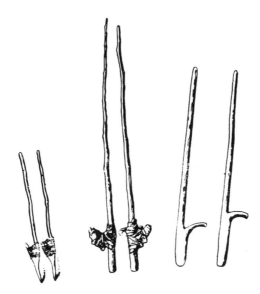

Figure 5.9. Stilts used by the Hopi, Zuni, and Shoshoni Indians. Photo used by permission of the Smithsonian Institution Press from *Twenty-fourth Annual Report of the Bureau of American Ethnology, 1902–1903*. Smithsonian Institution, Washington, DC, 1907.

implement with a handle). This game somewhat resembled today's game of badminton. Reporting on play among the Zuni at the turn of the century, John Owens (1891) stated that "they try how many times they can smack it [the shuttlecock] into the air while they count in their own language" (p. 39). Although acknowledging that it bore some resemblance to non-Indian games. Owens concluded: "I am inclined to think that we must give the Indians the credit of inventing this game rather than borrowing it" (p. 39). Stevenson (1903) reported that the game was played "as frequently by younger boys as by their elders, and always for stakes" (p. 492). Sample battledoors and shuttlecocks are shown in Figures 5.10 and 5.11.

Skin or Blanket Tossing

Blanket tossing as an activity for amusement was especially popular for both young people and adults in Canada and Alaska. In this activity one player would stand on a blanket or skin (usually made of walrus or buffalo skin) while many others around the perimeter of the skin took hold and tossed him or her into the air. The person on the blanket attempted to keep his or her balance while the others would try to throw him or her off balance. Individuals were tossed as high as fifteen to twenty feet into

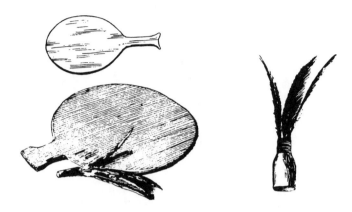

Figure 5.10. Battledoor paddles and shuttlecocks used by the Hesquiaht Indians in British Columbia. Photo used by permission of the Smithsonian Institution Press from *Twenty-fourth Annual Report of the Bureau of American Ethnology, 1902–1903.* Smithsonian Institution, Washington, DC, 1907.

Figure 5.11. Battledoor paddles used by Nimkish and Opitchesaht Indians in British Columbia. Photo used by permission of the Smithsonian Institution Press from *Twenty-fourth Annual Report of the Bureau of American Ethnology, 1902–1903.* Smithsonian Institution, Washington, DC, 1907.

the air. A photograph of this game with perhaps two dozen persons circling a large, circular hide is shown in Figure 5.12.

Originally, blanket tossing was used by hunters as a means of sighting game animals at faraway distances in the flat lands. However, it has more

Figure 5.12 Eskimo blanket tossing (Nulagatuk) in Barrow, Alaska. Photo taken in 1961 by Theodore B. Hetzel.

recently been used as a source of amusement or as a game of courage for young people. According to Ewers (1944), boys were divided into teams, and the boys of one side tossed a member of the opposite team as high as they could. "The object was to make him cry out that he had enough. If they could not do that, the other side was declared the winner" (p. 185). In another game one boy stood on the tightly-drawn blanket while the others tried to throw him off balance. If he remained standing after a period of time his side won. However, movement of the blanket back and forth and from side to side made it virtually impossible to retain one's balance. Blanket tossing is still a popular source of amusement among the Eskimos for both adults and children.

Ring and Pin

Widely played throughout the continent, the ring and pin game was more popular with adults than with children. Though usually played for general amusement, it was sometimes a game of serious consequences. Dorsey (1891) reported that for the Gros Ventres in Montana it was a "favorite pastime among young men and women, and so often called the matrimonial game" (p. 537). This activity was used by northeastern tribes to settle marriage proposals when two men were trying for the hand of one girl. The winner of the game was also the winner of the maiden. Sample ring and pin apparatus are shown in Figures 5.13 and 5.14.

Figure 5.13. Materials for the ring and pin game. Used by the Copper Eskimo in Alaska. Photo used by permission of the University Museum, University of Pennsylvania.

Figure 5.14. Materials for the ring and pin game. Photo used by permission of the National Anthropological Archives, Smithsonian Institution.

Equipment for this game included a pin perhaps six to twelve inches in length with a string that attached it to a target, which may be a ring, a cup, or some other item with holes or notches. While the player held onto the pin, he threw the target into the air and tried to spear it on the way down (i.e., to insert the pin into one of the rings or perforated areas). It was similar in performance to the ball-and-cup game widely practiced today in Latin American countries. In some variations, several rings were attached to a string; the idea was to toss the string of rings into the air and catch as many as possible on the pin as they fell downward.

Another variation of the ring and pin game involved attaching an animal skull to the end of the string and tossing it into the air. On the downward flight of the skull, an attempt was made to thrust the pin through a particular hole such as the eye, the nose, and so on. Different point values were assigned to different cavities. Conical bones were frequently joined together, and an additional target was also attached (see Figure 5.13). Chief Kah-Ge-Ga-Gah-Bouh (cited in Hamilton, 1972) of the Ojibway tribe referred to the ring and pin game as "bone play" because the articles used in his tribe were the hoof-joint bones of the deer, and he reported that "the ends are hollowed out, and from three to ten are strung together. In playing it, they use the same kind of sharp stick, the end of which is thrown into the bones" (p. 62).

Ball Juggling

Juggling was a very popular activity, particularly among the northern tribes and Eskimos. While walking along, individuals would frequently juggle two, three, or four small balls, stones, chips, or other objects. The object, of course, was to keep one or more balls in the air. A juggling race has been described in which women would run to a target area and return while juggling several balls. The winner of the race was the one who returned first without having dropped the ball or made any other error.

Hot Ball

In this activity a stone was put into the fire and heated until it became very hot. It was then taken out and thrown some distance into the woods. Young boys who were not allowed to see the ball thrown then went to search for it. The boy who first located the ball had first opportunity to pick it up and return it to camp. However, very frequently he had to drop the ball because it was too hot. If that happened, any other participant could seize the ball and run with it. The one who returned to camp with the hot ball was the winner and received a prize.

Pets

Children and adolescents frequently kept pets of various sorts, and the most common was the dog, which was one of the few domesticated animals. Wild animals such as foxes, bears, buffalo, deer, bees, and turkeys were also occasionally used as pets. Ohiyesa (cited in Hamilton, 1972) recalled his childhood:

> We had many curious wild pets. There were young foxes, bears, wolves, raccoons, fawns, buffalo calves and birds of all kinds, tamed by various boys. . . . I once had a grizzly bear for a pet and so far as he and I were concerned, our relations were charming and very close. But I hardly know whether he made more enemies for me or I for him. It was his habit to treat every boy unmercifully who injured me. He was despised for his conduct in my interest and I was hated on account of his interference. (p. 59)[2]

Talayesva (cited in Hamilton, 1972) emphasized that they were taught to treat animals with great respect whether they were pets or in their natural habitat, and he remembered that once he killed a small snake, "which was an awful thing to do" (p. 60).

The 1982 photograph (Figure 5.15) of three Innu Indian boys in northern Quebec shows that interest in caring for animals continues among Indian children today. These boys are holding two young birds that are to be cared for. Sensitivity to animals shows continuity with traditional life-styles, but the Boston Bruins cap perhaps reflects a dream of participation in modern sports in the National Hockey League. (Several Canadian Indian groups have sent a large number of players into professional ice hockey).

Storytelling

Storytelling was a favorite Indian youth activity. Older men were usually the best storytellers. Especially popular were stories about pranks and tricksters, and many of these stories referred to animals of long ago that had human powers. Like many of the fairy tales or fables among non-Indians, most Indian stories included a moral.

Storytelling was a well-developed and highly valued activity, and adults used its techniques as a means of instructing young people and propagating tribal traditions. Some older men developed reputations as excellent storytellers and were widely sought for this purpose. A favorite time for storytelling was after dark.

---

[2]From *Cry of the Thunderbird: The American Indian's Own Story*, edited by Charles Hamilton. New edition copyright © 1972 by University of Oklahoma Press.

Figure 5.15. Innu (Montagnais) Indian boys playing with young birds and perhaps contemplating a career with the Boston Bruins. This photograph was taken on the La Romaine, Basse Cate-Nord Reservation in northern Quebec. Photo by Serge Jauvin. Used by permission.

Summary

Childhood was a time for learning, for development, and for fun, but most of all it was seen as a period of preparation for adulthood. Compared to today's standards, the full responsibilities of adulthood came early.

During childhood, games for pure amusement and for development purposes were common. Children indulged much of the time in idle amusement for the inherent enjoyment of those activities. At other times, however, they engaged in semi-serious activity, mimicking the roles of their parents that they too would eventually assume. Adults always sought to ensure the development of sound physical characteristics as well as proper principles of moral behavior.

According to James Ewers (1944), Blackfeet boys who had reached their middle teens

> began to join war-parties and to take the part of men in hunting. In their early teens most girls married and settled down. Then they were men and women. Coasting, top-spinning, sliding on ice, and other children's games no longer interested them. Yet while they lasted, those childhood days in the winter camps were happy ones. (p. 197)

Chapter 6

Games of Chance

All games and leisure activities among traditional American Indians were categorized by Culin (1907) into either games of dexterity or games of chance. Games of dexterity included active physical contests of the type discussed in chapters 2 through 4. Games of chance, on the other hand, were activities similar to many of our table games of today. They were not dependent upon excellence in strategy but upon "pure chance" (p. 31). Games of chance focused on gambling and included the use of dice, sticks, and other objects as part of guessing exercises. Hand manipulation of these objects was frequently a part of the game.

The origin of games of chance is lost in antiquity; however, we do know that they were widespread, if not universal, at the time of the white man's first contact with the Indian. Roger Williams, founder of Rhode Island, had extensive, friendly contact with Indians of the New England area during the early and middle 17th century. William's writings (cited in Hallett, 1955) included substantial references to widespread play of dice games by Indians in the area, and he described both the implements used and the scoring systems. Beauchamp (1896) cited reports on dice games by de Brébeuf among the Huron Indians in 1636 and by LeJerome among the Iroquois in 1634.

As with sports and many other customs in Indian life, the practice of games of chance and gambling was dramatically altered during the 19th and 20th centuries. According to the value system of most non-Indians, Indian gambling had an evil connotation. Of course, there had been no such connotation in traditional tribal customs, but the non-Indian value system eventually prevailed because of the influence of colonial religious doctrine and the establishment of regulations by military and political leaders. Consequently, gambling related to games of chance and sports in general, which had been almost universal in the early 1800s, was almost nonexistent by the year 1900.

Games of chance were more widely represented than games of dexterity in Culin's (1907) extensive listing of tribal sports. Of approximately 250 tribes mentioned by him, 95% were specifically identified as engaging in one or more activities categorized as games of chance.

Betting on Games of Chance

As with games of dexterity, betting was customary in games of chance and was, in fact, usually more widespread and more intense than in sports activities because the spectators participated avidly in the gambling. Personal items such as clothing, jewelry, guns, horses, and the game implements themselves were wagered.

There is some evidence that the climate for betting varied from a casual and friendly setting to that of a much more serious nature involving significant materialistic goods. For example, according to Flannery and Cooper (1946), gambling on games among the Gros Ventre Indians was motivated for either "recreation" or "predatory" purposes (p. 392). Recreational betting was more friendly and was usually limited to family and close friends. Betting in these games simply added to the enjoyment of the activity. These were more casual games involving small or symbolic bets, with no one suffering serious financial setbacks. Nevertheless, bets involved such items as beads, pipes, dishes, or small pieces of jewelry. On more intimate occasions the losers were required to prepare a meal for the winners—something they would do for their friends anyway.

High-Stakes Betting

Games became more serious, or predatory, when they were played for larger stakes or for prestige. The term *predatory* suggests a more negative practice than most observers, including Flannery and Cooper (1946), actually reported. Even so, winners gained significant prizes such as guns, saddles, horses, or lodges. Though such losses were often felt severely by the losers, tradition demanded that they take it in good spirit; however, Flannery and Cooper reported that behavior often fell short of that goal by the late 19th century and that violence sometimes resulted.

One of the more lavish betting escapades for games of chance was reported among the Puyallup Indians near Tacoma, Washington. Culin

(1907) cited an 1885 report by Sammons in the *San Francisco Examiner* in which the trophies for a contest between two tribes that year consisted of

> 12 Winchester rifles of the latest pattern, 11 sound horses, 7 buggies, 100 blankets, 43 shawls, an uncounted pile of mats, clothing for men and women (some badly worn and some in good condition, but mostly worn), and $49 in money. (p. 250)

A few years earlier Eells (1877) noted a drop-off in the extent of betting among the Twana in Washington state when he reported that

> the Indians say that they now stake less money and spend less time in gaming than formerly. It is said that in former years as much as a thousand dollars was sometimes staked and that the players became so infatuated as to bet everything they had, even to the clothes on their backs. At present they seldom gamble anything except on rainy days when they have little else to do. (p. 88)

Controls on Gambling

Despite the fact that goods changed hands during games of chance, Flannery and Cooper (1946) argue that such gambling was not motivated by economic considerations. Rather, the practice was more a social custom, designed to promote friendliness and accord among groups. In fact, altruism and generosity were a significant part of this activity. Among the Gros Ventre, generosity was encouraged. These Indians were taught not to hoard property and not to accumulate wealth. Wins and losses tended to even out in these "pure chance" games, so no one consistently won or consistently lost. This view of friendly gambling is supported by Oren Lyons (personal communication, July, 1986), Faithkeeper of the Iroquois Confederacy in New York state. During the international lacrosse championships in 1986, he reported that Indian gambling involved "circular economics" and that all the goods remained within the community. Still, Flannery and Cooper speculate that the severe economic conditions encountered by most Indians during the late 19th century probably contributed to the decline of gambling.

There is little evidence of anyone suffering significant or permanent financial harm through gambling (Flannery & Cooper, 1946). Contrary to some reports, such as those of Sammons and Eells, Flannery and Cooper concluded that basic necessities of life were not wagered away, or rarely so. Whenever such problems did develop, losers were usually supported temporarily by family and friends. Excessive gambling and gambling for very high stakes was discouraged. Persons engaging in such behavior lost respect in the community and were not allowed to hold important positions. Consequently, the term predatory gambling appears to be misleading. There was no notion of destroying, or humiliating one's opponents. Furthermore, persons successful in gambling did not achieve recognition or prestige of the same type accorded to victors in sports, war, or hunting.

In addition to discouraging ruinously high stakes, there were other controls to prevent undue negative effects from gambling. For example, no gambling debts were allowed. That is, one could only bet what he or she had on hand at the time. Bets could not be based on promised goods to be delivered later. When one ran out of items to be wagered, he or she either had to stop or go out and get other goods and return with them, whereupon play could resume. Exorbitant debts were thus avoided.

In addition to the exchange of stakes, games of chance were, like sports, sometimes played for other purposes of social significance. Among these purposes was that of healing. Writing about a "game of dish" (a dice game in which a dish or bowl is used) in 1636, de Brébeuf (cited in Beauchamp, 1896) reported that the game

> is also in great credit in matters of medicine, especially if the sick man has dreamed it. . . . The whole company crowds into one cabin, and arranges itself on the one side and the other, upon poles raised even to the top. They bring in the sick man in a blanket, and that one from the village who is to shake the dish (for there is but one on each side appointed for this purpose) walks after, his face and his head enveloped in his robe. Both sides bet loud and firmly. (p. 271)

De Brébeuf pointed out that there was a great confidence that this activity would lead to the healing of sick persons.

Categories of Games of Chance

Games of chance may be grouped into four general categories: (a) in *dice games* a number of small stones, buttons, seeds, or other objects are tossed up, and the result is determined on the manner in which they fall; (b) in *stick games* the participant is required to guess the arrangement or the number of a group of sticks or to locate a particular one; (c) in the *moccasin* or *bullet game* the participant guesses the location of a bullet or other small item hidden under one of several moccasins or other concealing objects; and (4) in *hand games* the player attempts to guess which hand is concealing a particular object. The first of these, the dice game, required no participant activity except to hold the plate or dish and toss the dice. The other three games could be referred to as *guessing games*—participants were required to guess the location or position of objects.

Indian games of chance generally did not require mental calculations. Both Hamilton (1972) and Culin (1907) stated that games of chance requiring analytical skills (such as chess or checkers) were unknown to the Indians. Still, many players did not believe that the games were determined merely by chance. Rather, some believed that they had extraordinary perceptive powers that enabled them to make a correct guess even when no clues were available. These special, psychic powers were dependent upon one's relationship with the gods. In addition, many persons believed that they could use sleight of hand and other manipulative skills to deceive their opponents.

Dice Games

Stewart Culin (1907) identified dice games, or activities roughly described as such, among 130 different tribes. He observed that "from no one tribe does it appear to have been absent" (p. 45). Few activities were more universal than dice. There is some evidence, especially from implements recovered from ancient burial grounds in the southwestern United States, indicating that dice games have been played by Indians for more than 2,000 years. Indian dice games began to decline in popularity during the late 19th century. Daniel (1892) referred to the dice game as "a very ancient game of the Sioux Indians, played mostly by elderly women, although young women and men of all ages play also" (p. 215). Hoffman (1896) wrote that "the game of late is rarely seen" (p. 241), although he acknowledged its popularity in earlier times.

Culin (1907) included detailed reports on dice games from more than a hundred tribes covering all parts of the United States, Canada, and Central America. The playing implements, the organization of play, the counting systems, and the manner of betting varied from one place to another. No doubt the observers also varied in the accuracy and detail with which they reported these games. However, one undeniable point is that dice games were widespread, were deeply ingrained in the culture, and were very popular.

The game of dice was played by most Indian groups with no strategy or skill. The results of these games depended upon the random fall of the dice or sticks. There were at least two popular variations of dice games. In one type, also called a *bowl* game, dice were placed in a bowl or basket and tossed straight up into the air so that they fell again into the container. A count was then taken of the position of the dice in the bowl. In a painting by Mary Irwin Wright (Figure 6.1), a group of Menominee men are shown playing the dice game with a bowl.

In variation of the game, the dice were held in the hand and tossed against a blanket or hide, which was held perpendicular to the ground, and allowed to fall freely upon the earth or a blanket. Then a count was made, based on their position, of the dice on the floor or ground.

Figure 6.1 Menominee Indians playing dice game (also called bowl game). Painting by Mary Irwin Wright sometime prior to 1896. Photo used by permisssion of the National Anthropological Archives, Smithsonian Institution.

Figure 6.2. Wooden dice used by the Cherokee. Photo used by permission of the University Museum, University of Pennsylvania.

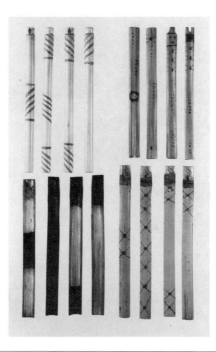

Figure 6.3. Stick dice. Probably used by the Pomo Indians in California. Photo used by permission of the University Museum, University of Pennsylvania.

Implements for dice games consisted of the dice themselves, a bowl or dish, and a hide or blanket. Whereas most persons are familiar with cubical dice having dots on each of the six sides, Indians played principally with *two-sided dice*. These flat dice were colored or had decorative markings on one side, but the opposite side was plain. They were made of bone, shells, split cane, wood, peach or plum pits, stone, pottery, and a variety of other materials. Dice were greatly individualized, and many had the appearance of various animals. They show little consistency or uniformity. Some dice had straight lines, some had zigzag lines, some had dots, and some had hand paintings. The consistent characteristic was that all dice had one plain side, usually light in color, and one side that was either dark or had colorful markings. As with heads and tails on today's coins, there was never confusion about which side was up. Indian dice are illustrated in Figures 6.2 through 6.4. As can be noted, practically every shape was used. Whereas two dice are used in today's popular gambling games, Indians generally used eight, although there were variations of the game with as few as four or as many as ten.

Bowls, dishes, or plates used for tossing the dice were usually made of woven material, wood, or pottery. It was necessary that the bowl be large enough and the bottom level enough so that the dice did not simply

Figure 6.4. Bone dice and basket. Photo used by permission of the National Anthropological Archives, Smithsonian Institution.

pile on top of each other. As with most implements in Indian play, these containers were carefully decorated.

Rules governing the game of dice varied somewhat from tribe to tribe. However, scoring was always dependent upon the number of dice falling upon the white, or plain side versus the number falling on the darkened, or decorated side. When the numbers of dice on each side were even, or nearly so, no points were gained. The greater the numbers falling on a single side, the greater the point value.

A typical dice game with a fairly standard scoring system played the Iroquois in New York state was described in 1851 by Morgan (cited in Culin, 1907).

> Eight buttons, about an inch in diameter, were made of elk horn, and having been rounded and polished, were slightly burned upon one side to blacken them . . . [and] a certain number of beans, fifty, perhaps, were made the capital, and the game continued until one of the players had won them all. Two players spread a blanket and seated themselves upon it, one of them shook the deer buttons in his hands and then threw them down. If six turned up of the same color, it counted 2; if seven it counted 4; and if all, it counted 20, the winner taking as many beans from the general stack as he made points by the throw. He also continued to throw as long as he continued to win. When less than six come up, either black or white, it counted nothing, and the throw passed to the other player. . . . The game ending as soon as the capital in the hands of either player was exhausted. (p.113)

A somewhat similar, though less precise, description of a dice game among the Chippewa in Wisconsin was provided by Carver (1796/1956).

> This game is played between two persons only. Each person has six or eight little bones not unlike a peach stone either in size or shape, except they are quadrangular, two of the sides of which are colored black, and the others white. These they throw up into the air, from whence they fall into a bowl or platter placed underneath, and made to spin round.
> According as these bones present the white or black side upward they reckon the game; he that happens to have the greatest number turn up of a similar color, counts 5 points; and 40 is the game.
> The winning party keeps his place and the loser yields his to another who is appointed by one of the umpires. . . . During this play the Indians appear to be greatly agitated, and at every decisive throw set up a hideous shout. . . . At this game some will lose their apparel, all the movables of their cabins, and even sometimes their liberty. (p. 23)

Although both men and women participated in dice games, they did so separately. Most writers reported that two persons played at a time, but some indicate that two to eight may play as long as there are equal numbers on each team. In addition, spectators became involved in games by placing side bets on the outcome. As with other games of chance, dice games often continued for long periods. According to Walker (1905), Sioux women often became totally absorbed in the game, "sometimes playing all day and all night at a single sitting" (p. 289). Other writers have reported games continuing for three or four days.

Although the playing of dice required no decision making by the participant, a variety of *guessing games* did require such a response, and the outcome of the game was dependent upon the accuracy of that choice. One simply observed the fall of the dice and realized whether the game was won or lost. In all guessing games, however, two or more options always existed that gave one the impression of controlling one's own destiny. In most of these games, though, the outcome was nothing more than chance (i.e., there were no helpful clues to aid the player in making a more accurate decision). The stick games, the moccasin game, the hand game, and the four-stick game were guessing games. Each will be discussed briefly.

Stick Games

Several varieties of stick games have been reported. Perhaps the most popular was one in which a large, *uneven* number of sticks were divided by one of the players. The opposing player then attempted to select either the even or uneven pile of sticks. (When an uneven number of sticks is divided into two piles, one pile will have an even number and the other pile an odd number.) According to Culin (1907), stick games usually involved from 20 to 100 sticks, and the person guessing was forced to make a rapid decision and was unable to count so many sticks before making the selection.

In another stick game the player attempted to guess the pile in which a specially marked stick was located. The particular stick was not visible to the participant. In still other games the player attempted to select the shortest or the longest of several sticks—one end of all the sticks would be concealed from the player. Depending on the game, sticks were either held openly in the hand or concealed in a leather pouch or some other container.

The sticks used in a game might be arrow shafts, straws, willow splints, reeds, or any other long, thin object. Such sticks were usually four to eight inches in length and were marked or painted colorfully. These decorative sticks were often kept in a leather pouch for protection. Illustrations of some gaming sticks are shown in Figure 6.5. In addition to the playing sticks, a pointer (a stick two to three feet in length) was used by the player either to separate the pile of sticks into two groups or to point to the pile of sticks being chosen.

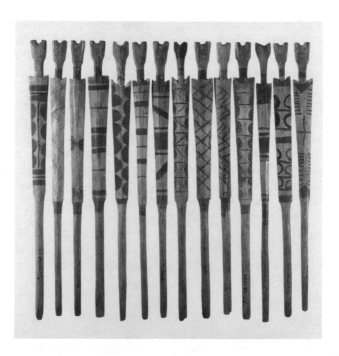

Figure 6.5. Gaming or counting sticks used by the Blackfeet Indians in Montana. Photo used by permission of the University Museum, University of Pennsylvania.

A fairly typical description of a stick game was presented by Nicholas Perrot in 1864 (cited in Culin, 1907). After observing a game among the Huron Indians in Ontario, he reported that

> they procure a certain number of straws or twigs of a certain plant, which are no thicker than the cord of a salmon net. They are made of the same length and thickness, being about 10 inches long. Their number is uneven. After turning and mixing them in their hands, they are placed in a skin or blanket rug. . . . Then he pushes the little pointed bone into the pile of straws and takes away as many as he wishes. His opponent takes those that remain on the rug and rapidly counts them by tens, making no errors. He who has the odd number of straws wins.
>
> This game sometimes lasts for three or four days. When a loser wins back everything and the former winner loses his all, a comrade takes his place and the game goes on till one side or the other has nothing left with which to play, it being the rule of the savages not to leave the game until one side or the other has lost everything. (p. 569)

Van Kotzebue (1821) observed the game at a mission for Indians in San Francisco:

> Two sit on the ground opposite each other, holding in their hands a number of thin sticks, and these being thrown up at the same time with great rapidity they immediately guess whether the number is odd or even; at the side of each of the players a person sits, who scores the gains and loss. (p. 281)

The Moccasin or Bullet Game

In this very old game, a small object was hidden under moccasins, wooden cups, cane tubes, leather patches, or other containers. The participant attempted to guess under which moccasin the object was hidden. The hidden object was often a bullet, stone, stick, die, or other small item. The moccasin game was the forerunner of the shell game and "Button, button, who's got the button?". It was played by most Indian groups long before the colonists arrived on this continent.

Although its exact origin is unknown, it is clearly one of the oldest of the Indian games. Eubank (1945, p. 138) recounted a Navajo legend describing how the game began and suggesting that the game dated back to the early days of Navajo oral tradition. According to the legend, long ago while the gods were creating the world, they sometimes grew tired of just being gods. On one such occasion they changed themselves into animals and birds. A dispute arose concerning the proper proportion of lightness and darkness in the world. Some wished the earth to be totally dark and others wanted it to be entirely light. To resolve this issue they organized themselves into two teams to play a moccasin game. Using a turquoise stone hidden under a pair of moccasins, they played the game for a long time, but it ended in a tie. Thus was it decreed that half the day would be light and half would be dark.

Early colonists on this continent adopted this game from the Indians and called it the bullet game because a bullet was usually the hidden object. In addition, they generally used caps to cover the bullet. It became so popular among the colonists that it became, according to Duncan (cited in Culin, 1907), "a recognized evil, and on the early statutes stands a law making gambling at bullet a finable offense" (p. 342).

The game of moccasin played by the Delaware Indians before 1879 was also described by Duncan.

Moccasin was a gambling game much practiced among the Delaware Indians, and was borrowed of them by the white settlers. As originally played, a deer skin was spread upon the ground and a half dozen upturned moccasins arranged in a semicircle within easy reach of the player. The latter, holding to view a good-sized bullet, then quickly thrust his hand under each moccasin in turn, leaving the bullet under one of them. This was done so skillfully as to leave the onlooker in doubt, and the gambling consisted in betting where the bullet was. This was called moccasin. (pp. 342–343)

Reuben Thwaites (1892) described a rather typical game among the Winnebago in Wisconsin.

The leader of the side that has the "deal" so to speak, takes a small bead in his right hand and deftly slides the hand under each moccasin in turn, pretending to leave the bead under each one of them; he finally does leave the bead under one, and the leader of the opposition side, watching him closely, is to guess which moccasin covers the bead. (p. 425)

A variation was reported by Dorsey (1888):

Sometimes it is determined to change the rule for winning, and then the guessor aims to *avoid* the right moccasin the first time, but to hit it when he makes the second trial. Should he hit the right one the first time he loses his stakes. (p. 339)

Several other authors reported games in which the purpose was to avoid selecting the moccasin covering the object for as long as possible.

Whereas the moccasin game was viewed primarily as an activity of pure chance, there was skill involved in the speed and sleight of hand used by the player responsible for hiding the object. That individual showed the object and then, in a series of rapid movements of both the object and the moccasin, hid the object under one of them. At the same time, bystanders were singing, beating a drum, or making noises that often distracted the individual trying to guess the location of the object. The guesser used perceptual skill and concentration in attempting to follow the object as it was being moved back and forth.

The playing of tambourines or drums and the singing of songs were used to add to the joy of the game as well as to distract the players. According to Baldwin (1969), Indians' facial expressions and body movements were also used to deceive the opposition. Ducatel (1846) reported that among the Chippewa in Wisconsin the hider performed "with a peculiar manner calculated to divert the attention of the one with whom he is playing, and with an incessant chant, accompanied by a swinging motion of the hand and trunk" (p. 367). Figures 6.6 and 6.7 show the moccasin game being played by the Menominee and White Earth Indians respectively.

In a Chippewa moccasin game, Flaskerd (1961) reported that the playing of drums and the singing and shouting of players and spectators made this a very exciting activity. He noted, however, that in recent times "singing has been discontinued due to the fact the songs have been forgotten" (p. 87).

Figure 6.6. Menominee Indians playing the moccasin game. From painting by Mary Irwin Wright, sometime prior to 1896. Photo used by permission of the National Anthropological Archives, Smithsonian Institution.

Figure 6.7. The moccasin game being played at the White Earth Reservation, perhaps around 1890. Notice the shotgun and lacrosse stick as wagers, and the drums for sound accompaniment. Photo used by permission of the National Anthropological Archives, Smithsonian Institution.

The Hand Game and the Four-Stick Game

Both the hand game and the four-stick game were guessing games entirely dependent upon chance. In the hand game the guesser attempted to identify which hand was holding one of two objects, which was specially marked or decorated. In the four-stick game the player tried to guess the location and position of four sticks placed under a blanket or other covering. The hand game was much more widely played than was the four-stick game.

Culin (1907) identified eighty-one different tribes from throughout the continent that played the hand game. It was primarily an indoor game, usually played in a lodge or shelter. The number of players varied from two upwards. Opponents sat facing each other, and the stakes were between the two sides. The two objects, usually bone or wooden cylinders, were similar except that one of them had a thong or string tied around the middle. The purpose of the game was to guess which hand was holding the unmarked stick. Several members of a team might hold a pair of the sticks in their hand. The side holding the bones chanted and swayed while the opponents attempted to guess the proper hand. When the correct hand was guessed, the bones went over to the opponent. Several observers reported that this game was played entirely by gestures, so individuals who only had sign language in common could play. These were festive games with a great deal of excitement. Singing and showmanship were commonplace. Both men and women played the game, but separately.

A typical hand game was described in 1892 by George Grinnell (cited in Culin, 1907) among the Blackfeet of Montana:

> Two small oblong bones were used, one of which had a black ring around it. Those who participated in this game, numbering from two to a dozen, were divided into two equal parties, ranged on either side of the lodge. Wagers were made, each person betting with the one directly opposite him. Then a man took the bones, and, by skillfully moving his hands and changing the objects from one to the other, sought to make it impossible for the person opposite him to decide which hand held the marked one. Ten points were the game, counted by sticks, and the side which first got the number took the stakes. A song always accompanied this game, a weird, unearthly air—if it can be so called but, when heard at a little distance, very pleasant and soothing. . . .The person concealing the bones swayed his body, arms, and hands in time to the air, and went through all manner of graceful and intricate movements for the purpose of confusing the guesser. The stakes were sometimes very high, two or three horses or more, and men have been known to lose everything they possessed, even to their clothing. (p. 269)

According to Flannery and Cooper (1946), the chief gambling games among the Gros Ventre were the two-button hand game and hoop-and-pole. The two-button game was played almost daily by many people. In this game two buttons were required, one long and one short one. Each would fit into the hand, and the objective was to guess which hand held the short one and which held the long one. Sides alternated as hiders and guessers. In the typical Gros Ventre game, twelve counting sticks were used, and one stick was awarded to the winner of each play. The game continued until all twelve sticks had been won by one side. The game could last for many hours, and some extended all day and all night.

Culin (1907) identified only a half dozen tribes that played the four-stick game; it was very popular among the Klamath and several other tribes in the Northwest. In this game the four small sticks were arranged out of view of the guesser who had to describe their arrangement. Paul Kane (1859) reported how the Clackama in Oregon played the four-stick game.

> The game consists of one of them having his hands covered with a small round mat resting on the ground. He has four small sticks in his hands, which he disposes under the mat in certain positions, requiring the opposite party to guess how he has placed them. If he

guesses right, the mat is handed round to the next, and a stick is stuck up as a counter in his favor. If wrong, a stick is stuck up on the opposite side as a mark against him. This, like almost all Indian games, was accompanied with singing; but in this case the singing was particularly sweet and wild, possessing a harmony I never heard before or since among Indians. (p. 196)

Summary

A thorough review of the mode of life among the traditional American Indian must include a look at their games of chance and the related betting activities. Clearly, these activities were a prominent and important part of community life. Much leisure time was devoted to the games by both men and women. Children too, according to Stevenson (1903), engaged in such games, including betting. She reported, however, that betting among children was discouraged by parents. Perhaps there was concern that children were not mature enough to keep these games in proper perspective. Early colonists adopted several of the games of chance, particularly the dice and moccasin games.

Betting on games of chance was never viewed by Indians as an ethical or moral issue. Rather, it was part of the tradition and social life of the community. Although the ethics of gambling was never raised, the Indians did discourage excesses.

Gambling did redistribute the wealth somewhat, but it all remained within the community. Care was taken to avoid impoverishing an individual or a family. The accumulation of great wealth, through game play or otherwise, was not a high priority for Indians. It is interesting to note also that many non-Indians observed those gaming practices and did not discuss them in terms of good or evil. Roger Williams, a prominent minister and founder of Rhode Island in the 17th century, wrote about the gaming practices in some detail but apparently did not condemn these activities. It is possible, however, that general condemnation by non-Indians in the late 19th and early 20th centuries, along with a multitude of "civilizing" efforts, contributed to the decline of the games.

Part II
The Emergence of Indians in Modern Sport

Chapter 7

Early Sports Exchange: Pre-20th Century

American Indians have interacted with non-Indians since the white man first arrived on this continent. Columbus and other explorers who followed wrote about their contacts with the Indians. Relationships were more firmly developed with colonists who came to this continent to establish permanent homes. During the early colonial period, contacts were usually friendly, involving such activities as trade, the sharing of techniques for farming, hunting, fishing, and other measures for general survival. In addition, sports and games were among the social activities and festivities they shared.

The early entrance and subsequent prominence of Indians in modern sports[1] were related not only to informal social interaction but more specifically to school attendance and school-related activities. Whereas school sports were not played or were discouraged in colonial times, during the last century schools encouraged play and sports. As Indians were brought into the public school system during the past century, games were viewed as an integral part of their adaptation to the dominant culture. For most Indian children, the school provided the first opportunity to become acquainted with those sports that were growing in popularity in the non-Indian community. This review of early American sports provides

---

[1]The terms *modern sports* or *non-Indian sports* are used here to refer to activities popular in the non-Indian community. These included football, basketball, baseball, and others that were either imported to this country or developed by non-Indians

important information about the merging of the Indian and non-Indian cultures and the emergence of Indians on the popular sports scene.

Distinctions Between Indian and Non-Indian Sports

It is important to note that Indian sports were not encumbered by some of the inhibitions that were a part of non-Indian culture. Perhaps most important of these was the Puritanical attitude of colonists toward play. According to the strong work ethic of the early settlers, play was a waste of time at best, and at worst, actually evil. This attitude, although somewhat diminished, continued well into the 20th century.

Another distinction between Indian and non-Indian sports during the 19th century was that unsavory persons were often sponsors of major, professional contests in the non-Indian world, and persons attending these events were usually not associated with polite society. Consequently, raucous behavior, along with bribing and the "throwing" of contests, was rather commonplace at boxing matches, cockfights, horse races, baseball games, and other sporting activities. In contrast, sports were held in high esteem within the Indian community. They were widely supported and respected by all members of society, and a respectable level of behavior was expected among both players and spectators.

Non-Indians often displayed class bias in sports. Crew, tennis, and golf were adopted by the upper class, and baseball, boxing, and certain of the ethnic sports from Europe were for the lower strata of society. There is no evidence that Indian sports interest or participation were reflections of social class.

Several early authors referred to occasions when white persons joined in the Indian games, though with a lack of success. Their awkwardness in these unfamiliar activities was often a source of amusement for the Indians. Conversely, the Indian sometimes engaged with similar clumsiness in unfamiliar white man's games. Usually such participation was not taken seriously by either group and consequently was short lived.

Had the climate remained friendly between Indians and non-Indians during the 18th and 19th centuries, the exchange of sports and other social activities would, no doubt, have developed more rapidly. However, strife and hostility escalated during this period. Obviously, intergroup play could not flourish in such a climate. Consequently, very limited sports interaction between Indians and non-Indians took place prior to the last decade of the 19th century, at which time open hostilities began to subside.

The Development of Non-Indian Sports in America

Early immigrants to this continent brought with them sports from their native country. Ancient football, skittles, gymnastics, wrestling, cricket, billiards, card playing, and horse racing, among others, attained early popularity. However, the development of the Puritan philosophy along with an evangelical temperament hampered the growth of sport and shaped the attitude of subsequent generations. For example, sports participation on the sabbath was particularly prohibited.

In addition to those sports imported from their native country, colonists quickly adopted lacrosse, shinny, canoeing, archery, and several other games from the Indians. Culin (1907) stated that playing cards and a few table games were the only sports the Indians adopted from non-Indians. (Within a few years of his report, however, it was clear that Indians had adopted, and were excelling in, the non-Indian games of football, basketball, and baseball.) On the other hand, Culin reported that a great number of the native American games were taken into the non-Indian culture. In fact, he reported that non-Indians had adapted practically all the Indian games in the Southwest and in Mexico, but had applied Spanish names to most of them.

During the 19th century, sports popularity among non-Indians was aided most by the development of (a) professionalism, (b) athletic clubs, and (c) college athletics. Each of these stimulated interest within a different clientele.

Professional Sports

Professionalism was particularly popular in prize fighting, horse racing, footracing, cockfighting, and rowing. Interest in boxing was brought to this country by the British, among whom it had gained popularity as early as the 18th century. Before the middle of the 19th century, it had become very popular in this country. However, bare-knuckle fighting was very brutal and thus was widely condemned by the Victorians and most others in polite society. In addition, the rowdy behavior of the spectators prevented it from achieving respectability. Boxing did not begin to attain some respectability among society in general until gloves were required and the Marquis of Queensberry rules were established in 1867.

Professional sport had its beginning in commercial spectacles during the early and middle 19th century. Such activities as footraces, horse races, boxing matches, and billiards were highly publicized, brought large crowds, and usually envoked heavy betting. However, during this era there were no regular schedules of contests. Conferences and leagues to promote sustained play were nonexistent. Promoters and entrepreneurs waited until there appeared to be sufficient interest in the contest before scheduling it. The first professional sport to capture the sustained interest of the public was baseball. Though it was established and attained some degree of popularity prior to the Civil War, its intense and widespread popularity came after the war. By 1870 baseball had become a national game. The Civil War served to popularize the game in a larger geographical area than had been the case prior to the war. Semiprofessional and professional baseball developed rapidly in the 1870s.

In 1869 the Cincinnati Red Stockings baseball team became the first truly professional team. The team traveled to all major cities east of the Mississippi River and played fifty-eight games with no losses and one tie. The National League (the so-called Senior Circuit) was established in 1876, the American League, or Junior Circuit, was established in 1901, and these two leagues have dominated baseball to the present day. Several other major leagues were established and died out during the last quarter of the 19th century. As with boxing, horse racing, billiards, and other professional sports, baseball was often plagued by gambling among spectators and an undisciplined life-style among the players. Consequently, suspicions were frequent regarding the integrity with which the games were being played. Nevertheless, baseball was the first professional sport to capture the imagination of the American public, the first to prosper as a substantial commercial enterprise, and the first to establish respectability within general society.

Horse racing attained a great deal of popularity in the early 1800s, especially in Maryland and New York. Rader (1983) reported that in 1823 the "race of the century" (p. 38) was held at the Union Course on Long Island and was witnessed by 50,000 to 100,000 spectators. Heavy betting on the race was reported. The Pimlico Race Course in Maryland was developed during the early 1800s. Interest in horse racing has been sustained by betting.

Pedestrianism (walking races) was very popular during the early part of the 1800s; thereafter, running races began to replace them. Rader (1983) reported that John Cox Stevens, the premier promoter of New York City's professional sports in the early 19th century, sponsored a variety of sporting events, providing an avenue for his gambling interests. Footraces, horse races, and yachting were his primary interests. In 1835 Stevens offered $1,000 to any runners who could race ten miles in less than one hour. Twenty thousand spectators came to the Union Race Course on Long Island to witness this event. Henry Stannard, a farmer from Connecticut, was the only one to receive the prize, finishing in 59 minutes and 48 seconds.

Another race took place in 1844 at the Beacon (Horse) Race Course in Hoboken, New Jersey, where 30,000 attended. John Steeprock, a Seneca Indian, competed against thirty-seven other American, English, and Irish runners. Rader (1983) quoted one reporter: "It was a trial of the Indian against the white man on the point in which the Red man most boasts his superiority'' (p. 410). Steeprock did not win the race but was beaten by John Gildersleeve, a New York chairbuilder. Following this race, a reporter stated that during the subsequent ''ten to fifteen years there were more athletes competing and more races than ever before. People in virtually every state in the union attended professional footraces'' (p. 40). Indians from the northeastern part of the United States, and Canada, were frequently successful in these activities. The outstanding runners of the southwestern tribes were generally not involved in 19th century professional races.

One Indian who did attain success and considerable fortune in regular competition against non-Indians during the 1850s and 1860s was Louis ''Deerfoot'' Bennett. Bennett, from the Seneca nation near Buffalo, New York, successfully competed in races for small purses during the 1850s. After attaining considerable fame as the best runner in this country, he was invited to go to Britain in 1861, where the races were more formally organized and the prize money was greater. Bennett was equally successful against the professional runners throughout Great Britain, attaining times in distance races (from four to twelve miles) that would be the envy of most runners today. His running exploits were frequently featured in the *London Times* of the early 1860s. (Further discussion of Deerfoot Bennett is included in chapter 11.)

In 1876 Big Hawk Chief, a Pawnee Indian, ran the world's first recorded sub-four-minute mile at the Sidney barracks in Nebraska. Though this race was timed by two army officers with stop watches and the track was later meticulously measured with a steel tape, it remains unofficial.

Athletic Clubs

A major social development in the middle and late 19th century was the formation and expansion of athletic clubs. Though originally developed to promote athletic participation, especially in golf and cricket, these clubs quickly evolved into centers for social activity, catering to persons from a particular national background or social class. For example, the Cricket Club was primarily oriented to serve the sporting and social interests of the English settlers. The Turnverine (gymnastic) societies served the German Americans. The Caledonian (track and field) clubs served the Scottish decendents. As those clubs developed, however, they took on status implications as well as ethnic character.

Indians were not members of these athletic clubs. Neither the club organizers nor the Indians saw the desirability of such involvement. Although exhibitions in running or in other sports were viewed as appropriate for spectators, the close, personal associations characteristic of athletic clubs were not extended to Indians. However, these clubs served as the primary outlet for sports interests for many ethnic groups.

Intercollegiate Sports

In colleges, sports developed prominently in the late 19th century and flourished in the early 20th century. At first these athletic activities were played within the institution (intramural) and later between institutions (intercollegiate). A few colleges developed physical exercise and sports programs primarily for health purposes even earlier. For example, Georgetown University began promoting sports and games for the health of students as early as 1798. Prominent games included fencing, swimming, handball, and crew. A handball court was constructed there in 1814. Several other colleges promoted sports on an informal basis for both men and women prior to 1850. After around 1850 these informal activities began taking on a more organized character both within and outside the institution.

Rader (1983) refers to crew as "the first intercollegiate sport" (p. 71). Just prior to 1850, both Harvard and Yale had small, informal clubs that engaged in intramural contests. The first American intercollegiate match was held in 1852 between Harvard and Yale. During the remainder of the century, many other regattas matched the prominent colleges in the northeastern United States.

The first intercollegiate baseball game was played on July 1, 1859, with Amherst beating Williams by a score of 73 to 32. However, the real dawn of intercollegiate sports is often thought to have been the first intercollegiate football game, which was held on November 6, 1869, between Rutgers and Princeton. The game was actually much closer to soccer than to today's American football. However, the game rapidly evolved, and by the turn of the century, football had attained great popularity and became recognizable as the sport we know today. Colleges and universities throughout the Northeast and Midwest made great efforts during this period to develop prominent athletic teams, particularly in football. School officials even at that early date realized the value of athletics in promoting the name of the institution, in developing school spirit and loyalty, and in recruiting new students.

Practically no Indians attended regular colleges and universities during the 19th century. The earliest Indian involvement in college athletics came in the last decade of the century when Indian students at the Training School at Carlisle, Pennsylvania, organized a football team and began competing against schools, sports clubs, and colleges in the area. It was not until after the beginning of the 20th century that national prominence was attained. This success led to more widespread athletic involvement for students at Carlisle, Haskell, and other Indian schools, and it also facilitated the entry of Indians into regular (non-Indian) colleges.

Indian–Non-Indian Sports Exchange

Because of the strained relations during the 19th century, social interaction between Indians and non-Indians was limited. Prior to the last decade of the century, practically all Indian participation in non-Indian sports was restricted to boarding schools. Such activities as football, baseball, boxing, basketball, and bowling were played first among the Indians themselves, then between Indians and non-Indians.

While Indians were beginning to participate in games of the dominant society, non-Indians were beginning to adopt Indian games. Lacrosse, shinny, archery, kayaking, and canoeing were becoming popular among non-Indians during the middle and latter parts of the 19th century. Lacrosse was especially popular in the northern part of the United States and in Canada. In fact, it was so widespread and popular in Canada that it was designated as the national sport in 1869. The game of shinny, though played to a lesser extent in non-Indian society, was gradually adapted into the games of field hockey and ice hockey. Other sports that had previously been a part of both cultures (i.e., footraces, swimming, wrestling, etc.) continued to be played separately, and when sports interaction began, Indians and non-Indians played together.

General acceptance of Indians into the mainstream of American sports was given its greatest impetus by the success of Jim Thorpe and other football players of the Carlisle School. In addition, Charles Bender and John Meyers of major league baseball fame did much to extend this acceptance by their success in the national pastime. Indians had not yet had widespread success in individual sports such as running, and they did not participate at the center of the national sports scene.

Indian participation in non-Indian sports took two forms during the years immediately prior to, and following, the year 1900. First, Indians competed as members of teams representing their own tribe or school. This was a continuation of the traditional system whereby players represented their extended family or their tribe against an opposing tribe or a neighborhood group. This practice continued into the 1920s when an all-Indian football team, the Oorang Indians, competed professionally in Ohio. (The team was composed mostly of former members of the great Carlisle teams of earlier years.) Second, during the early part of the 20th century, Indians began joining college or professional teams as minority members of those teams.

Early ventures of Indians into unfamiliar sports were not especially successful. Commenting on the quality of football play at the Carlisle School around 1890, Steckbeck (1951) described it as a "jumbled mess, as all types of players tried to acquaint themselves with the white man's game" (p. 127). At that time a formal program of instruction and competition was first attempted by a local instructor for two or three years. An intramural school league was then established to further acclimate the Indians to the new sport.

Early Indian and non-Indian sports interaction was far from smooth. First, most non-Indians were rather isolated socially and geographically from Indians. The Indian image—either hostile or warlike—did not encourage fraternization. When Indians began to play the sports of the white man during the later 19th century and early 20th century, verbal abuse was commonplace and physical abuse happened occasionally. For example, when Louis Sockalexis, a Penobscot, began playing baseball with the Cleveland team in the 1890s he encountered heavy abuse and "was greeted at each game with war whoops, 'Ki Yi's,' insults, and threats. Although batting .413, Sockalexis, after two months in the league, was suspended for drunkenness" (Rader, 1983, p. 120). (*The Official Encyclopedia of Baseball* [Turkin & Thompson, 1951] reveals that in 1897 Sockalexis batted .331 in 66 games.) It is ironic that in 1916 when the fans of Cleveland were given an opportunity to select a nickname for the team, they selected *Indians* as a tribute to Sockalexis who had played nearly twenty years earlier.

Shortly after the beginning of the 20th century, Indians did achieve prominence in competition with non-Indians, particularly in football, track, and baseball. Most distinguished among these successes were the football and track teams from the Training School for Indians at Carlisle, Pennsylvania. Between 1900 and 1915 sports teams at this small school achieved great acclaim by competing successfully against the nation's best college teams. To a somewhat lesser extent, the Haskell Indian School in Lawrence, Kansas, attained national recognition during the 1920s and early 1930s. In addition, Indian schools in Oklahoma, Washington state, and other parts of the country achieved local or area recognition in sports at the grammar or secondary school level during the early part of the century.

Summary

Although the performances by John Steeprock, Deerfoot Bennett, and Big Hawk Chief were outstanding and occurred in the presence of and against non-Indian competition, they did not signal a flood of Indian–non-Indian competitions. Neither did they lead to any significant entry of Indians into popular sports of the late 19th century. It was not until the emergence of the team sports of baseball and football, with their regularly scheduled competitions, that Indians began to attain visibility as athletes. Nevertheless, Indian participation in these mainstream sports (whether on special teams, e.g., Carlisle football, or as individuals, e.g., Chief Bender with the Philadelphia Athletics) provided impetus for the Indian heyday in sports during the first quarter of the 20th century.

Chapter 8

Role of Early Indian Schools

Indian education is as old as Indian life. In traditional times the education of children was viewed as a serious enterprise not only for the immediate family but also for the broader community. In addition to the father and mother, grandparents, uncles, and other relatives within the clan became closely identified with the training of the child. Adults of the extended family usually assumed teaching roles consistent with their particular interest or talents (e.g., hunting, farming, crafts, warfare, survival, and so on). One of the most valued techniques for instruction was storytelling.

Sports, too, were an important part of the training program for Indian children. The physical demands, the strategies, and the moral strengths required in sports were viewed as important virtues. It was assumed by the adults that these assets would transfer to other life situations. Consequently, the lessons of sport were carefully taught.

The broad range of work and survival skills varied widely in different parts of the country. That is, skills for food gathering, house construction, or general prosperity differed greatly from the Eastern Woodland Indians to those of the Southwest or the Plains. Sports, too, varied among different tribes, though there were some common activities. The education of children, therefore, was a multifaceted endeavor, including many persons, a diversity of skills to be learned, and a range of media through which it took place. This traditional approach to education differed widely from the formal school setting that existed in non-Indian society during the late 19th century.

Non-Indian involvement in Indian education began soon after the arrival of the white man on this continent. The Spanish initiated programs to educate the Indians in the southwestern regions and in Florida during the 16th century, and the English colonists did the same soon after their arrival in Virginia and in New England early in the 17th century. The primary purpose of these early ventures, whether individual and informal or the more organized mission schools, was to convert the Indians to Christianity. When the federal government began assuming a major responsibility for educating Indian children near the beginning of the 19th century, the primary objective evolved toward preparing the Indian for citizenship in the larger society.

Early Colonial Assistance

The efforts of English colonists to educate the Indian took the form of day schools, boarding schools, colleges, and informal individual instruction in colonial homes. Support for these efforts came from a variety of sources, including private initiatives, missionary societies, charities, and colonial land grants. One of the first non-Indians to make a concerted effort to educate the Indian was Reverend John Elist who arrived in Massachusetts in 1631. While he served as a pastor in Boston for fifty-six years, he founded the Roxbury Latin School and served as overseer of Harvard College. In addition, he published books for the Indian, preached to them, and taught the children to read and write English.

Formal efforts of non-Indians to educate Indians were highlighted by the establishment of special programs at Harvard (under the leadership of Reverend Elist) immediately after its founding in 1650 and later at William and Mary in 1691 and Dartmouth in 1769. These institutions were established with a strong orientation toward the education of Indian youth (Adams, 1946; Fuchs, 1970; and Ryberg & Belok, 1973).

Despite the apparently noble intentions of the colonists, there was considerable Indian resistance to these overtures. Conversion to the white man's religion and larger culture was slow to a point that seemed to mystify the white man. For example, the Virginia Company Charters in 1606 and in 1609 specifically emphasized the conversion of Indians, and provided ten pounds as an inticement to any colonial home that provided instruction for an Indian boy. However, the colonists complained that "they could not obtain many Indian children in a peaceable manner because the parents were so deeply attached to them" (Adams, 1946, p. 15).

Resistance to the white man's education was based on more than religious grounds. In general, there was a lack of conviction that this education led to a superior way of life. One incident illustrates the reluctance of Indians to send their young men off to college (Beatty, 1941). In a letter to Benjamin Franklin in 1744, the Chief of Six Nations declined an invitation to have six young men sent off to the College of William and Mary. In explaining his reasons the chief stated:

We are convinced . . . that you mean to do us good by your proposal, and we thank you heartily. But you, who are wise, must know that different nations have different conceptions of things; and you will not therefore take it amiss if our ideas of this kind of education happen not to be the same with yours. We have had some experience with it. Several of our young people were formally brought up at the colleges of the Northern provinces; they were instructed in all your science; but when they came back to us, they were bad runners, ignorant of every means of living in the woods, unable to bear either cold or hunger, knew neither how to build a cabin, take a deer, or kill an enemy, spoke our language imperfectly, were therefore neither fit for warriors, hunters, nor counselors; they were totally good for nothing. (p. 61)

Programs at Harvard, William and Mary, Dartmouth, and several other institutions continued with mixed results. Although some Indians converted to Christianity, became conversant in the English language, and learned other academic and social skills for living in a "civilized" society, these programs did not catch on in the Indian community in the manner anticipated.

Following the *removals* (the forced evacuation of Indians from their homelands) and other disruptions during the 1830s, tribes began developing their own schools. For example, the Choctaws established twelve log schoolhouses in 1833. A more elaborate school system was developed by the Cherokees; they had twenty-one schools and two academies with an enrollment of 1,100 by 1852. The development of these tribal schools was prompted by a growing dissatisfaction with mission and sectarian schools as well as programs at major universities.

Mission Schools

The Franciscans began establishing mission schools in southern California late in the 18th Century. The first such mission school for Indians was opened in San Diego in 1769, and by 1823 twenty mission schools had been established south of San Francisco (Adams, 1946). These schools were located in densely populated Indian communities.

The federal government began assuming partial responsibility for educating the Indians early in the 19th century as a condition of treaty agreements. Funds for this purpose were first appropriated in 1819. From then until late in the 19th century, this money was allocated to religious groups to implement the educational programs for Indians. However, in the face of growing public resistance to the idea of giving money to religious groups, this practice was stopped in 1900.

The overall impact of the mission schools on Indian education was somewhat short of spectacular. The primary purpose of these schools was to Christianize the Indian, a process that met some resistance in Indian communities. It seemed to the Indian that conquest was being followed by forced religious conversion. This basic mistrust of the white man's motives thwarted the success of the mission schools.

Boarding Schools

In the 1870s the federal government began accepting full responsibility for Indian education. Many mission schools were replaced by government boarding schools. The government favored these schools because of the absolute control possible in a school environment. For example, instead of using the bilingual mission school approach, the language could be restricted to English. In addition, student appearance, behavior, and daily routine could be made to conform to specific rules. Unlike the narrower, religiously oriented programs of the mission schools, federal authorities wished to promote a broader range of vocational skills.

There were strong differences of opinion about whether the federal boarding schools should be on or near the reservation or whether they should be more remote. Some argued that the schools would be more effective if they were far removed because children would be completely disengaged from tribal influences for the duration of the school experience. Others believed that some contact with the home and family would provide needed support for the child and thus would permit a more gradual weaning from the traditional Indian life-style. As it turned out, most boarding schools did remove the children from all home influence and force them to live a non-Indian life.

Most boarding schools were restricted to the lower grades. Parents were pressured to give up their children, who were then transported to schools in distant areas. For example, the Carlisle School in Pennsylvania was thousands of miles away from the homes of most of the children attending that school. Furthermore, students were held as virtual prisoners during the school term, or longer. Home visits were infrequent and brief. In fact, some children never returned home after leaving for boarding school at an early age until they completed high school training. Then, as indicated in the letter from the tribal chief to Benjamin Franklin (Beatty, 1941), serious problems were often encountered in readjusting to the life and language of the Indian community. Consequently, these educated young people did not easily fit into either the Indian world or the non-Indian community.

Purposes of Federal Schools for Indians

During the last quarter of the 19th century, it became official federal policy to *assimilate* Indians into the majority society. This was seen as the most appropriate solution to the "Indian Problem." Whereas the mission schools had been conducted to Christianize Indians, government schools aimed to "civilize" them. To prepare the child for a useful role in the dominant society, Indian youth were taught many basic skills, especially to read, write, and speak English. In high school, boys were taught agricultural or other vocational skills, and girls were taught homemaking and related trades. In addition, some effort was made to acquaint Indian students with the social mores and life-styles of the non-Indian society. The Carlisle School publication, *The Red Man and Helper*, carried this slogan: "There is only one way: To civilize the Indian, get him into civilization; to keep him civilized, let him stay" (Newcombe, 1975, p. 62). That philosophy of Lieutenant Richard H. Pratt, the schools' founder, was no doubt reflected in other schools that were established during that era for Indians.

School practices included the prohibition of the use of native languages, the elimination of traditional hair styles and clothing, and often the substitution of new religious customs for old ones. In addition, children were given anglicized names. Figures 8.1 and 8.2 provide evidence of dramatic changes in clothing, hair styles, and postures among Indian children soon after their arrival at the Carlisle School. Figure 8.1 shows a group of Chiricahua Apache immediately upon their arrival at the school, and Figure 8.2 shows another group of Apaches after having spent some time there.

One of the first federal educational programs for Indians was established during the 1870s by Lieutenant Pratt, a U.S. Army Officer stationed at Fort Sill, Oklahoma (in Indian territory). Pratt was given orders to transport young Indian prisoners to the Spanish prison in St. Augustine, Florida. During this travel and his subsequent supervision of the Indians in Florida, he developed a fondness for the boys and accorded them more lenient treatment than was customary. In fact, contrary to regulations, he allowed them to leave the prison during the day for employment in the vicinity and to return to prison each night.

Figure 8.1. Group of Chiricahua Apache children immediately after their arrival at the Carlisle School. Photographer and date not recorded, but probably in the early 1880s. Photo used by permission of the National Anthropological Archives, Smithsonian Institution.

Figure 8.2. Apache children several months after their arrival at the Carlisle School. Photo used by permission of the National Anthropological Archives, Smithsonian Institution.

Pratt soon began teaching the young Indians to read, write, and speak English, and he later contacted several Eastern schools in an attempt to have the Indian youth accepted into those institutions. The only receptive response was from the Hampton Institute in Virginia, a school for black youth. In 1878 a special program for the Indian boys was established at Hampton and continued for several years, during which time more than 400 Indians were trained in agriculture and related trades. Adams (1946) reported that Indians continued to be enrolled at Hampton until 1912. Though most reports concluded that this program was successful, McDonald (1972) stated without qualification that "the mingling of the two races did not prove successful" (p. 61). Regardless, authorities

Table 8.1 Government Off-Reservation Schools Established Prior to 1900

Locations	Dates of opening
Carlisle, PA	November 1, 1879
Chemawa, OR	February 25, 1880
Chilocco, OK	January 15, 1884
Genoa, NE	February 20, 1884
Albuquerque, NM	August, 1884
Lawrence, KS (Haskell Institute)	September 1, 1884
Grand Junction, CO	1886
Sante Fe, NM	October, 1890
Fort Mohave, AZ	December, 1890
Carson, NV	December, 1890
Pierre, SD	February, 1891
Phoenix, AZ	September, 1891
Fort Lewis, CO	March, 1892
Fort Shaw, MT	December 27, 1892
Perris, CA	January 9, 1893
Flandreau, SD	March 7, 1893
Pipestone, MN	February, 1893
Mount Pleasant, MI	January 3, 1893
Tomah, WI	January 19, 1893
Wittenberg, WI	August 24, 1895
Greenville, CA	September 25, 1895
Morris, MN	April 3, 1897
Chamberlain, SD	March, 1898
Fort Bidwell, CA	April 4, 1898
Rapid City, SD	September 1, 1898

Note. From *Identification of Unique Features in Education at American Indian Schools* (p. 67) by C.E. Jackson, 1965. Unpublished doctoral dissertation, University of Utah.

Table 8.2 Government Off-Reservation Schools as of 1964

Name of school	Location
Flandreau School	Flandreau, SD
Wahpeton Indian School	Wahpeton, ND
Pierre Indian School	Pierre, SD
Haskell Institute	Lawrence KS
Chilocco Indian School	Chilocco, OK
Cheyenne-Arapahoe School	Concho, OK
Concho Demonstration School	Concho, OK
Riverside Indian School	Anadarko, OK
Wingate Vocational School	Fort Wingate, NM
Aneth Boarding School	Aneth, UT
Albuquerque School	Albuquerque, NM
Institute of American Indian Arts	Santa Fe, NM
Intermountain School	Brigham City, UT
Seneca Indian School	Wyandotte, OK
Sequoyah Vocational School	Tahlequah, OK
Phoenix Indian School	Phoenix, AZ
Sherman Institute	Riverside, CA
Chemawa Indian School	Chemawa, OR
Stewart Indian School	Stewart, NV

Note. From *Identification of Unique Features in Education at American Indian School* (p. 55) by C.E. Jackson, 1965. Unpublished doctoral dissertation, University of Utah.

concluded that off-reservation education for Indians could prove successful. Subsequently the Training School for Indians at Carlisle, Pennsylvania, was opened in 1879 and was immediately judged a success.

Growth of Off-Reservation Schools

Initial reports of the educational program at the Carlisle program were so positive that Congress appropriated funding for additional boarding schools for the training of Indian youth. During the twenty years following the opening of the Carlisle School in 1879, twenty-five other off-reservation schools were established for Indians. Table 8.1 includes a list of those schools established prior to 1900. Each of these schools was begun as a grammar school but later evolved into a high school. Table 8.2 shows the list of off-reservation schools as of 1964. It can be noted that several schools, such as Haskell, Chilocco, and Chemawa, remained through the years.

Programs at the Indian boarding schools were similar in that all were designed to prepare the children for life off the reservation. The children were taught basic English and arithmetic skills and were given vocational training assumed to be necessary to help them earn a livelihood off the reservation. In addition, they were taught the social skills viewed as proper for citizens in polite society. Figures 8.3–8.7 show examples of academic and vocational training at several of these schools. Figure 8.8 proudly shows "the finished product," the Carlisle graduating class of 1915.

Figure 8.3. Indian children receiving training in fractions at the Carlisle School. Note the formality of both teacher and students. Photo from National Archives and Records Administration.

Figure 8.4. Boys at the Carlisle School receiving training in cobbling, under the watchful eye of the instructor. Photo from National Archives and Records Administration.

Figure 8.5. Wagonmaking at the Riverside Indian School in California. Photo from National Archives and Records Administration.

Figure 8.6. Girls in mending class at the Carlisle School. Photo from National Archives and Records Administration.

Figure 8.7 Military drill at the Phoenix Indian School in 1907. Photo from National Archives and Records Administration.

Figure 8.8. The Carlisle graduating class of 1915. Photo from National Archives and Records Administration.

At the time of rapid development of boarding schools for Indians (in the 1880s), Congress also appropriated money for educating the native Alaskans. It should be noted that those Indian groups not holding a trust relationship with the federal government were sometimes provided special schools by the state government. For example, the Lumbee Indians in North Carolina, after a fifty-year period without schools, were provided a grammar school in 1887. This school, located in Pembroke, North Carolina, evolved into a high school, a junior college, and then, in the 1930s, a four-year college for Indians. Until it desegregated in the 1950s, it served as the only four-year Indian college in the country.

Sports at Indian Schools

Traditional Indian sports were not a prominent part of programs in Indian schools for two apparent reasons. First, the very reason for the existence of these special schools was to acculturate Indian students, that is, to adapt them to the dominant society. Consequently, school officials responsible for the curriculum selected activities that were most prominent in the dominant society. For example, rigid exercise programs similar to those in non-Indian schools of the period were established in the Indian schools. Some of these are shown in Figures 8.9–8.11. At the same time, school administrators sought to extinguish those experiences and behaviors (including sports) that were traditionally Indian.

Second, there were usually no available teams within the locality against which these schools could compete in traditional Indian sports. It can be noted, however, that there was no serious resistance among the students to the introduction of football, baseball, basketball, or other non-Indian sports. In fact, they welcomed these new sports and performed them exceedingly well. Figure 8.12 shows Indian boys attired for baseball play at the Hampton Institute.

The heyday of Indian sports in modern times occurred during the first three decades of the 20th century. A high level of achievement and attention was attained by Indian athletes in football, baseball, track, lacrosse, and boxing. Foremost among the Indian schools receiving sports recognition were those at Carlisle in Pennsylvania and, later, the Haskell Institute in Kansas. No other Indian school approached their levels of success. This may be due to the fact that these two institutions apparently recruited promising young athletes from other Indian schools, leaving those schools largely depleted of talented athletes.

During the period of greatest success at the Carlisle and Haskell schools, the respective superintendents were especially supportive of the athletic programs, perhaps for the developmental values of the activities but probably more for the recognition it brought to the school.

Figure 8.9. Physical exercises in the classroom at the Camp Verde Indian School in Arizona. Photo from National Archives and Records Administration.

Figure 8.10. Girls gymnasium exercises at the Haskell School. Photo from National Archives and Records Administration.

Figure 8.11. Formal exercises on the school grounds at Camp Verde, Arizona. Photo from National Archives and Records Administration.

Figure 8.12. Indian students at the Hampton Institute in Virginia. Photo is probably from the 1880s. Photo used by permission of the National Anthropological Archives, Smithsonian Institution.

Summary

Indian education has gone through several phases over the past four centuries. First, traditional Indian education involved a variety of persons and approaches in teaching Indian youth the skills necessary for survival and success. Next, special programs at the first, and subsequently most prestigious, colleges (Harvard, William and Mary, and Dartmouth) were initiated during the colonial period. Though they reflected noble intentions (i.e., elevating the quality of life for Indians), these programs were not widely accepted and supported by the Indians themselves.

The mission schools were established by churches essentially to convert the Indians to Christianity and to lead them away from the traditional life-style, which was viewed by the churches as heathen and savage. Though supported by the federal government through much of the 19th century, the mission schools, too, fell short of their goal. While recognizing some values in this education, Indian leaders objected to a system designed to destroy their total life-style.

In addition to federal schools located on reservations, at least two dozen off-reservation government boarding schools were established during the last two decades of the 19th century. The primary purpose of these schools was to prepare the Indians for life in non-Indian society. Therefore, training in the English language, vocational trades, and a non-Indian life-style were emphasized. At the same time, Indian youth were prevented from using traditional Indian languages and dress or engaging in familiar sports. New habits, including sports, were taught that essentially duplicated programs at non-Indian schools. In general, the Indian youth accepted and even excelled at the new sports. Students at the Carlisle and Haskell schools were particularly successful, often to the distraction of non-Indians. Sports programs at these two schools will be dealt with in the following chapter.

Chapter 9

Sports Programs at the Carlisle and Haskell Schools

Hundreds of schools have been devoted to the education of the Indian since the white man first settled on this continent. These schools have been sponsored by the federal government, state governments, tribal organizations, missionary groups, and other organizations and individuals having a range of interests. Schools for Indians have varied widely not only in terms of the purpose for which they were established but in several additional characteristics. For example, some schools have been restricted to the elementary grades whereas others extended to the college level. Some have been located on reservations; others were quite remote from the reservation. Some schools have been restricted to Indians only (sometimes limited to members of a single tribe), and others have integrated Indians with one or more races. Some Indian schools have been short lived, but others have survived much longer (e.g., Haskell celebrated its centennial in 1984).

Indian schools have also varied widely in the attention devoted to sport and play. In general, the early schools, especially those prior to 1875, allowed little time during the school day for play or other activity viewed as frivolous by (non-Indian) school authorities. A recess period was provided, but the traditional Indian concept of sport as a serious and integral part of life and as an important developmental activity for young people was not generally adopted by the non-Indian society. Indeed, the lingering effects of Puritanism and the work ethic curtailed a full appreciation of the role of sport well into the 20th century. Still, most Indian schools late in the 19th century initiated programs of physical activity that were similar to those in non-Indian schools. One reason for this was to develop within Indian children the skills that were characteristic of the dominant society. These activities were formal and stilted, as were physical activity programs at non-Indian schools of that period. However, these programs were different from the more informal play of Indian children or the games and sports of Indian adults.

Despite the great number of Indian schools and their quick adoption of the white man's sports, only two attained significant acclaim in the area of athletics. These were the Indian Training School in Carlisle, Pennsylvania, and the Haskell Institute (now the Haskell Indian Junior College) in Lawrence, Kansas. After some initial success and increased visibility of these institutions, school administrators seized upon sports as a means of bringing important recognition to the school. Potentially outstanding athletes were actively recruited to Carlisle and Haskell in the belief that a prominent sport program would reflect well on the institution and would also attract talented students in other areas. Because of their demonstrated excellence in sports and the resulting public acclaim, these programs will be presented in some detail.

The Carlisle Indian School

After opening in 1879, the Indian Training School at Carlisle, Pennsylvania, survived only thirty-nine years before being closed in 1918 following a damaging congressional investigation. Nevertheless, during its short life it attained a level of fame in athletics that would survive long after its demise as an institution. Though the school was established for the purpose of teaching Indian youth the white man's ways, it came to be known best for its athletic prowess.

Origin of the School

Following the initial success of the Indian education program at the Hampton Institute (see chapter 8), Lieutenant Richard H. Pratt began searching for a more expanded opportunity for special Indian education. He concluded that a special Indian school would best meet this need. Being familiar with the recently vacated army barracks at Carlisle, Pennsylvania, he appealed to Congress and to the War Department (it was then responsible for Indian programs) to obtain those facilities to be used as a separate school for Indians. This request was rapidly approved,

Figure 9.1. Facilities at the Indian Training School housed in the U.S. Army barracks at Carlisle, Pennsylvania. Photo taken in 1909. Photo from National Archives and Records Administration.

and according to Steckbeck (1951), the first governmental, nonreservation school for Indians was established at that site in 1879. A photograph of the school facilities, taken in 1909, is shown in Figure 9.1. The first students at Carlisle were all from the Midwest or Great Plains regions. Lieutenant Pratt (later promoted to the rank of General) served as superintendent from the school's opening until 1905.

The overriding motivation for establishing the Indian school was one of helpfulness. Superintendent Pratt and his supporters believed that to prepare Indians for a fruitful life in this country, they must first be detached from the exclusivity and life-style that were a part of the Indian culture. They must be placed in an educational program similar to that used for white children. The barracks at Carlisle, Pennsylvania, geographically removed from the reservations of the West, were viewed as a desirable location for these children.

In the beginning, students were given the most rudimentary academic training and were taught simple trades. As the school developed, the curriculum broadened and improved. However, it was never more than a trade school, perhaps at the mid–high school level. Although some of the students remained in school through their teen years and even into their early twenties, it was never considered an institution of higher learning.

One important feature of the Carlisle program was the *outing* system, which placed Indian boys and girls in the homes of white families in the neighboring communities. The purpose was not only to work on the farm, in the home, and at various trades but also to absorb the white culture by living within it. The students worked side by side with successful farmers and tradesmen. In addition, they were paid nominal wages for services rendered.

From the beginning, students were encouraged to take part in play and games of skill. They were allowed to engage in some familiar activities such as running, jumping, and individual skills of physical prowess, and they were also taught the white man's games. Most common among these were baseball, soccer, football, and formal track events. Basketball also became very popular at Carlisle after its origination in 1892. Indian youth proved to be enthusiastic participants in these activities and before long began to excel in them.

The Early Years in Football

The spectacular success of the Carlisle football teams, both in achievement on the field and in general popularity, was unexpected. The Indians did not have a history of playing football. The school had neither traditions nor influential alumni to promote the program or the school. Indeed, there was little reason to believe that this small and loosely organized program could compete with local high schools, let alone the major universities of the nation. Whereas Eastern colleges started competing in football in the 1870s, the Carlisle School did not begin formal competition until 1893. In that year two games were played: one with Harrisburg High School and another with the Educational Home of Philadelphia. There was little indication at that time that within six years (1899) the Carlisle School would win nine games while losing only two in a schedule that included wins over the University of Pennsylvania, Columbia University, the University of California, and smaller colleges in Pennsylvania and New York. The two losses in 1899 were to Harvard University in Cambridge by a score of 20 to 10 and to Princeton in New York by a score of 12 to 0.

Football began as an informal sport on the Carlisle campus around 1890. Pickup games were arranged in which different departments would enter teams in a loosely organized schedule leading to a school champion. Steckbeck (1951) reported that in 1890 a single game was played against a team from Dickinson College, which was also located in Carlisle, Pennsylvania. However, one of the Indian players suffered a broken leg in the game in what the school newspaper, *The Indian Helper*, referred to as "one of the most serious accidents to ever happen at our school" (cited in Steckbeck, 1951, p. 12). Pratt saw fit to abandon the sport for two or three years.

In 1894 Mr. Vance McCormick, a resident of nearby Harrisburg and a former all-American quarterback at Yale University, began coaching a team of Carlisle players on a volunteer basis. Having no playing field at that time, they played all games away from home, a practice that was generally true throughout the life of the school. In 1894 the schedule was expanded to nine games; Carlisle won only one game while losing six and tying two. Their opponents included a high school team (their only win), two athletic clubs, a YMCA, and five colleges. Their win-loss record was undistinguished, but there were several hopeful signs. Despite losing to the

Pittsburgh Athletic Club 8-0, the *Pittsburgh Post* reported that "certainly no more superb tackling has ever been seen in Pittsburgh, than that displayed by everyone on the Indian team. They feared nothing and whenever they got their hands on a runner he went down in his tracks" (cited in Steckbeck, 1951, p. 14). The greater experience of most of their opponents appeared to be the vital difference.

In 1895 the record of the Carlisle Indians improved to four wins and four losses. All the losses were to college teams; two of the four wins were against YMCA teams and one was against an athletic club. In 1896 a significant improvement in the football program was noted. A new coach was employed, and the schedule was upgraded to include Yale, Harvard, Princeton, Pennsylvania, Brown, Connecticut, Wisconsin, Penn State, Dickinson, and the Duquesne Athletic Club. Such scheduling seemed ambitious, if not foolhardy, for this small training school. Still, Carlisle won six games while losing only four. The University of Wisconsin game was played at night in Chicago's Coliseum on December 19, 1896, with 16,000 persons in attendance. It has been widely reported that this was the first night football game ever played.

In 1897 Carlisle again had six wins and four losses and in 1898 had five wins and four losses. This unexpected success against the nation's best football teams led to a great deal of national recognition for the Carlisle School.

These early successes in football heightened the interest and involvement of Superintendent Pratt. According to Newcombe (1975), Pratt contacted Indian agents around the country and asked that they be on the lookout for Indians gifted physically and otherwise. He requested young men "swift of foot or qualified for athletics . . . to help Carlisle compete with the great universities on those lines" (p. 85). During the early years of Carlisle football, student athletes were recruited from Haskell Institute and as far away as the Sherman Institute for Indians in California. Pratt saw that football and other athletics could bring valuable recognition to Carlisle. Furthermore, he appreciated the value of athletics in providing helpful travel and social experiences for the student athletes.

Superintendent Pratt expended great effort to encourage fair play on the part of the Indians. He insisted that Carlisle not fight back even when abused. During his administration Carlisle teams won recognition for sportsmanlike play.

Although the football team received much greater public attention, the track and field team was no less impressive. For example, during the years from 1910 to 1912, typically only three or four persons on the Carlisle team won points in track meets. Still, they were usually victorious. Jim Thorpe often won five events, Louis Tewanima usually won the two long distance events, and Joe Guyon won one or two sprints. Thus, with just a few second place finishes, the Carlisle team accrued enough points to win. This aspect of the athletic program received little attention prior to

Thorpe and Tewanema's success at the 1912 Olympic Games. The game of football simply had much greater public popularity.

Influence of Pop Warner

Glenn S. "Pop" Warner began his long coaching career at the Carlisle School in 1899. Pratt hired Warner at the suggestion of Walter Camp, who was the coach at Yale University and generally recognized as the country's foremost authority on football. Warner remained at Carlisle as the head football coach from 1899 through 1914 except for three years (1904–1906) when he returned to coach at his alma mater, Cornell. Under Warner's leadership Carlisle attained great success on the field and widespread recognition. It was during his tenure that several players from Carlisle achieved All-American status, led by the legendary Jim Thorpe.

All major football games played by Carlisle were at the site of the opposing institution, which makes their highly successful record even more astounding. Carlisle was a much-traveled team, a circumstance consistent with the philosophy of school officials who believed that traveling was a valuable educational experience. This was assumed to be especially enlightening for Indian youth, who were seen as needing to experience more of the nonreservation culture. Thus, the 1899 team played games in New York state, New England, and as far west as Chicago. In addition, after their last scheduled game on November 30 against Columbia in New York City, they were invited to San Francisco to play the University of California in the East-West Championship. Pop Warner took them to California by train, and Carlisle won the game 2–0 on Christmas Day. Steckbeck (1951) reported that only the eleven starters and three substitutes made the trip.

Apparently the players did not object to this extensive travel. In fact, both Newcombe (1975) and Steckbeck (1951) report that they viewed athletics and travel as a welcome relief from the military style routine and restrictions of the Carlisle campus. Steckbeck cites numerous travel anecdotes of the football team indicating the young men engaged in the frivolity and practical jokes that might be expected of any group of young men.

Under Warner's leadership and in the absence of external controls or nationally established standards, Carlisle frequently played more than the customary ten games. The 1903 schedule called for fourteen games, including play on December 25 and on New Year's Day in California. At one time during the season three games were played within a period of one week. There were occasional comments that these extensive schedules and travel were disruptive to the educational program for the players, making them virtually full-time athletes. However, this was not viewed as improper by Warner, and Pratt apparently supported these broadening experiences.

One reason for the extensive schedule was the financial guarantees made by opposing institutions. The excellence of the Carlisle teams and their novelty as an all-Indian team made them an attractive draw. It was not unusual for them to be paid $10,000 or even $15,000 for a game at Harvard, Columbia, Chicago, or another major university. This money was controlled by Warner who used it for a variety of purposes related directly or indirectly to athletics.

The coaching career of Warner at Carlisle was marked by great success on the football field and notoriety in the sports pages. He was an intense, hard-driving coach who used strong measures to force players toward the limits of their abilities. Warner's success at Carlisle was attributable as much to his attention to conditioning and discipline as to his tactical skills. Warner undoubtedly had a very fertile mind, and he was innovative in developing equipment, drills, formations, strategy, and even new rules.

In his relations with Indian athletes, Warner has been described as profane and hard driving, without compassion. He is reported to have resorted to intimidation and, occasionally, physical abuse. According to Newcombe (1975), Indians were more offended at his language and abusive manner than were the non-Indians Warner coached at other institutions. During congressional hearings into problems at Carlisle in 1914, several players expressed the feeling that Warner's derisive remarks were intended to humiliate them. Actually, he did tone down his behavior from time to time because many Indian athletes chose to stay away from practices if abused. Gus Welch, a popular student leader and football captain, acknowledged that Warner was a skilled coach but described him as a man of low moral character (Newcombe, 1975).

It must be stated in Warner's defense that his techniques later became commonplace at other institutions and were in fact used effectively by him after leaving Carlisle. His hard-driving, win-at-all-cost style was a prototype for football coaches at major universities and even at the professional level. Vince Lombardi's "winning is everything" and Leo Durocher's "nice guys finish last" are expressions of this orientation. Whereas Warner did not intend his comments to be taken personally, they were so received by the young, sensitive Indians, who were not accustomed to this general or individual condemnation.

Kendall Blanchard (1981) has reported similar Indian reactions to such coaching tactics in the 1970s. In studies among the Navajos (Blanchard, 1974) and among the Choctaw (Blanchard, 1981), he found that Indians rejected the aggressive, dictatorial type of coaching leadership and that they responded better to a more democratic style. It is probable that Warner did not comprehend this trait in the Indian character.

Warner was sometimes accused of searching for ways to circumvent the rules. His style of play often bordered on illegality. More favorable observers reported that he was simply an imaginative individual who took advantage of any lack of clarity in the rules. Warner "was never malicious but was clever enough to outwit the smartest opponent" (Steckbeck, 1951, p. 65). His teams were often described as tricky. The high code of sportsmanship under Pratt during the 1890s was not adhered to under Warner.

As an example of Warner's creative style, he successfully instituted the hidden-ball play in a 1903 game at Harvard (Steckbeck, 1951). The play was first used at the beginning of the second half when Harvard kicked off to Carlisle.

Upon receiving the ball, the Indians clustered together, and for a moment the pigskin was concealed in their midst. Harvard's players dashed into the Indian huddle but found that it was like looking for the proverbial needle in a haystack. Before the mystery could be solved, big Dillon, the Indian guard, was plunging half way down the field with the ball securely tucked up under the back of his sweater. The crimson team tried to stop him, but too late. Struggling to remove the ball from beneath his jersey, Dillon was aided by his teammate Johnson, who removed it and touched it down for a score. The cleverness of this "hidden ball" play has never been disputed. The sewing of an elastic band in the bottom of the Indian players' jerseys can be credited to the craftiness of Coach Warner. (p. 44)

On another occasion, Warner used an exaggerated version of a "psyching" technique that has become rather commonplace in the latter part of the 20th century. Prior to playing a very tough Syracuse team in 1908, Warner bemoaned the sad condition of the Carlisle team. According to him, the players were badly injured, fatigued, and sick. This claim seemed valid when the players appeared for warm-ups heavily bandaged prior to the game and went through lethargic and seemingly painful exercise. However, all signs of injury and fatigue disappeared when the game started. The Syracuse team, which had beaten Yale the previous week, was overwhelmed 12-0. This technique of "playing possum" was common in Indian folklore but had not been widely used in college sports.

Another deceptive technique used by Coach Warner was to have emblems the size, shape, and color of footballs sewn onto the front of the jerseys of all Carlisle players. This made it difficult for opponents to distinguish the player holding the ball from those with only the emblem of the ball on their jersey. This trick was used in a game against Syracuse in 1906. The following week Harvard heard about the incident and objected to the use of the same jerseys. Warner argued that the rules did not prohibit jerseys so decorated. Not until the Harvard coach had produced game balls painted crimson to match the Harvard jerseys did Warner agree to have the football patches removed.

The Carlisle Team: National Football Power

The Carlisle team in 1906 achieved a record of nine wins and two losses against the best colleges in the East and Midwest. While scoring 244 points to their opponents' thirty-six, they were beaten by Harvard 5–0 and by Penn State University 4–0. In the *Outing Magazine*, Casper Whitney (1907) ranked the 1906 Carlisle team as the fifth best in the nation for that year.

The 1907 season marked the entry of Jim Thorpe into the Carlisle football picture. However, it was his first year in football and he was not on the first team. The team was led by several others including Frank Mt. Pleasant, who achieved the status of Honorable Mention on Walter Camp's All-American Team. This 1907 team earned a record of ten wins and only one loss, beating such teams as Harvard, Syracuse, Villanova, and the Universities of Chicago, Minnesota, and Pennsylvania. The single loss came against Princeton University. According to Steckbeck (1951), the Minnesota game (next to last game of the season) ''was considered decisive of the championship of the country'' (p. 72). However, at that time there were no official rankings for a number one team in the country.

The team of 1908 played thirteen games and was only slightly less spectacular, losing only to Harvard and the University of Minnesota and tying the University of Pennsylvania with a score of 6–6. The Carlisle touchdown against the University of Pennsylvania was the only one scored against that team all season. The 1909 and 1910 teams, in the absence of Jim Thorpe, had good, but not spectacular, seasons. The 1909 team played twelve games, winning eight, losing three, and tying one. The 1910 team scheduled an incredible fifteen games, winning eight, losing six, and having one cancelled.

In 1911 Jim Thorpe returned to the team after having dropped out of school for two years. This team won eleven of twelve games; the only loss was a 12–11 defeat by Syracuse. The team scored 298 points to their opponents' 49. The following year, 1912, was hardly less successful when they won twelve games, lost one and tied one. The only loss was to the University of Pennsylvania by a score of 34-26. They were tied by the Rose Bowl–bound Washington and Jefferson team. Jim Thrope achieved First Team All-American status both in 1911 and 1912. In one often-reported incident during the 1912 season against the Army Team at West Point, he returned a kickoff the full length of the field for a touchdown only to have the play nullified because of a rule infraction. Army was again forced to kick off, and once again Thorpe received the ball and ran the full length of the field for a touchdown, which counted. Dwight Eisenhower, the future president, played for the Army team.

The Carlisle players were almost always smaller than players on the opposing teams. For example, the biggest player on the 1912 team was guard Elmer Bush who weighed 186 pounds. No other player weighed more than 180 pounds. Jim Thorpe was reported to be the tallest player at six feet even. Steckbeck (1951) cited the *Carlisle Evening Sentinel* on October 27, 1913, as stating that the University of Pennsylvania team out-weighed the Carlisle team by an average of eleven pounds per man. The success of the Carlisle team was most remarkable in view of their size differential, and it was based on speed, skill, determination, and the coaching strategy of Pop Warner.

The last team at Carlisle to achieve significant success was in 1913. This team finished with a record of ten wins, one loss, and one tie despite the fact that most of the players were relatively new. Two players, Elmer Busch and Joe Guyon, were selected by Walter Camp for Second Team All-American honors.

Decline of the Carlisle Football Prominence

In 1914 a senatorial investigation was launched into activities at the Carlisle School. Criticism had been forthcoming about laxity in the academic pro-gram, overemphasis on athletics, abuse of students, handling of athletic funds, inflated school attendance records, and the general lack of disci-pline. The investigation was initiated at least in part by the students. Gus Welch, a student leader and prominent football player, was one of the persons calling for an investigation. Two hundred students signed the petition. The cloud that accompanied the investigation and related activi-ties never lifted. The long and troublesome probe resulted in the eventual closing of the school in 1918.

The decline in the football program during and after the investigation was dramatic. The schedule was severely downgraded. The discipline usually characteristic of Coach Warner's program was no longer evident. In 1914 the team won only four games, thus achieving the poorest record since the team of 1901. Coach Warner left the school at the end of 1914 to assume the head coaching position at the University of Pittsburgh. His teams won a total of 103 games, lost 40, and tied 8 during his time at Carlisle. After leaving, he went on to several other universities and achieved one of the most outstanding coaching records of all time.

In 1915 the Carlisle team won only three games while losing six and tying two. They were held scoreless in five games and were badly beaten by several teams, including a loss to the University of Pittsburgh by a score of 45 to 0. In 1916, disbanding the team was seriously discussed. Only five games were played, none against major opponents. The sched-ule, in fact, looked much as it did during the first year of Carlisle football in 1894.

The plight of the football program was reflected in a game between Carlisle and the Conshohocken Athletic Association in 1916. The first half was marred by poor play and even poorer sportsmanship. The Carlisle coach withdrew his team from the competition after the first half because of alleged brutal play on the part of the opponents. The coach wound up in jail for refusing to return the money guaranteed the Indians to play the game. The 6–6 score at the end of the first half was recorded as the final score of the game. In the five-game schedule during that year, the Indians won only one game while losing three and tying one.

In 1917, with the end in sight, an ill-advised nine-game schedule was played. In the last seven games, Carlisle scored only once. They were badly beaten on most occasions, including a 98–0 loss to Georgia Tech. This was the last football at Carlisle, and the school closed in August of 1918.

Football at the Carlisle School reached a level of success and visibility that had never before (or since) been attained by an Indian school. The extraordinary achievements of the team from this very small training school against major universities was astonishing, and this success captured the imagination of a large segment of the American public. The decline of football at Carlisle was as quick and complete as had been its birth and success. The deterioration and termination of the athletic program and, indeed, the school was through no fault of the Indians. The collapse of the program resulted not from a deterioration of skill or a lack of interest—the closing of the school was largely a mystery to them. Their day in the sun was removed suddenly, and without apparent reason.

It has never been made entirely clear why the Carlisle School was closed. It may be assumed that federal officials concluded that the program was no longer "civilizing" the Indians in an acceptable manner. In the years immediately preceding World War I, furthermore, the "Indian problem" was no longer a popular social issue. There was a lessening of interest in moving the Indian students a long way from western reservations to the Pennsylvania site. It is also probable that authorities concluded that the prominence of the football program and other excesses had diverted attention from the primary purpose of the school, to prepare Indian youth for life in the non-Indian society. The congressional investigation, beginning in 1914, and the resulting publicity exposed and apparently exacerbated the problems at the school. Therefore, it is probable that the investigation accelerated the closing of the school.

Haskell Indian Junior College (Formerly Haskell Institute)

In view of the success of the Carlisle School, in 1882 Congress authorized the expenditure of $150,000 for the building of three additional Indian industrial schools, to be located in Kansas, Nebraska, and Oklahoma. Dudley C. Haskell, a prominent citizen and congressman from Lawrence,

Kansas, went to Washington to encourage the establishment of one of these schools in Lawrence. At that time Haskell was chairman of the Congressional Committee on Indian Affairs. He pointed out that "the Indians living in the area are themselves educated, and they would be very helpful in gaining acceptance with the Indian parents who might send their children to school" (Haskell Institute, 1959, p. 13). From all indications, Lawrence did prove to be a good choice for locating the Institute.

Haskell Institute USA 1884–1959, published in 1959 to commemorate the 75th anniversary of Haskell, noted that

if Mr. Haskell had operated completely without hometown prejudice, and perhaps he did, a more nearly ideal site for an Indian school to serve both the Indian people and the people of the Unites States' major culture could not have been selected. (p. 4)

Unlike the Carlisle School, which was far removed from most reservations from which students were brought, Haskell was reasonably close to large Indian populations. This fact seemed to lend stability to this program, particularly during the early years. When Mr. Haskell died in 1883 at the age of forty-one, plans for the Indian school were well underway. The buildings were completed and the school opened in September, 1884 with only twenty-five students in attendance. However, by January, 1885 the enrollment had reached 400.

At the dedication service for the Haskell Institute, Chancellor Lippincott of the University of Kansas, also located at Lawrence, stated that "when one Indian boy or girl leaves this school with an education, the 'Indian problem' will forever be solved for him and his children" (Haskell Institute, 1959, p. 16). This statement was noble in intent and indeed reflected the prevailing sentiment of the time. However, it has hardly proven accurate over the past 100 years.

The program for boys included farming and certain trades such as blacksmithing and wagon and harness making, which were useful in an agricultural community. (It was also noted in *Haskell Institute USA 1884–1959*, that the blacksmithing and harness skills were helpful in making and repairing shoes, pads, uniforms, and other equipment for the football team.) The girls were taught housework, cooking, and sewing. In addition, both boys and girls spent three to four hours each day in formal education, learning English, arithmetic, and history. Approximately equal amounts of time were spent in formal education and in working to learn a trade.

Initially, five grades were included in the program at Haskell. This increased to nine grades by 1894, and the first "normal school" program, which prepared students to become teachers at the completion of high school, started in 1895. McDonald (1972) stated that in the early 1920s

Haskell advanced the curriculum to twelve grades, including a four-year high school. Shortly thereafter, in the mid-1920s, two years of post-high school work was offered, giving the Institute junior college status.

Haskell's Role in Assimilation

It was clear that the purpose of Haskell was to ease the movement of the Indian population into the majority of society. The seventy-fifth anniversary publication (Haskell Institute, 1959) expressed satisfaction with the first years of the school and indicated that "the American culture went on record as believing that cultures can be assimilated through education" (p. 22). The program was designed to enable "the Indians to make their way in the social and economic life of the country" (p. 22).

The principal architect of the Haskell program, including athletics, was H.B. Peairs. He arrived at the Institute in 1887, only three years after its opening. Peairs came to Haskell as a disciplinarian but soon became superintendent, a role he held until his retirement in 1930. He was very cognizant of the recognition that athletics had brought to Carlisle and was hopeful that the same thing could occur at Haskell. This goal was accomplished to a large extent during the 1920s with the great success of athletic teams and the building of the great stadium in 1926. Mr. Peair's enthusiasm for establishing prominence in athletics was apparent to McDonald (1972), who reported that when he took the widely acclaimed football recruit, John Levi, into the superintendent's office, "Mr. Peairs could not have welcomed the commissioner of Indian affairs more wholeheartedly" (p. 11) than he welcomed John Levi.

As recently as 1952, Superintendent Solon Ayers reiterated the aim of the federal government and of Haskell. In a written report that year (cited in Haskell Institute, 1959), he stated that "assimilation is the dominant goal of federal Indian policy" (pp. 22-23). He then went on to point out the contribution that Haskell was making to that goal.

> The effectiveness of the assimilative efforts of Haskell is indicated in the number of Haskell alumni who actually participate in the modern social and economic life of the nation. . . . It may also be noted that 50 percent of the 346 married graduates chose non-Haskell spouses and that 23 percent married non-Indians. (p. 22)

Records of recent students were given to indicate that nearly 100 percent of graduates over a recent five-year period had attained off-reservation employment. Reflecting with pride on Chancellor Lippincott's 1884 statement that "For that boy or girl the 'Indian problem' will forever be solved," the *Haskell Institute USA 1884–1959* concluded that this goal had been attained.

It should be noted that the 1983 *Student Handbook* (1983) reflects a clear departure from the assimilation philosophy that had been so strongly articulated as late as the 1950s. The more recent publication insists that the college "recognize and appreciate the cultural and historical backgrounds of Indian students and the needs of the Indian Community so as to serve the larger community and to help students establish identity and perspective" (p. 5).

The first objective of the general education programs, as reflected in the 1983 *Student Handbook*, is that the Indian students "understand their own heritage as well as the cultural heritage of a larger society" (p. 5).

A Native American cultural program at the college has been developed

1. To help students examine and understand their cultural past and present, to express their personal and cultural identity, and to comprehend the needs and problems of Indian communities.
2. To provide through curricular and extra-curricular activities more understanding between Indian and non-Indian cultures, using resources from Indian communities and individuals.

A discussion with the college president, Dr. Gerald Gipp, in 1984 revealed that Haskell College today makes a determined effort to support students in their ethnic identity. An observation of the facilities, as well as the curricular and social activities of students, reveals this to be the case. The College's commitment to Indian identity is also reflected in its housing and promotion of the American Indian Athletic Hall of Fame. Despite this interest in Indian heritage, students are prepared for working and living in the broader society. These two missions are viewed as complementary.

Evolution of Programs at the Haskell Institute

According to the publication *Haskell Institute USA 1884–1959* (1959), work, play, study, and social training were part of the school program from the beginning. During playtime the Indian youth engaged in a wide variety of activities. The children "loved competitive games and were unusually good at them. However, they also enjoyed recreation of a type that approached hard work" (pp. 15-16). Activities included "music groups of every kind, dance, athletic associations, hiking clubs, riding clubs . . . and a club where Indians may learn to shoot the bow and arrow" (p. 16).

During the early part of the 20th century, Haskell evolved from a primary emphasis on farming and homemaking to much broader vocational training. Specializations changed from wagon making and blacksmithing to automobile mechanics, plumbing, and electricity. In 1917 all primary grades at Haskell were discontinued, and no new students under fourteen years of age were enrolled. Though the school was now essentially a high school, older (college-age) students often attended. Students interested in studying agriculture were referred to other schools after about 1934. The course of study for girls was expanded from homemaking to include clerical work, retailing, and a variety of service occupations. Although the collegiate program had ended in the 1930s after a controversy over the athletic program, by around 1970 Haskell again began offering post–high school work and became once more a junior college.

Athletics at Haskell

Haskell was second only to Carlisle in athletic acclaim among Indian schools. In fact, its success and resulting recognition between 1920 and the early 1930s led to its being known as "The New Carlisle of the West." Although basketball was introduced soon after its development in the 1890s (see Figure 9.2), prominence at Haskell was particularly evident in football and track. The football teams achieved their greatest success over a ten-year period between 1920 and 1930. The track team at Haskell attained prominence a few years earlier than the football team. According to *Haskell Institute USA 1884–1959* (1959) the school paper reported in 1917 that the track meet against the University of Kansas proved to be a "walkaway for Haskell" (p. 35). The local newspaper in Lawrence

Figure 9.2. Boys basketball team at Haskell around 1900. Photo from National Archives and Records Administration.

reported that the athletic team "has been denied membership in the Missouri Allied Conference because the Haskell teams outclass the others" (cited in Haskell Institute, 1959, p. 35).

Football prominence began around 1920, when the Haskell football team first beat Oklahoma A & M by a score of 33-7. In 1926 a new football stadium was constructed and the team won all games played that year. Figure 9.3 shows football play at the school prior to the opening of the new stadium. John Levi, Haskell's most famous athlete, made the All-American team in football in 1923. Other prominent Haskell athletes of that period included Philip Osif, who was the national champion in the 1,000-meter run and also was a member of the U.S. Olympic team of 1932; Mayers McClain, a fullback, who scored 253 points for the 1926 football team; "Tiny" Roebuck (six feet six inches and weighing 280 pounds), a prominent football player for Haskell in 1926; and Louis "Rabbit" Weller, a great running back. Weller, Oron Crow, and David Ward, all of Haskell football fame, went on to play professional football, as did Roebuck. Wilson "Buster" Charles, an outstanding football, basketball, and track performer, made the Olympic team in 1932 as a decathlon participant.

Without question, the greatest of all Haskell athletes was John Levi, an Arapahoe from Oklahoma who attended Haskell from 1921 to 1924. There was no better authority on Levi's skill than Jim Thorpe. He said

Figure 9.3. Football play at Haskell during the early 1900s. Photo from National Archives and Records Administration.

of Levi: "He is the greatest athlete I have ever seen. He is the greatest athlete in America right now, and in another year he'll hold more championships than I ever thought of winning" (cited in McDonald, 1972, p. 16). In 1924 Levi made the All-American team as a fullback from Haskell. He beat out the great Ernie Nevers of Stanford to share the first team backfield with Red Grange. "Matty" Bell came to Haskell in 1920 and coached football for two years before moving on to greater acclaim at Texas Christian, Texas A & M, and Southern Methodist Universities. Although he coached Levi only during his freshman year, Bell stated, "I would place him in the same category with Bobby Wilson '35, Doak Walker '47-48, and Kyle Rote '48—three of the greatest who played on my championship teams here at Southern Methodist University. They could do it all" (cited in McDonald, 1972, p. 11).

Like Thorpe, John Levi was a multi-talented athlete, playing football, basketball, baseball, and participating in track at Haskell. During the spring he participated in baseball and track and took part in spring football practice. During a baseball game with Drake University, Levi also participated in a track meet against Baker University between innings, winning the shotput, discus, and high jump while in a baseball uniform (McDonald, 1972). Plans to play professional baseball with the New York Yankees prevented him from trying out for the 1924 Olympic team. Levi did go to spring training with the New York Yankees in the spring of 1925 and was assigned to the minor league team in Harrisburg, Pennsylvania. Though hitting over .300, he returned to Haskell in August because he did not wish to move away from his people. Levi remained at Haskell for several years as a coach.

The junior college program at Haskell was abolished in 1932 and this ended the era of major intercollegiate athletics for the Haskell Indians. At that time the Indian commissioner's office ordered that "there must be no return to big time football" (Haskell Institute, 1959, p. 41). As a result there was less attention to and visibility for sports. In addition, greater adherence to eligibility rules, along with a prohibition against recruiting athletes from other schools, became part of a de-emphasis in Haskell athletics. Officials at the school desired to avoid the abuse and overemphasis problems that had been reported from Carlisle and that had been suggested at Haskell.

Haskell Institute USA 1884–1959 (1959) explained that

the controversy regarding school athletics has been a big quarrel for many years. . . . Whatever may be the stand of the individual in the raging and unresolved controversy, the early-day Indian athlete gave Haskell, Sherman, and Carlisle great publicity. His athletic prowess and spirit were fantastic, and amazed the world. . . . Haskell teams played nearly every famous team in the nation and won a majority of the games. The contests were hard fought and the fame and publicity allowed the Indians to plunge Haskell onto the school map of the continent. (p. 16, 20)

Despite being cut back to high school-level competition, Haskell continued a tradition of athletic excellence. For example, the 1944 football team won all its games and the 1946 team won all but one. Boxing emerged as a prominent sport, and many championships were won in amateur competition. Among these was the National Championship in Golden Gloves competition won by Chester Ellis in 1939.

In 1956, led by Billy Mills, the cross-country team won the state high school championship. Mills then went on to the University of Kansas where he immediately established a national record for freshmen in the two-mile run. He later won the gold medal in the 10,000 meters at the 1964 Olympic Games in Toyko.

The Great Homecoming

One of the major events in the history of the Haskell Institute took place on October 30, 1926, when the new 10,500-seat stadium was opened and dedicated. This was at the height of football interest at Haskell, and indeed that team went through the season undefeated. During the fund-raising campaigns of 1925 and 1926, $185,000 was raised for stadium construction and, according to Dolph Simmons, "every dollar came from Indians" (cited in McDonald, 1972, p. 22).

Dedication of the stadium provided an opportunity for a major homecoming festival and attracted many thousands of Indians from all over the country. Many Indian chiefs leading large tribal contingents came to take part in the powwows, dances, plays, buffalo barbeques, fellowship, and, of course, the football game. According to McDonald (1972) the local press reported that 125,000 visitors were attracted to the festivities and that "the occasion brought together the most colorful group of Indians ever seen in this area of our country and attracted the most visitors, Indians and others, that the city of Lawrence had ever seen, regardless of the event" (p. 69). Representatives from more than seventy tribes were registered.

The football game was relatively insignificant in relation to the overall homecoming and related ceremonies. In the game, however, Haskell defeated Bucknell College by a score of 36–0. "No team in the country could have beaten Haskell on that day . . . the Pennsylvanians were tossed about like a tiny craft on an angry sea" (McDonald, 1972, p. 80).

McDonald noted with some pride and satisfaction the congeniality apparent in the meeting of Indian leaders who had not seen each other for many years. It was noted that earlier meetings were not always under such happy circumstances. One Lawrence newspaper reported that Chief White Buffalo and Chief Bull Calf met for the first time in twenty-seven years. Bull Calf was quoted as saying, "White Buffalo acts like he doesn't know me, but he does alright. I shot him in the ear in a war many years ago" (cited in McDonald, 1972, p. 68).

At the conclusion of the four-day ceremony, there was obvious joy as well as sadness as they departed.

> When the Blackfeet shook hands with their former adversary, the Cheyenne, they had mixed emotions. The old Indians knew that they would never meet again. To them this great event was a reunion the like of which they had never seen before (McDonald, 1972, p. 84).

As in earlier centuries, an athletic contest (and stadium dedication) brought together the Indian community as perhaps nothing else could have done. The importance and appropriateness of athletics as a major social event for Indians was still apparent well into the 20th century. However, it was no longer the Blackfeet against the Cheyenne or the Cherokee against the Sauk and the Fox. Rather, all Indians joined together against a common foe (i.e., non-Indians). The elders, too, recognized that they were no longer each other's enemies. It was clear that a new day had arrived.

Summary

The coming together of Indian youth from different tribes at boarding schools such as Carlisle and Haskell marked a new phase in Indian relations. The different Indian groups had lived separately before the schools were established and had competed against each other in games or in social strife. Even in conflict with non-Indian officials or citizens, separate tribes generally functioned separately. Consequently, being thrust together in schools was a new experience for these diverse groups.

The experience of combined Indian teams competing against non-Indians on a regular basis was also new. The pooling of Indian resources (athletes) against non-Indians in a nonwarring activity led to extraordinary success at the Indian schools, particularly Carlisle and Haskell. Strong sports interests, a tradition of participation, and the enthusiasm generated in these new games, led to unanticipated success.

Despite the protests from the Indian players, Pop Warner established himself as the prototype of the intense, authoritarian football coach. His drive, ingenuity, and willingness to push the rules of athletics to the limit, enabled him to establish a powerhouse at the small Indian school. The great success of the Carlisle football and track teams between 1895 and 1915 seems to have been a factor in the closing of the school by federal officials in 1918. The success of the Haskell Indian School in the 1920s was only slightly less dramatic.

The athletic teams at Indian schools provided a morale boost and rallying focus for the total Indian population. In addition, a cohesion among Indian tribes was affected by these visible successes. The spirit of the total Indian community was lifted by sports success at Indian schools as well as by individuals who excelled in individual sports or as members of non-Indian teams. Evidence of the social impact of these activities was shown with the raising of $185,000 among Indians to build the Haskell Stadium in the mid-1920s. The fact that this was in support of sports activity was surely a major contributing factor.

Another bit of evidence of sports as a unifying force for Indians was the success of the great homecoming to celebrate the opening of the Haskell stadium with a football game in 1926. The earlier successes of Carlisle, along with more contemporary successes of Haskell, no doubt, contributed to this interest. McDonald (1972), a non-Indian observer, stated that former tribal enemies who had fought many battles in the past came together in this venture of common interest. It was clear that the common Indian schools and the unified sports teams were contributing to the reduction of intertribal friction.

It is noteworthy that the federal government's response to athletic and other abuses at Indian schools was to close the school (as was done at Carlisle) or to seriously curtail the level of activity (as at Haskell). Why this never occurred at non-Indian institutions, which have encountered serious academic irregularities, professionalism, and drug abuse problems over the years, is worth speculating. Such speculation leads to the conclusion that the government is quicker to determine what is good for Indians, and is more prone to initiate actions to control their destiny.

Chapter 10

The Legendary Jim Thorpe

Although Jim Thorpe was never described as a particularly complex man, the social issues surrounding his life have made him seem so. Thorpe's life and times focused attention on such diverse issues as the meaning of amateurism in sports, abuse in college athletics, exploitation of heroes, alcoholism, and a multitude of federal government–Indian and white–Indian questions. On the positive side he provided a genuine sports hero image and, according to Arthur Daley of the *New York Times*, was "Frank Merriwell come to life" (cited in Bernstein, 1972, p. 28).

The mention of Jim Thorpe's name often brings to mind visions of the naive, stoic Indian who is unable to adapt to the complexities and contradictions of white society; the sad and innocent young athlete caught up in the hypocrisy of the Olympic ideal of amateurism; or the abused and frequently exploited sports hero. However, first and foremost, Jim Thorpe was an athlete, perhaps the greatest of the 20th century. Consequently, this discussion will focus on his sports achievements rather than the confusing and often distressing events surrounding his life following those athletic exploits.

Jim Thorpe's athletic achievements tend to defy belief. Even though the quantitative measures of his performance (speeds, distances, scores, etc.) are extraordinary enough, even more impressive is the clear margin of superiority he exhibited over opponents in a wide variety of activities. As was consistent in Indian sports traditions (as discussed in chapter 1)

Thorpe strived only to *win* in each contest, giving no attention to the margin of victory. There was never any indication that he sought to humiliate an opponent by the magnitude of the score. On the contrary, he was criticized by some of his more demanding coaches as performing just well enough to win. Still, that standard was good enough to earn him the title of the Greatest Athlete in the First Half of the 20th Century. This title was accorded him by the Associated Press, which in 1950 conducted a major poll of sportswriters and reported that Thorpe easily outpolled Babe Ruth, Jack Dempsey, Ty Cobb, and a host of other well-known athletes from a variety of sports (Wheeler, 1979, pp. 216–217).

Jim Thorpe was never an extraordinarily impressive physical specimen. Measurements at the Olympic Games in 1912, when he was twenty-four years of age, reveal that he was five feet eleven inches tall and weighed 181 pounds. He had a 15.9-inch neck, 32.2-inch waist, 39.7-inch chest, and a 72.5-inch reach. He was described as having fairly narrow shoulders. Though frequently referred to as "Big Jim," his playing weight was rarely listed as more than 180 pounds. His greatest assets were not in physical dimensions but in speed, endurance, versatility, and a tenacious, competitive spirit.

The Early Years: Family Background

Some confusion has existed concerning Thorpe's exact date of birth. Wheeler (1979) quotes a statement written by Thorpe himself that places his birth date as May 28, 1888. However, *World Book Encyclopedia Volume 19* (Wolfe, 1978) reports that he was born in 1886, and Newcombe (1975) states that he was born on May 27, 1887. Subsequent references to Thorpe's age in this chapter will be consistent with Wheeler's claim of 1888.

James Francis Thorpe was born as a twin (with brother Charles) into the Sac and Fox clan along the North Canadian River near Prague, Oklahoma. He is assumed to be a direct descendent of the great Sac war chief, Black Hawk. The Indian name given to Thorpe at birth was Wa-Tho-Huck, meaning Bright Path. However, this name was not consistently used because it was general practice at the time in Indian schools and in other government interactions to drop Indian names as part of the "civilizing" process.

Thorpe was born about twenty years after the Sac and Fox clan had been forcefully relocated from Kansas into Potowatomie County in Oklahoma. A few years earlier (in the 1840s) a large segment of the Fox clan had moved from Iowa to Kansas. Precise lineage within the Thorpe family is difficult to verify. According to Newcombe (1975), the Sac and

Fox tribe was one in which mixed bloods, orphans from friendly tribes, and distant relatives were warmly accepted into a family lodge as sons or daughters. In addition, he reported that a form of polygamy was often practiced within the community. Precise records of the lineage of Thorpe's parents have not been available. Jim Thorpe has been described as from one-eighth to three-fourths Indian blood, but was most probably three-eights Potawatomi and two-eighths Sac and Fox.

The name Thorpe came into the clan when Jim's paternal grandfather Hiram G. Thorpe, an Irishman, married a Sac and Fox woman and lived among the group as a blacksmith. Out of this union Jim's father, Hiram P. Thorpe, was born around 1850. Hiram P. Thorpe married Charlotte Vieux, a woman of French-Potawatomi mixture. To this marriage a son, George, was born in 1881, and Jim and Charles in 1888. Jim Thorpe was born into the Sac and Fox clan and reared as an Indian. During his early childhood years, Thorpe lived on a 160-acre allotment of land near Prague, Oklahoma.

It is significant that Thorpe's family makeup is not clear and distinct. According to Newcombe (1975), Jim's father married five wives and fathered at least nineteen children. This large family included many half-brothers and sisters covering a wide range of ages along with an extended family of blood relatives. It appears that Jim hardly knew some of the older and younger children of his father. As a matter of fact, Jim did not live continuously at home after around the age of six or seven, and his period at home did not overlap that of the majority of his brothers and sisters. In addition, the nineteen children fathered by his father lived in several different households.

By all accounts Hiram P. Thorpe, Jim's father, was physically very impressive. He was described as large and heavily muscled. Newcombe (1975) described him as "over six feet and about 225 pounds" (p. 27). According to Wheeler (1979), Jim was proud of his father's athletic accomplishments and stated with pride that "my father was the un-disputed champion in sprinting, wrestling, swimming, high jumping, broad jumping, and horseback riding" (p. 11). Jim grew very close to his father and emulated his athletic pursuits and his hunting interests. Reports of family and friends indicate that Jim spent more time with his father than did any of the other children because of these common interests and a genuine personal fondness.

Struggles With Early Schools

Jim had a close and stable relationship during his early years with his twin brother Charles. According to Wheeler (1979), they were inseparable, sharing a common interest in hunting, games, and a multitude of outdoor activities. Their early life was characterized by a maximum of freedom to roam the farm and woods around their home in Oklahoma. However, in 1893 the boys were virtually captured and taken to the mission boarding school approximately twenty miles to the north of their home.

Though described by some writers as a heavy drinker and a runner of whiskey to the Indians, Jim Thorpe's father was a strong believer in schooling. Having attended a Methodist school during his youth in Kansas, Hiram P. Thorpe was one of a very few Sac and Fox Indians who could read and write English. He welcomed the opportunity to have the school assist in the training and disciplining of his children. However, this was little consolation for Jim; he quickly grew weary of the bells and other evidences of control at the school. He reported that bells were used as the signal for getting up, eating, going to class, reporting to work, going to bed, and practically all other daily routines. Jim and Charles did not easily accept this strict regimentation, which was in sharp contrast to their earlier life on the reservation.

Newcombe (1975) reports that on one occasion after being delivered to the school by his father on wagon, Jim broke away and raced his father back home. Nevertheless, this was the beginning of the formal education process that was to be a part of his life, off and on, for the next eighteen to twenty years. The reality of being removed from his home and placed in a boarding school was resisted from the start and, in fact, was disrupted by frequent absences ranging from a few days up to 2 years. Later Jim was relocated to two other schools, Haskell and Carlisle, which were a far greater distance from home than were the early grammar schools.

In addition to developing "civilizing" skills such as reading and writing English and teaching common vocational skills, schools even dictated the games to be played. Traditional Indian games were prohibited. Newcombe (1975) quotes an observer who inquired about the lack of enthusiasm with which some of the children played the unfamiliar games during a play period: "I asked [the supervisor] if he had tried Indian games; with a blank look he said the government rules specified what games were to be played. Perhaps it never occurred to him that Indians have games of their own" (p. 42).

Although Jim was a leader in active games such as running, wrestling, follow-the-leader, and chasing, he was far from an ideal student. Newcombe (1975) reports that at the age of 9, school records described twin brother Charles as "nice" and "gentle," but Jim most often received only a "fair" rating and was even described as "incorrigible" by one teacher. His school record showed an attendance gap of two weeks when he ran away from school. He was said to be interested only in outdoor activities and diversions. The twin boys' close relationship provided mutual support in their life away from home. However, at around the age of ten, Charles got sick and died of pneumonia. This provided the first great tragedy in Thorpe's life. A second occurred when his own first-born son died before reaching his fourth birthday. Whereas the loss of his Olympic medals in later life was often viewed as a contributing factor to many of Thorpe's problems, it may be more reasonable to assume that the loss of his brother, his closest kin and friend, at the age of ten shaped his psychological makeup to a much greater extent.

Following the death of Charles, Jim once again ran away from school with the desire to drop out. His father grew weary of this truant behavior and, according to Newcombe (1975), told him, "I'm going to send you so far you will never find your way back home" (p. 49). In 1898, at the age of ten, Jim was sent to the Haskell Institute in Lawrence, Kansas, 300 miles from his home.

Haskell Institute, which had been opened fourteen years earlier, was patterned after the program at the Carlisle School. Classroom education, manual training, and military style discipline were the order of the day. Young Jim tolerated the strict discipline and work routine at Haskell for about three years and it was there he first encountered the game of football. However, the sport was for the older boys, so Thorpe, as an eleven- and twelve-year-old, did not receive instruction or engage in formal competition. During his first year at Haskell, the Carlisle football team visited on their return from California, where they had engaged in an East-West championship game and had defeated the University of California. The Haskell boys were duly impressed with the more famous players from Carlisle.

Jim left Haskell in the summer of 1901 at the age of thirteen. After spending a short time at home and, according to Newcombe (1975), not getting along well with his father, he left home for about a year. During this period he traveled through Texas, mainly working on ranches as a farmhand. His mother died and his father remarried while he was away. After returning home, Jim attended a one-room school nearby but again did not distinguish himself in his studies.

After a year of sporadic school attendance and a growing lack of discipline, Jim had caused his father a high level of frustration. Newcombe (1975) quotes a letter from the elder Thorpe to the U.S. Indian agent in Oklahoma territory requesting that arrangements be made to send Jim to Carlisle or Hampton, both in the East, "so he cannot run away" (p. 60). The letter further stated that "he is 14 years of age and I cannot do anything with him and he is getting worse every day and I want him to go and make something of himself and he cannot do it here" (p. 60).

The Indian agent arranged for Jim to be admitted to the Carlisle Indian Industrial School, where he arrived in February, 1904, at the age of fifteen. Thus toughened in life and work, he began his nine years (including a two-year absence) at this school. School records show that he was five feet five inches tall, certainly not an impressive size for a young man approaching his sixteenth birthday. He was to add about six inches to his height over the next three years.

The Carlisle Years

The Carlisle School was somewhat similar to Haskell in its program of activities and general philosophy. Carlisle's published motto was "There is only one way: To civilize the Indian, get him into civilization; to keep him civilized, let him stay." Some young Indians, such as football players Albert Exendine and Gus Welch, both from western Oklahoma, actively sought entrance to Carlisle, which had achieved some distinction both in football and as a training school. Given the limited options available to Indians, Carlisle was viewed as a good choice. Jim Thorpe, however, was a reluctant recruit.

Encountering the "Civilizing" Process

A special feature of the Carlisle program, and one that perhaps delayed Thorpe's entry into athletics, was the *outing* experience. During their period at Carlisle, all students were assigned to families, usually farmers, in Pennsylvania and neighboring states. In this program students lived and worked with the assigned family for three months per year or longer. These assignments might occur at any time of the year, but practically all students lived off-campus during the summer months.

Lieutenant Richard H. Pratt, founder of the Carlisle School, established the outing program to enable students to learn skills related to farm work and the proper techniques for running a farm. He also hoped that the civilizing process would be enhanced by the proper models that had been selected for the students. Though students were paid at least nominally for their services, they were encouraged to become a part of the family rather than hired hands. Host families were encouraged to aid in the education and supervision of the students and to send in reports about the behavior, manners, and work habits of the students. Host families therefore became surrogate parents and the faculty for the school.

The value of the outing experience was largely dependent upon the "luck of the draw," (i.e., the nature of the assigned family). An assignment with reasonable work responsibilities, a caring and compatible family, and adequate pay usually resulted in a pleasant experience, which was both educational and financially profitable. Of course, such was not always the case. Jim Thorpe's first assignment, in mid-June of 1904, soon after his arrival, was not a good match. He was sent to the farm of A.E. Buckholz along the Susquehanna River, not a great distance from the school. His work responsibilities were to clean the house and help out in the kitchen. Nothing could have been more incompatible with his interests. Further, he was required to eat in the kitchen and was paid only $5 per month, which was sent to Carlisle and held in trust for him. Despite his requests for an outside job, he was restricted to inside chores. Finally, when he could tolerate this humiliation no longer, he walked away from the farm and returned to Carlisle.

According to Newcombe (1975), Thorpe was sent out three additional times over the next two years but none of the outings proved particularly satisfactory. However, many other students enjoyed the outing experiences, finding it a pleasant relief from the confinement and routine of the campus. Some, especially the girls, developed close family attachments. Others, such as All-American football player Albert Exendine, reported that the outing assignments proved to be among their richest learning experiences.

During his first three years at Carlisle, Thorpe did not distinguish himself in school, and his behavior reflected his lack of interest in academic matters. He resisted equally the restrictions imposed by the tight militaristic regimen at Carlisle and the demands of the courses. The outing experiences provided little relief from those constraints, and his frequent truancies seemed to be his only relief from that climate. There is no indication that he engaged in any seriously mischievous behavior at any point but simply sought to shed the restrictions imposed by the schools. Except for his one-year travels through Texas at about the age of fifteen, his run-away escapades were short-lived.

Entrance Into Athletics

A side effect of the outing assignments for Thorpe was that they probably prevented him from training or competing for any of the athletic teams during his first three years at the school. Students who were members of varsity teams were usually put on a protected list, and they were not to be sent out on assignment, at least not during the playing season. The title of Newcombe's (1975) book, *The Best of the Athletic Boys*, is based on the students' designation of ball players as "the athletic boys." These students were known to receive special privileges during the Pop Warner years. Not having been on a varsity team during his first three years, Thorpe was available for an outing assignment at any time. As it turned out, however, he later developed into the very best of the athletic boys.

There are some references to Thorpe's playing on an intramural team on the campus during his first few years. However, because the varsity football team played most games away from the campus, there was little opportunity for other students to see them play or for the coaches to observe the intramural matches. Apparently, Thorpe did not try out for any varsity team prior to the spring of 1907, when he competed very briefly with the track and field team. Actually, it was coincidence that enabled him to be available at that time. During that spring he had been assigned to a family on a vegetable farm near Trenton, New Jersey. However, he became weary of that work and returned to Carlisle. Newcombe (1975) quotes from a letter by a friend of Thorpe: "I am sorry to say that

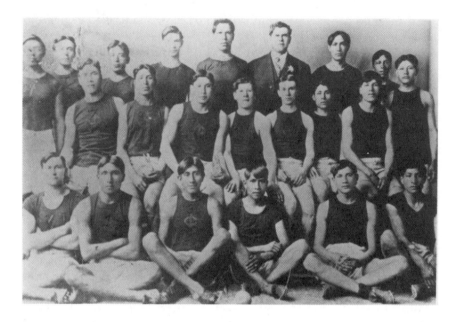

Figure 10.1. Jim Thorpe (center of middle row) as a member of the 1907 track team at Carlisle. At the time Thorpe was nearly nineteen years of age. Photo used by permission of Cumberland County Historical Society, Carlisle, PA 17013.

James Thorpe is in the guard house for running away from his country home'' (p. 95). Apparently he chose the guardhouse over the frustration of being away from school and his friends, some of whom were on the athletic teams. Wheeler (1979) reports that when Thorpe returned to Carlisle in 1907, ''he had grown to 5 feet 9¼ inches and 144 pounds'' (p. 50). Of course, this is still not an impressive size for one nearly nineteen years of age who is about to commence a career in football. (Note Thorpe's smallish size in Figure 10.1.)

A frequently reported incident occurred in the Spring of 1907 which led to his formal entrance into the athletic program. Jim and several of his friends walked past the track where the high jumpers were practicing. After noticing that the jumpers had consistently failed to clear the bar at five feet nine inches, Jim—in full work clothes—asked if he could try. Without warm-up he took a short approach and cleared the bar on the first try, establishing a school record at the time. Though not having seen this incident, Coach Warner heard about it and invited Thorpe out for the track team. He subsequently entered a few meets during that spring.

In the summer of 1907 Thorpe was put on the protected list by Pop Warner, who was not only the football coach but the track and baseball coach as well. Not being forced to go off campus, nineteen-year-old Thorpe was able to go out for the football team for the first time in 1907.

Thorpe had never practiced or competed with the varsity team before. However, he did have some rather informal experience in an intramural program in which he played with his department (the tailors) against teams from other departments at the school. His talent in speed and power were obvious to Warner, but the skills of football were sorely lacking. He worked hard and learned quickly during both the training period and the season. He had much to learn, however, and did not make the starting lineup during that season. Despite his considerable talent, there was nothing particularly noteworthy in his performances at this time.

After becoming one of Coach Warner's athletic boys, Thorpe's life at Carlisle changed in a very positive way. He began receiving recognition for his considerable success in sports. Further, he established a relationship with a strong adult personality, Coach Pop Warner, who provided support, guidance, and supervision. Warner also gave Thorpe and the other athletes small amounts of money for clothing and expenses from his athletic slush fund. Up to this point Thorpe had been hard pressed financially because he had not received the allotment money due him from the Indian agent in Oklahoma. Perhaps most important, he was no longer required to observe the school's strict regimen that so irritated him. In addition, a great deal of time was spent in travel away from the campus, and this added variety to Thorpe's life.

With things looking up in his life, Thorpe showed improvement in his school work and general behavior. He communicated effectively in oral and written English and, in fact, typed letters to the Sac and Fox agent back in Oklahoma. He became more involved socially and established a relationship with a female student at the school, Iva Miller, who was later to become his first wife. On more than one occasion, Thorpe won dancing contests at social events at the school. Newcombe (1975) cites several examples of his extraordinarily courteous behavior toward teachers whom he admired. During Thorpe's days at Carlisle, he was not a problem drinker, although some of the athletes were and also engaged in raucous behavior. Actually, the saloon keepers in town were not legally permitted to sell whiskey to Indians, but it seemed to happen nevertheless.

Football Play at Carlisle

Jim Thorpe "arrived" as a superb football player in 1908, his first season as a regular member of the starting team. His play during the season was so outstanding that he was selected on Walter Camp's third-string All-American team, the only member of the Carlisle team so selected. By this time he had filled out to 175 pounds and was around five feet eleven inches. Thorpe excelled in kicking (punting and field goals) and in running. Over the next dozen years, in college and professional play, it was generally conceded that he was the nation's premier performer both in running and in kicking. During the 1908 season his long distance drop-kicking drew even more attention than did his running.

Thorpe did not play football during the 1909 and 1910 seasons. During the summer of 1909 he dropped out of school and, among other things, played "professional" baseball for Rocky Mount and Fayetteville in the Eastern Carolina Baseball League. This activity was to cause him problems that would remain an issue with him for most of the remaining years of his life. (The forced return of his Olympic medals, which resulted from this professional play, is discussed later in this chapter.)

By the summer of 1911, the Eastern Carolina Baseball League had disbanded, and Thorpe was uninvolved with any sports or other fruitful activity. At this point he was receptive to Coach Warner's letters that encouraged him to return to play football at Carlisle. Thorpe was also encouraged by former Carlisle teammate, and fellow Oklahoman, Albert Exendine. Consequently, he returned to Carlisle in September 1911 after a two-year absence to resume his football play and schooling. Upon his return he became the dominant figure in college football and remained so for the next two years. Evidence of his superiority was based more on verbal descriptions than on statistical accounts. Several truly noteworthy performances occurred against the major competition of that era.

The 1911 team proved to be among the most successful in Carlisle's history, winning eleven games while losing only one. The loss was to Syracuse University by a score of 12 to 11. Thorpe easily made the All-American team.

Prior to the football season of 1912, Thorpe won international acclaim as a result of his dramatic victories in the decathlon and pentathlon in the Olympic Games at Stockholm, Sweden. He was offered $10,000 to go on tour to capitalize on his newly won fame. However, Coach Warner persuaded him to return to Carlisle for his last year of football, saying that he would be an even greater attraction after another year.

During the 1912 football season, Thorpe again played brilliantly and the team lost only one game, to the University of Pennsylvania, though Carlisle outgained them 400 yards to 177 yards. Against an outstanding Springfield college team in 1912, Thorpe scored four touchdowns, three extra points, and one field goal in a 30–24 win. The following week he scored all thirty-two points in a win over Brown University. It was practically routine for him to dropkick field goals from any place under 50 yards and to gain 200 yards on long distance runs during a game. He again made Walter Camp's All-American team for the 1912 season.

Track and Field

Jim Thorpe's participation in track was limited to four years at Carlisle (1907, 1908, 1909, and 1912) plus the Olympic Games in 1912. In contrast,

Table 10.1   Some Highlights of Jim Thorpe's Football Record While Playing at Carlisle

1907—substitute halfback
1908—Walter Camp's All-American team as a third team halfback
1911—Walter Camp's All-American team as a first team halfback
1911—Harvard-Carlisle game—scored all the points in 18–15 victory
1911—Dickinson-Carlisle game—scored 17 points in 17 minutes
1911—scored 4 field goals against Harvard, one from just inside the 50-yard line
1911—kicked punt more than 70 yards against Lafayette
1912—Walter Camp's All-American team as a first team halfback
      Long runs—60 yards, 75 yards, 85 yards for touchdowns against
          Pennsylvania
          —53 yards, 45 yards, for touchdowns against Pittsburgh
          —70 yards, twice against Brown
          —40 yards, for touchdown against Georgetown
1912—Harvard-Carlisle game—Thorpe gained 173 of the 334 yards gained by the Indians through rushing
1912—Army-Carlisle game—he ran almost 200 yards to score a touchdown (offside penalty)
1912—Pittsburgh-Carlisle game—scored 28 of 34 points.
1912—Army-Carlisle game—scored 22 of 27 points
1912—scored 6 conversions in one game against Pittsburgh
1912—scored 198 points (never equaled by a major school)
1912—kicked punt more than 70 yards against Pittsburgh

Note.   Adapted from *Jim Thorpe—Carlisle Indian* (p. 23) by W.J. Gobrecht, 1969, Carlisle, PA: Cumberland County Historical Society and Hamilton Library Association. Copyright 1969 by Cumberland County Historical Society, Carlisle, PA 17013. Reprinted by permission.

his football play extended over a twenty-year period. However, his legendary performances in track at Carlisle and at the Olympic Games, the controversy surrounding the revocation of his medals, and efforts to get them returned perhaps earned him equal recognition.

Although Thorpe undoubtedly took part in informal running activities in his early years, he did not engage in any varsity competition or receive any formal coaching until 1907, when he was nearly nineteen years of age. During that spring, after his unauthorized return to Carlisle from his outing assignment near Trenton, New Jersey, and after being released from his stay in the guardhouse, he was inadvertently discovered by Pop Warner, who coached both football and track. Thorpe joined the varsity team late in the season and entered only two meets, earning a total of nine points for the team.

The spring of 1908 was Thorpe's first full season with the track team. As one of Warner's protected athletes, he was able to eat at the athletes' training table and to be relieved of certain other distracting chores that were a part of the routine at the school. Further, he would not be assigned an outing experience away from the school during the season. Under these favorable conditions, he was able to train and compete on a more regular basis. The only major distraction for track was that he also played on the baseball team, which competed during the same season. In baseball he played outfield and pitched. In his first start as a pitcher, Thorpe hurled a no-hitter against a team from Hagerstown, Maryland, and at the end of the season he pitched a shutout against Millersville State (Newcombe, 1975).

Thorpe's exploits in track and field at Carlisle are not as carefully chronicled as were his performances in football. Track was viewed as less important in terms of general interest. Whereas performances at the Olympic Games were meticulously recorded and reported, such was not always the case in Carlisle's competition with college teams. Nevertheless, the diversity and endurance of Thorpe's performances were astounding and led to reports that defy belief. It was not unusual for him to enter, and win, five or more events in the same meet. Louis Tewanima, who also went to the 1912 Olympic Games, performed on the Carlisle team at the same time as Thorpe. Tewanima excelled in the long-distance races. In addition, Gus Welch, a football player, ran the shorter sprints.

Thorpe performed in most of the field events and also ran short races and the hurdles. With unlimited entries possible, these three performers made Carlisle competitive against squads of thirty or more. Stories got around that Carlisle only took three or four performers to dual track meets. Bernstein (1972) reported that Carlisle took a team of five members in 1909 to meet a forty-five-member Lafayette College team in Easton, Pennsylvania. However, Newcombe (1975) claims that Carlisle actually took eight performers to that meet (p. 182). At any rate, Thorpe won six events, Welch and Tewanima won two each, and Sam Burd one. With a few second place finishes by others, Carlisle easily won the meet. Bernstein states that later in the 1909 season "against an even stronger Harvard team, Thorpe competed in eight events and won all eight" (p. 31).

Other Sports at Carlisle

If there ever existed an all-around athlete, Jim Thorpe seems to have been the one. In addition to football, track, and baseball, Jim Thorpe participated in other sports as time permitted. According to Daniel J. Colombi (1983), Thorpe earned varsity letters in eleven different sports at Carlisle. In addition to those previously discussed, his letters were earned in boxing, wrestling, lacrosse, gymnastics, swimming, hockey, handball, and basketball (see Figure 10.2).

Figure 10.2. Thorpe as a basketball player at Carlisle in 1912. Photo courtesy of Robert W. Wheeler.

Bernstein (1972) has stated that Thorpe golfed in the 70s and regularly bowled in the 200s. Costo (1982), a long time friend of Thorpe, has stated that he not only won All-American recognition in football and track but in lacrosse and basketball as well. Costo also points out that Thorpe excelled in boxing, gymnastics, rowing, and billiards.

The Olympic Games

The single athletic feat for which Thorpe has been most widely recognized and remembered over the years was his performance at the 1912 Olympic Games in Stockholm. Although the Olympics at that time did not captivate worldwide attention to the same extent as do today's games, Thorpe's performances were widely acclaimed. The versatility in his performances and the magnitude of his victories were certainly contributing factors.

Early in 1912 it occurred to Pop Warner that Jim Thorpe, Louis Tewanima (from the Hopi tribe in Arizona), and Gus Welch had excellent chances to participate in the Olympic Games that were to be held in Stockholm, Sweden, during the summer of that year. He began training them for that purpose in February and March. Though facilities were less than adequate, an indoor and outdoor training program was established.

From most accounts, Thorpe trained seriously for the diversified events in the pentathlon and decathlon. Although Warner was not a technically skilled track coach, he did provide basic conditioning, which was helpful. Prior to the regular spring schedule, Warner entered Thorpe in indoor meets in Boston, Trenton, and Washington.

Thorpe, Tewanima, and Welch were well conditioned and had an excellent competitive season at Carlisle during the spring of 1912. As there were no Olympic trials in the pentathlon and decathlon, Thorpe made the Olympic team in these events on the basis of his performance records during spring meets. Tewanima made the team on the same basis, but Welch was forced to drop out of the spring competition because of illness. Thorpe and Tewanima, along with Warner as coach, boarded the ship in New York in late June for the long journey to Stockholm. Contrary to prevalent reports of laxity in training, there are indications that the two athletes trained seriously during the ocean journey. Wheeler (1979) quotes Ralph Craig, who won two gold medals for the United States in the 100- and 200-meter races, to refute the oft-repeated claims that Thorpe refused to train during the ocean journey. According to Craig,

> it has been fifty years since that journey . . . but I can certainly remember running laps and doing calisthenics with Jim every day on the ship. In fact, Jim and I nearly overdid it on more than one occasion because we were always challenging one another in the sprints. (p. 100)

The Pentathlon

The pentathlon was scheduled early in the program. The five events in this competition were held in one day. Thorpe easily won the pentathlon, finishing first in the 200-meter dash, the 1,500-meter run, the broad jump, and the discus throw and finishing third in the javelin (see Figure 10.3). His score (based on his cumulative place of finish for the five events) was 7. A perfect score would have been 5. The second-place finisher was Ferdinand R. Bie of Norway, with a score of 21. Thorpe's low cumulative score of 7 was never equalled up to the time the event was eliminated after the 1924 Olympics. The performance most closely approaching that of Thorpe was a score of 14 earned by E.R. Lehtenen of Finland in 1920 (see Table 10.2).

According to Newcombe (1975), Thorpe's performance in the pentathlon received scant notice in the press in this country because three other Americans had finished one, two, and three in the more popular 100-meter dash (p. 184). Still, the Europeans were duly impressed because this event was supposed to be their forte, particularly athletes from Scandinavian countries.

Table 10.2   Jim Thorpe's Winning Performances in the Pentathlon at the 1912 Olympic Games in Stockholm, Sweden

Long jump: *first* at 23 feet 2¼ inches
Javelin: *third* at 153 feet 2 inches
200 meters: *first* in 22.9 seconds
Discus: *first* at 117 feet 3 inches
1,500 meters: *first* in 4 minutes 44.8 seconds

Total (low points win): 7 points
(Second-place finisher was Ferdinand Bie of Norway with a score of 21.)

Note. From "Jim Thorpe's Olympic Medals are Restored" by G. Eskenazi, 1982, *The New York Times*, October 14, pp. A1, B18. Copyright © 1982 by The New York Times Company. Reprinted by permission.

Figure 10.3.   Start of 1,500-meter run in the 1912 Olympic pentathlon. Thorpe is second from the left. Avery Brundage, future president of the International Olympic Committee is on the far right. Photo courtesy of Robert W. Wheeler.

The Decathlon

There were six days between the pentathlon and the beginning of the decathlon, which was spread over three days. Twenty-nine competitors were entered in the decathlon. Although Thorpe was considerably off his personal best for single events, he still won the overall competition handily. He finished first in four of the ten events and no lower than fourth in any event. His total score of 8,413 was nearly 700 points more than Hugo Wieslander of Sweden, the second-place finisher (see Table 10.3). Thorpe's score was not surpassed in Olympic competition until

Table 10.3 Jim Thorpe's Winning Performances in the Decathlon at the 1912 Olympic Games in Stockholm, Sweden

100 meters: *third* in 11.2 seconds
Long jump: *third* at 22 feet 3¼ inches
Shot put: *first* at 42 feet 3½ inches
High jump: *first* at 6 feet 1¾ inches
400 meters: *fourth* at 52.2 seconds
Discus: *third* at 121 feet 4 inches
110-meter hurdles: *first* in 15.6 seconds
Pole vault: *third* at 10 feet 8 inches
Javelin: *fourth* at 149 feet 11 inches
1,500 meters: *first* in 4 minutes 40.1 seconds

Total: 8,413 points
(Second-place finisher was Hugo Wieslander of Sweden with a score of 7,724.)

Note. From "Jim Thorpe's Olympic Medals are Restored" by G. Eskenazi, 1982, *The New York Times*, October 14, pp. A1, B18. Copyright © 1982 by The New York Times Company. Reprinted by permission.

1932. These combined victories astounded European experts, who viewed Americans as specialists (i.e., excelling in only one or two events). Furthermore, their argument that all outstanding American athletes were recent immigrants from the continent was refuted. Such a claim could hardly be made about Thorpe.

Thorpe's performances in the pentathlon and decathlon led King Gustav V of Sweden to accurately say to Thorpe at the Awards Ceremony, "Sir, you are the greatest athlete in the world." Thorpe's widely reported response was simply, "Thanks, King" (Wheeler, 1979, p. 110). His performance was eventually recognized by the American press, and he received great acclaim when he returned to this country after the games.

Like all decathlon performers, Thorpe exhibited a high level of endurance and versatility. In addition, his skill in certain of the individual events challenged the specialists in those activities, as indeed was shown in many of the dual meets in which he participated while at Carlisle. On separate occasions Thorpe ran the 100 yard in 10 seconds flat, the 220 yard in 21.8 seconds, and the mile in 4 minutes 35 seconds; he jumped 6 feet 5 inches, long jumped 23 feet 6 inches, put the shot 47 feet 9 inches and pole vaulted 11 feet (Powers, 1969).

Triumphant Return

Jim Thorpe's return to this country was met with parades and ceremonies. He did not expect the intense personal attention bestowed upon him and he did not have any idea how to respond. Adulation had begun to build aboard the ship on the return trip to this country. The *Carlisle Arrow* (September 13, 1912) quoted the *New York American* as stating that on the voyage to the United States after the Olympic Games, Thorpe "was the hero of the big ship, but he refused to act his part" (p. 7). Furthermore, the *New York World* ("Carlisle Honors," 1912) reported that in the New York parade honoring Thorpe and Tewanima,

> Jim Thorpe, the big Carlisle Indian and Champion all-around athlete of the world, sat alone in an automobile in embarrassed silence. He was perhaps the chief attraction in line, but he pulled his panama hat over his eyes, chewed gum, pinched his knees and seldom lifted his gaze. Piled in front of him in the car were his trophies, above which fluttered the Carlisle pennant. (p. 8)

According to the *Carlisle Arrow* ("Carlisle Honors," 1912), the student newspaper, the hometown (Carlisle) celebration honoring Thorpe and Tewanima was "the most unique and greatest celebration of its kind ever witnessed in the old town" (p. 1). Congratulatory letters from President William H. Taft, the Secretary of Interior, and the Commissioner of Indian Affairs were all read to him. The *Carlisle Arrow* ("Carlisle Honors," 1912) included President Taft's letter, which stated in part:

> You have set a high standard of physical development, which is attained only by right living and right thinking, and your victory will serve as an incentive to all to improve those qualities which characterize the best type of American citizen. (p. 33)

His return to Carlisle included parades through the town, fireworks, a great reception with music, a dinner, and speeches. According to Newcombe (1975, p. 284) the extent of Thorpe's speech at the reception was, "All I can say is, that you showed me a good time." This was followed by Tewanima's speech, which is reported to have been even shorter, "Me too." There is no reason to believe that this attention had any important impact on Thorpe. In the dance that followed the formal ceremonies, Newcombe (1975) reported that from 9:00 p.m. until 1:45 a.m., Thorpe was "seldom off the floor" (p. 286).

Loss of the Olympic Medals

One of the most widely discussed and hotly debated issues related to Jim Thorpe was the revocation of his Olympic awards (gold medals for the decathlon and pentathlon championships) and efforts to get them returned. In January, 1913, seven months following the Olympic Games and after the completion of his last year of intercollegiate football, the *Worcester Telegram* in Massachusetts reported that Thorpe had played minor league baseball in North Carolina prior to the Olympic Games. The paper noted that this may have voided his amateur standing and could therefore invalidate Thorpe's victory in the Olympics (cited in Newcombe, 1975).

The United States Amateur Athletic Union (AAU), eager to preserve the sanctity of the amateur code, moved quickly to investigate the charges. During the investigation, Thorpe sent a letter (drafted by Coach Warner) to the AAU in which he requested excusal for the violation because of his ignorance of the technicalities of the rules. Further, he truthfully argued that he played because he enjoyed the activity, not for the money. Still, the AAU erased Thorpe's name from the records and returned the medals to the Swedish Olympic Committee. They were awarded to the second-place finisher in each event. The medals were returned to the committee by Pop Warner, to whom they had been entrusted for safe-keeping by Thorpe. Though officials of amateur athletics determined upon investigation that it was commonplace for college athletes to play base-ball for pay in the summer and for football players to play on Sunday afternoon for pay (usually under assumed names), the publicity surround-ing the Thorpe issue was too great to ignore. Thus the AAU succumbed to the pressure for pure (if misguided) amateurism.

Despite the scorn and ridicule heaped on the AAU and the international committee, the decision held fast for almost three-quarters of a century. Not until January 19, 1983, exactly seventy years after the story broke in the *Worcester Telegram*, were replicas of the medals returned, posthu-mously, to Thorpe. Some felt that Avery Brundage, long-time president of the International Olympic Committee, resisted the return of the medals partially because, as a participant in the 1912 Olympics, he had finished far behind Thorpe in both the pentathlon (fifth place) and decathlon (four-teenth place). However, it must be noted that Brundage consistently assumed a position in support of the traditional interpretation of amateurism until his retirement after the 1976 Olympics.

Much discussion has taken place regarding the effect of the loss of the medals on Jim Thorpe. He actually had little to say about the matter either then or later. His quiet acceptance of the rebuke was either one of quiet hurt or the assumption that it really mattered very little. Still, many ob-servers believed that the difficulties he encountered in later life were at least partially attributable to pain he bore from this incident. In support of this view, Ritter (1966) quoted Chief Meyers, the great New York Giant catcher, who was a Mission Indian from Oklahoma and a roommate of Thorpe. Thorpe was, he said, a

proud man. Not conceited, he was never that. But proud.
I remember very late one night Jim came in and woke me up. I remember it like it was only last night. He was crying and tears were rolling down his cheeks.

"You know, Chief," he said, "the King of Sweden gave me those trophies, he gave them to me. But they took them away from me... They're mine, Chief, I won them fair and square." It broke his heart and he never really recovered. (p. 175)

Professional Football

Although some form of professional football had been played practically since the turn of the century, it was not until after Thorpe left Carlisle in 1913 that it began developing any consistent fan support. Thorpe's entrance into the game as a major attraction was, in fact, one of the primary reasons why professional football developed as a popular enterprise during the late teens and early 1920s.

The Early Years (1913-1919)

By the time Thorpe left Carlisle in 1913, a modest level of interest in professional football had been developed in the Midwest, especially in Ohio. Communities sponsoring these teams (Canton, Massillon, Toledo, Columbus, and Youngstown) realized that the addition of familiar names of current or former college players would add immensely to the appeal of the game. During this period Thorpe was clearly the most attractive "draw," and in 1915 he was recruited to play for Canton, probably the strongest professional franchise at that time. The World Champion 1920 team is shown in Figure 10.4.

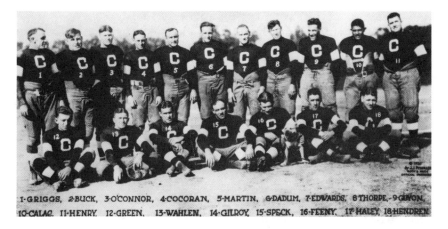

1-GRIGGS, 2-BUCK, 3-O'CONNOR, 4-COCORAN, 5-MARTIN, 6-DADUM, 7-EDWARDS, 8-THORPE, 9-GWON, 10-CALAC, 11-HENRY, 12-GREEN, 13-WAHLEN, 14-GILROY, 15-SPECK, 16-FEENY, 17-HALEY, 18-HENDREN

Figure 10.4. Thorpe (No. 8) with the World Champion Canton Bulldogs in 1920. Photo courtesy of Robert W. Wheeler.

Figure 10.5. Thorpe at the peak of his professional football playing career with the Canton Bulldogs, around 1920. Photo courtesy of Robert W. Wheeler.

In addition to playing sporadically for several teams during the 1913–1919 period, Thorpe also served as a coach for college and professional teams. In 1913 and 1914 he was hired as assistant football coach at Indiana University in Bloomington. At the same time, he played and coached with the Pine Village team at Lafayette, Indiana, the site of Purdue University. He was initially paid $250 per game to play. Over the next several years (until 1920), his superb play and magnetic name raised the awareness and interest in professional football throughout the Midwest. Even though he was not under the strong and disciplined leadership of Pop Warner, Thorpe's natural talent and love for the game enabled him to continue as the dominant player throughout this period (see Figure 10.5).

The National Football League

By 1920 interest in professional football had expanded beyond the tight pocket of small towns in Ohio. Larger cities, over a wider geographical area, were now interested in having teams. In addition, there was a need for the establishment of standards and controls to maximize benefits and to prevent incidents such as the "Black Sox" scandal, which had seriously damaged the credibility of baseball during the 1919 World Series.

Professional football itself had been dealt a near death blow by an alleged "fix" in a three-game series between Canton and Massillon in November, 1906. At that point in the season, the two teams were clearly the dominant powers in football: Canton had scored 287 points to none for its opponents, and Massillon had averaged 55 points per game. Amid rumors of a fix, along with heavy betting, Canton won the first game at home by a score of 10-5 and Massillon prevailed in the second one at their home field by a score of 13-6. Massillon's newspapers, the *Independent* and *Evening Gleaner* both alleged a gambling plot. Newcombe (1975) reported that a third, "clean" game was then scheduled for Cleveland. He quotes the *Evening Gleaner* as stating that

> many who saw the game Saturday were surprised to see the hitherto daring Hayden [Jack Hayden, Canton's quarterback from Penn] apparently deliberately shirk several scrimmages with Massillon. Whether the former Tiger quarterback had cold feet, rheumatic joints or avoided the contact with Tiger beef from pure politeness is not known. In Canton Saturday night it was rumored Hayden had sold out. (p. 220)

After the game a major brawl broke out among the betting Canton fans that required the intervention of the police. Newcombe (1975) stated that "the brawl signaled the beginning of the end of pro football in the two cities for a period of time" (p. 221).

Along with the rapidly developing public interest in professional football between 1915 and 1920, there were also business interests in promoting the sport. There was also interest in developing credibility and standardizing competition. To meet those concerns the American Professional Football Association was formed in September of 1920. Jim Thorpe was established as president to bring both visibility and credibility to the league. Within two years the name of the league was changed to the National Football League (NFL), a name that has continued to the present time.

Team membership in the new league fluctuated greatly during the first few years. However, during the early 1920s the Chicago Bears (under George Halas), the Acme Packers of Green Bay, Wisconsin (under Curley Lambeau), and the Chicago (now St. Louis) Cardinals were established and have continued to this day. Other towns with teams were Canton, Cleveland, Buffalo, Rochester, and Akron. It is generally assumed that Thorpe was established as first president of the league not so much for his administrative skills but for the popularity of his name. He remained as president for only one year.

Thorpe continued to play football through the mid-1920s until advancing age and an undisciplined life-style began to diminish his skills noticeably. He retained his kicking skills longer than his running effectiveness, and so he was relied on more for kicking than for running. In the early 1920s he was still the premier punter and field goal kicker in the game.

Figure 10.6. Thorpe with the New York (football) Giants around 1925. Photo courtesy of Pro Football Hall of Fame.

Newcombe (1975) reports that Thorpe would routinely warm-up before games by placing the ball on the fifty-yard line and kicking it through the goalposts at one end of the field. Then he would place the ball at the same spot and kick it through the goalposts at the other end. Note Thorpe's kicking style (Figure 10.6) from a photograph taken around 1925 when he played with the New York Giants.

Jim Thorpe continued to play sporadically through the 1920s with a variety of teams in the National Football League. In 1922 and 1923, he assembled an all-Indian team called the Oorang Indians (after the Oorang Dog Kennels) in La Rue, Ohio. This team, composed primarily of former players from the Carlisle teams of many years past, attained only modest success. The group also sponsored Indian dancing prior to the games. They were neither skilled at marketing the Indian image nor disciplined or cohesive as a football team. Still, the old friends had a good time but disbanded within two years. Subsequently, Thorpe played with Cleveland, New York, Chicago, Rock Island, and Toledo. He last played in 1928 at the age of forty-one. Highlights of Thorpe's football career are presented in Table 10.4.

Baseball

Jim Thorpe's baseball skills did not match his abilities in football or in track. In fact, it would be erroneous to claim that he was a great baseball

Table 10.4 Some Highlights of Jim Thorpe's Professional Football Playing Career

---

1915—Helped reorganize and was player–coach of Canton Bulldogs.

1920—Elected president of the American Professional Football Association (forerunner of the NFL).

Played with the following pro teams:
Canton Bulldogs—Oorang Indians—Cleveland Indians—Rock Island Independents—New York Giants—St. Petersburg—Portsmouth, Ohio—Chicago Cardinals—others.

Thorpe's drawing power dominated professional football from 1915 until 1925 when "Red" Grange entered the game.

Brought the modern concept of offensive football, which he learned from Warner, to the professional game.

Longest Punt—90 yards with Canton.

Longest Field Goal—75 yards with Canton.

Note. From *Jim Thorpe—Carlisle Indian* (p. 24) by W.J. Gobrecht, 1969, Carlisle, PA: Cumberland County Historical Society and Hamilton Library Association. Copyright 1969 by Cumberland County Historical Society, Carlisle, PA 17013. Reprinted by permission.

player when compared to the major league stars of his era. However, he was talented enough to play successfully for parts of six seasons in the major leagues, mostly with the New York Giants, and an equal amount of time in the minor leagues.

In defense of Thorpe's modest record in major league baseball, it is important to point out that, as with the other sports, he had little preparation or training prior to the age of nineteen, his first year on the varsity at Carlisle. Second, he was never able to play baseball as a single sport interest. For example, while at Carlisle he played baseball and competed in track during the same season. From 1913 through 1919, while playing major league baseball, he also played professional football and frequently coached at the college and professional levels. After leaving major league baseball, he continued to play in the minor leagues from time to time. In 1920 he played with the Akron Internationals and batted an impressive .365.

The "Professional" Baseball Experience in North Carolina

Although Thorpe earned a salary for several years playing baseball, one could rightly argue that the game caused him more harm than good. Aside from the stress of interacting with John McGraw, the overbearing New York Giants baseball manager, and his inability to achieve real stardom in the major leagues, it was his earlier baseball play in the minor leagues (in 1909 and 1910) that led to the revocation of his Olympic medals.

After two years of successful play at Carlisle, Thorpe got the wander-lust. With fellow Carlisle students Jesse Youngdeer and Joe Libby, he traveled to North Carolina, where in 1909 they played baseball for Rocky Mount, a minor league team in the Eastern Carolina League. It was a rather common practice for baseball players still in college to play during the summer with a minor league team. According to Wheeler (1979), Libby has confirmed that Coach Warner actually sent the three players to Rocky Mount to further develop their baseball skills. The practice of college athletes playing for pay continued for many decades. In fact, while a college student in 1951 I played baseball for pay in Rockingham, North Carolina, more than forty years after Jim Thorpe's experience. It is even alleged that the same thing occurs today under slightly revised conditions.

Inasmuch as the practice of playing baseball for pay (usually around $2–$3 per day) was technically illegal for amateur college players, most played under assumed names during that period. However, Thorpe used his real name for the record. There has been much debate about why he did this. Perhaps he did not think of the hazards (regarding his college eligibility) or he may have had no intention of returning to Carlisle (in which case the amateur question would have been moot). It is possible that he simply assumed that he was following his coach's directions and thus believed that everything was proper. It is also possible that his sense of pride, as well as honesty, prevented him from using an assumed name. Whatever the reason, this experience was to cause him a great deal of anguish in later years because it was the basis for nullifying his Olympic victories and for returning his medals. It had made him a professional player, thus (retroactively) rendering him ineligible to compete in the Olympic Games. This issue served as the source of much societal debate over the next several decades concerning the meaning of amateurism.

Thorpe had played baseball from time to time in his early school life and also at Carlisle. He showed versatility both at this time and later in his professional career, playing the infield and outfield and pitching. In his play at Rocky Mount and later at Fayetteville, North Carolina, he was primarily a pitcher. According to Newcombe (1975), he had a strong but "untrained" (p. 144) arm and in his first year won nine games and lost ten. As an outfielder he batted around .250, and many of the hits were the result of his extraordinary speed in running to first base.

In minor league baseball play during 1909 and 1910, Thorpe found free-dom from the routine of the Carlisle school, a subsistence level of pay, and joy in playing the game on a regular basis. In addition, the adulation of the local townspeople was satisfying. Consequently, plans to return to Carlisle faded as a priority, and he did not return for two years. In-stead, he returned to Oklahoma to spend the winters. Although he was once visited by Coach Warner during the football team's trip to Haskell, he was not yet ready to get back into that life-style. He remained at home and in the spring of 1910 returned again to Rocky Mount, North Carolina, to play baseball.

Figure 10.7. Thorpe with the New York (baseball) Giants around 1918. Photo courtesy of Robert W. Wheeler.

Major League Play

At the height of Thorpe's Olympic fame, and after he had completed his play at the Carlisle School, he signed a contract in the spring of 1913 to play baseball with the New York Giants (see Figure 10.7). The Giants were managed by the famous John McGraw. It has been speculated that Thorpe would have developed more fully as a baseball player had he been "farmed out" to the minor leagues for additional training. This was not done, however, for the first year or so because of the public relations value of having this Indian hero as a member of the Giant team. Thorpe clashed with the dictatorial style of manager John McGraw, and this clearly affected his general disposition, his performance on the field, and his general enthusiasm for the game of baseball. Sitting on the bench and observing the more talented regulars did little to lift his spirits. Thorpe and others have contended that his baseball skills would have developed more fully if he had been afforded the chance to play for another manager.

Thorpe's best season in the major leagues was in 1919 when he batted .327 in sixty games while playing for Boston. In the minor leagues (triple-A) he batted .360 with Akron in 1920, .358 with Toledo in 1921 (including three home runs in one game), and .308 with Portland in 1922. His versatility in baseball was evident because he was a pitcher and an infielder in the minor leagues and an infielder and outfielder in the major leagues.

How Good Was He: Reality and Myth

Reports of the athletic prowess of Jim Thorpe often defy belief. One may assume that many of the feats described have improved with the passage of time and with the translation from one generation to the next. As with any legendary figure, reality and myth become intertwined. Some of his contemporaries claimed, however, that it was impossible to exaggerate Thorpe's performances. Still, one often wonders, just how good *was* he?

Comparing Jim Thorpe to more recent athletes is an exercise in speculation. Changes in activities, practices, and attitudes over the years has made exact comparisons in performance standards practically meaningless. In recent years the practice of rating the relative strength of athletes has become fashionable. This practice has assumed a semblance of scientific authenticity with the meticulous collection and analysis of quantifiable data. In track-and-field activities we tabulate performances to the nearest hundredth of a second in time or to the nearest millimeter in distance. Whereas these comparisons may apply to performances by Thorpe in track and field events, the same cannot be said for his performances in team sports.

Unlike the playing days of Thorpe, we now keep a record of the number of tackles, even the number of assists, made by defensive football players. Record is also kept of the number of "sacks" of the quarterback and the number of "hurries." In baseball, the base-on-balls and strikeout ratio is tabulated, as are the numbers of wins and saves and the earned run average. In basketball, shooting, rebounds, assists, and steals are catalogued. Such statistics allow us to make some *general* comparisons (e.g. football players Joe Montana versus Dan Marino, baseball pitchers Fernando Valenzuela versus Dwight Gooden, and basketball players Magic Johnson versus Larry Bird). Although data of the type mentioned do not tell the whole story about one's performance, they do serve as a basis for negotiation on subsequent contracts. However, we are not able to compare Jim Thorpe to contemporary players by using these kinds of measures.

During Thorpe's era sports statistics were limited to rather gross measures, such as win-loss records or total points scored, except in track-and-field performances, where the types of measurement (times and distances) were similar to those of today, albeit not with the same degree of precision. Consequently, much of our estimation of his relative skill is based on how good people *said* he was. These reports are supplemented by the recognition and honors bestowed upon him, including All-American teams, Hall of Fame designations, and "all-time best" selections. (Figure 10.8 shows Thorpe as a superbly conditioned athlete while still at Carlisle.)

Figure 10.8. Thorpe as a well-conditioned young athlete at Carlisle. Photo courtesy of Pro Football Hall of Fame.

Some Phenomenal Feats

Descriptions of Thorpe's athletic exploits began to approach legendary proportions early in his career at Carlisle. For example, early in November of 1911, prior to his Olympic exploits and even before his most notable football feats, the following report was published (cited in Newcombe, 1975) in the *Muskogee Times-Democrat* in Oklahoma:

> The 1911 season has brought into the public eye a young Indian student at the Carlisle School who promises to become the greatest athlete the world has ever seen. James Thorpe, a Sac and Fox from Oklahoma, came to Carlisle in 1908 with no knowledge whatever of athletics. . . .The world of college trainers has been astonished by his achievements. He is not only a basketball player at which game he fills the center post with truly remarkable skill, but he is a baseball player of great talent and covers any of the sacks or outfields with as much credit as a professional. He can put the 16-pound shot 43 feet, broad jump 22 feet 10 inches, run 100 in 10 seconds. The high hurdles are pie for him in 15⅘ seconds, while the 220 hurdles he negotiates in 26 seconds. The youthful redskin hunts, plays lacrosse,

tennis, indoor baseball, handball, hockey all with equal skill and can fill almost any position on a football team with superlative credit. As a football halfback he is probably seen best, whirling, twisting, dashing and plunging, bewildering his opponents with little panther-like leaps. Thorpe, who is only 22 years old, is 6 feet tall and averages about 178 pounds in weight. (p. 162)

The following story of Thorpe's overall speed and football savvy was reported (cited in Newcombe, 1975) in the *Pittsburgh Dispatch* following a game between Carlisle and the University of Pittsburgh on October 21, 1911:

On two occasions, Thorpe, who kicked wonderfully well for Carlisle, got down the field under his own booting, capturing the ball each time. Once he kicked a beautiful long spiral almost into the midst of five Pitt players and got down the field in time to grab the pigskin, shake off three or four would-be tacklers and dart 20 yards across the line for a touchdown. (p. 158)

His "bootings" on that day were reported to be "from 50 to 70 yards every time his shoe crushed the ball" (p. 158).

Many reports of Thorpe's kicking skill were astounding. For example, Leo Lyons, as reported by Wheeler (1979), described Thorpe's punting with the Canton professional team:

Whenever the Canton team played, Jim would give an exhibition of punting. In this particular game, he stood in the end zone. . .a photographer and newspaperman marked the distances. He kicked the old football one hundred yards on the fly twice out of five tries. The other three traveled eighty to ninety yards and bounded over the goal line. (p. 262)

George Krafton, who played with and against Thorpe in the professional league, described an incident from a Canton–Hammond game in 1919. According to Krafton (cited in Wheeler, 1979), "Canton got the ball and Jim standing in his own end zone punted the ball out of bounds at the other end of the field on the one-yard line. The kick went all the way in the air" (p. 276).

Another interesting kicking feat is reported by Newcombe from a Canton game against Massillon in 1919. Thorpe punted the ball from his five-yard line through the opponent's end zone and against a fence beyond, and was credited with a ninety-five-yard punt! Gobrecht (1969) reported that he once kicked a seventy-four-yard field goal while playing for the Canton Bulldogs! If true, this would remain a record even today.

Recognition and Honors

The nature of the honors received by Thorpe for his athletic accomplishments provide some indication of the esteem with which he was held by those who observed him. During his playing years at Carlisle, he was selected on Walter Camp's All-American first teams in 1911 and 1912 after having been selected for the third team in 1908. Grantland Rice, the most widely respected judge of football for the first half of the century, selected Thorpe on both his All-Time All-American (College) football team as well as his All-Time All-Professional team. Among his other football honors, he was inducted into the Professional Football Hall of Fame in the first year of its existence. In addition, in 1955 the Most Valuable Player Trophy for the National Football League was named the Jim Thorpe trophy.

Thorpe's greatest personal recognition came as a double-barreled triumph in 1950. The Associated Press conducted a poll of 391 sportswriters and broadcasters to determine the greatest football player of the half-century (1900–1950). The results of that poll are presented in Table 10.5. Like all polls, the votes are based on opinion and do not really prove anything except that most sports newspeople *believed* that Thorpe was the best player up to that time.

Shortly thereafter, the Associated Press announced the results of a similar poll to select the Best Male Athlete of the first half of the 20th century. Thorpe won this balloting with an overwhelming margin over Babe Ruth, Jack Dempsey, and others. The fact that Thorpe had excelled not only

Table 10.5 Results of the Associated Press Poll to Select the Greatest Football Player 1900–1950

Player	College	Votes
James Thorpe	Carlisle	170
Harold "Red" Grange	Illinois	138
Bronko Nagurski	Minnosota	38
Ernie Nevers	Stanford	7
Sammy Baugh	Texas Christian	7
Don Huston	Alabama	6
George Gipp	Notre Dame	4
Charles Trippi	Georgia	3

Note. From *Jim Thorpe: World's Greatest Athlete* (p. 216) by R.W. Wheeler, 1979, Norman: University of Oklahoma Press. Copyright 1979 by University of Oklahoma Press. Reprinted by permission.

Table 10.6   Results of Associated Press Poll to Select the Best Male Athlete 1900–1950

Name	Points
1. Jim Thorpe (252)[a]	875
2. Babe Ruth (86)	539
3. Jack Dempsey (19)	246
4. Ty Cobb (19)	148
5. Bobby Jones (2)	88
6. Joe Louis (5)	73
7. Red Grange (3)	57
8. Jesse Owens (0)	54
9. Lou Gehrig (4)	34
10. Bronko Nagurski (1)	26
11. Jackie Robinson (2)	24
12. Bob Mathias (0)	13
13. Walter Johnson (1)	12
14. Glenn Davis (0)	11
15. Bill Tilden (0)	9
16. Glenn Cunningham (0)	8
17. Glenn Morris (0)	8
18. Cornelius Warmerdam (1)	7

Note. From *Jim Thorpe: World's Greatest Athlete* (pp. 217–218) by R.W. Wheeler, 1979, Norman: University of Oklahoma Press. Copyright 1979 by the University of Oklahoma Press. Reprinted by permission.
[a]Numbers in parentheses refer to first place selections

in football but in track, baseball, and several other sports no doubt aided his case. The results of this poll are reported in Table 10.6.

Commenting on this recognition, Gayle Talbert (cited in Wheeler, 1979), of the Associated Press said that

> Jim Thorpe, that almost legendary figure of the sports world, had additional laurels heaped upon his leathern brow today when the nation's sports experts named him the greatest male athlete of the half century.
>
> Previously voted the No. 1 football player of the past 50 years, the wonderful Sac and Fox became the only double winner in the Associated Press poll when 252 out of 393 sports writers and radio broadcasters accorded him the ultimate honor. (p. 217)

Despite the impressiveness of Jim Thorpe's athletic exploits, there nevertheless existed conditions that limited the magnitude of his accomplishments. Among these conditions were (a) the lack of formal coaching or participation in organized athletics until he was nearly nineteen years of age, (b) rather limited formal preparation for the 1912 Olympic Games, (c) his participation in a broad range of activities rather than specializing in one or two, (d) the unavailability of strenuous competition in most activities, (e) the unavailability of a knowledgeable track coach, and (f) his tendency to put forth just enough effort to win—not pushing himself to his ultimate capacity. While not wishing to apologize for Thorpe's athletic performances, one can only speculate on the magnitude of his performances had he been given the relatively ideal training and competitive conditions of today or even the more advantageous conditions of some performers of his day.

The legend of Jim Thorpe was probably aided by the widespread assumption that he didn't try very hard. That is, he was viewed as so talented that even a half-hearted effort on his part produced results that were superior to the best of the other athletes. An example of this attitude was reported in a 1911 edition of the Philadelphia *Inquirer* (cited in Newcombe, 1975).

Thorpe is probably the most indifferent athlete we have ever had. He makes no special preparation for his efforts, and simply meanders carelessly up to his tasks and does them in an unconscious way that paralyzes the spectators. There is nothing showy or suggestive of extreme effort in his work. (p. 163)

This public attitude, which was really a type of compliment, continued throughout his playing career and beyond.

Life After Sports

Efforts to exploit Jim Thorpe as a sports hero, particularly an *Indian* sports hero, continued throughout his life and even after his death. As an Indian he was seen as an anachronism, a curiosity of a bygone era. As his athletic prowess waned and the vividness of his exploits dimmed, his image as a genuine sports hero diminished somewhat. Still, the fascination with who he was and what he had done continued throughout his life. He continued to be a recognizable figure and was frequently believed to be pining his life away, consumed by the loss of his Olympic medals. Thus, ''Poor old Jim'' became an easy reference for writers who wished to place him in their own contexts. Many who knew him have suggested that the deaths of his first-born son at the age of three and of his twin brother Charles at age ten had a much greater impact on his life.

Figure 10.9. Jim Thorpe in a 1952 photograph (at the age of sixty-four). Photo courtesy of Robert W. Wheeler.

Following Thorpe's permanent retirement from football in 1928, he lived in several places around the country. Winters were usually spent around Yale, Oklahoma, where he hunted raccoon, fished, played pool, and visited with friends. When he died on March 28, 1953, at the age of sixty-four he was living in a trailer park in California. Figure 10.9 shows a photo taken the year before his death.

During his later years, Thorpe was periodically in the news usually because of his misfortunes with alcohol, illness, or being discovered in some demeaning job. In addition, he was frequently visible as part of a promotion of some event or product. Late in World War II, Thorpe served briefly in the Merchant Marines after being rejected by the other branches of the armed services because of his age. He had bit parts in several Hollywood movies and, in fact, lived to see a very successful movie made of his life, *Jim Thorpe—All American*, starring Burt Lancaster in the title role. Figure 10.10 shows the famous painting by Charles Banks Wilson, which stands at the bottom of the grand staircase in the rotunda of Oklahoma's capitol building. A reasonable facsimile of this painting, featuring Burt Lancaster, was used as the focal publicity piece for the Jim Thorpe movie.

Return of the Olympic Medals

Over the years pleas to return the Olympic awards to Thorpe and, after 1953, to his descendants were based on arguments about Thorpe's

Figure 10.10. Charles Banks Wilson's painting of Jim Thorpe as an athlete at the 1912 Olympics. Photo used with permission of the artist. Copyright © State of Oklahoma.

naivete, on the meaning of amateurism, on emotion, and on general humanitarian reasons. Such arguments were usually met with firm resistance and the statement that ignorance was no excuse. It was not until 1973 that the Amateur Athletic Union, which had initially taken Thorpe's medals and returned them to the Swedish Olympic Committee, reestablished his amateur status as of the time of his Olympic competition. But this had no influence with the International Olympic Committee. Thus the medals were not returned, and official Olympic records still showed the second-place finishers (Ferdinand Bie in the pentathlon and Hugo Wieslander in the decathlon) as the gold medal winners in those events.

A new and more determined effort to win the restoration of the medals was initiated in 1982 when Robert W. Wheeler, a long-time admirer and biographer of Jim Thorpe, and his wife Florence Ridlon founded the Jim Thorpe Foundation. The Foundation was ''Dedicated to the Restoration of the Olympic Honors of Jim Thorpe.'' Composed of some influential political and sports persons including several prominent Indians, the Foundation commenced both scholarly and political efforts to accomplish their goal.

In preparing this case Wheeler (1979, p. vii) uncovered several facts that subsequently proved both morally persuasive and legally binding. First, a teammate of Thorpe at Carlisle confirmed that Coach Pop Warner had actually sent Thorpe and two other players to Rocky Mount, North Carolina, to gain additional playing experience and to make fruitful use of their time. This would mean that Thorpe was responding to a request of his superior and did not initiate the venture himself. Second, the Amateur Athletic Union (AAU), not the International Olympic Committee (IOC), had stripped the medals from Thorpe. The AAU had restored his amateur status in 1973, thus seeming to clear the way for the IOC to do the same. Third, Thorpe was a ward of the government in 1913 and as such should have had a lawyer provided to defend him. He did not.

These findings, however, were not adequate to convince the IOC. A more legally binding argument was needed. The convincing discovery was reported by Wheeler (1979).

> Finally, researching the general regulations of the 1912 Olympiad in the Library of Congress, my wife found what we needed. Rule 13 read: ''Objections to the qualification of a competitor must be made in writing, and be forwarded without delay to the Swedish Olympic Committee. No such objection shall be entertained unless accompanied by a deposit of 20 Swedish Kronor and received by the Swedish Olympic Committee before the lapse of 30 days from the distribution of the prizes.'' The newspaper story that led to Jim's disqualification did not appear until nearly seven months after the games.

These facts combined with the resolutions of United States Representative James J. Howard and Senator Don Nickles and more than 250,000 signatures on the foundation's petition enabled us to convince longtime Jim Thorpe supporter William E. Simon and United States IOC Representatives Julian K. Roosevelt and Douglas F. Roby that Thorpe's case had legal merit. The foundation's petition had been distributed by American Indian organizations, the Southwestern Wax Museum, the Junior Chambers of Commerce, the Benevolent and Protective Order of Elks, and many concerned individuals.

After meeting with William E. Simon, IOC President Juan Antonio Samaranch proposed the restoration of Jim's amateur status at the October 13, 1982 meeting of the nine-member executive committee in Lausanne, Switzerland. The resolution passed unanimously and on January 18, 1983, seventy years after Jim had been accused of professionalism, duplicate gold medals were returned to his children by President Samaranch in Los Angeles.

In 1913 the AAU had told Jim Thorpe, "Ignorance is no excuse." In 1976 the then IOC president, Avery Brundage, again told me, "Ignorance is no excuse." This time my wife and I were able to tell the IOC: "Gentlemen, with all due respect, ignorance of the general regulations for the 1912 Olympics was no excuse for illegally divesting Jim Thorpe of his awards." (vii-viii)[1]

Jim Thorpe was a product, and perhaps a victim, of his Indian heritage, his early family life, his schooling, and the extraordinary pressures that persisted throughout his life. He was a gentle and a trusting man. His naivete and kindness made him a soft touch for a real, or created, sob story. But all in all, he can best be described as a sportsman, and for a period in history he was certainly "the greatest athlete in the world."

---

[1]From *Jim Thorpe: World's Greatest Athlete,* by Robert W. Wheeler. Revised edition copyright © 1979 by the University of Oklahoma Press.

Chapter 11

Prominent Indian Athletes Prior to 1930

Over the past century many Indian athletes have achieved prominence in a variety of modern sports. Their greatest recognition was evident during the first three decades of the 20th century. Although some competed successfully as individuals in boxing, long-distance running, and other non-team sports, the majority attained recognition as members of teams at the school, college, or professional level. The greatest notoriety came to those who attended and participated at the Carlisle and Haskell Indian schools. However, a number of Indian athletes attended non-Indian colleges and participated in football, basketball, or baseball. Still others achieved prominence in professional sports, with or without having first attended school or college. This was true especially for several who played major league baseball during the early part of the century.

With two exceptions this review of prominent Indian athletes dates back only to the 1890s. Although the Carlisle Indian School had been developed in 1879, and others shortly thereafter, it wasn't until the late 1890s that Indian success in athletics was noted in the non-Indian community. The focus of this chapter is on those Indian athletes achieving prominence prior to 1930. More recent athletes will be presented in chapter 13.

Exclusion of "Legendary" Performers

Most discussions of notable sports performers prior to the 1890's are based on limited information or legend. For example, in the 1830s George Catlin (1841/1944) reported that Tullock-chish-ko (He Who Drinks the Juice of the Stone) was "the most distinguished ball-player in the Choctaw nation" (p. 142). To have achieved this prominence among a large tribe recognized for their strong tradition in lacrosse was certainly significant. In fact, Catlin was so impressed that he produced a painting of Tullock-chish-ko in full competitive costume (see Figure 1.6). Still, there is no way of establishing just *how* great a player he was. Neither was there any interest within the Choctaw culture in quantifying his individual prominence.

The two exceptions (predating 1890) are the cases of Louis "Deerfoot" Bennett and Big Hawk Chief, both runners. Bennett's domination in long-distance running in both this country and Britain during the 1850s and 1860s has been well documented. Big Hawk Chief's breaking the four-minute mile barrier was described in detail by an army officer and reported by several writers. There have been many other isolated reports of superior athletes and performances. However, verification has proven to be troublesome.

Another extraordinary running performance by a Zuni Indian (unnamed) was observed and reported separately by Owens and Hodge in 1891 (cited in Culin, 1907), who described a race over a measured twenty-five-mile course. They both stated that the twenty-five-mile course was run in two hours, and Hodge stated that it was "exactly two hours" (p. 686). If accurate, this would remain a record today because none of the marathon runners (26 miles, 285 yards) have attained a pace that would reach the twenty-five-mile mark in two hours. Such excellence in running by Indians during the 19th century and before is altogether believable by those who were well acquainted with the running life-style among many Indian tribes. Still, because of the lack of corroborating evidence and the lack of additional data about the participants, those athletes are not included in this review. Since the beginning of the 20th century, Indian athletes have been performing in what is essentially a different forum.

The time of this review of prominent Indian athletes closely follows their emergence in formal sports for non-Indians in this country. In fact, it was not until the last quarter of the 19th century that intercollegiate and professional team sports became established at all. For example, the first official intercollegiate football game was played between Princeton and Rutgers in 1869. It was another fifteen or twenty years, however, before college teams began participating in intercollegiate football on a widespread and consistent basis. Baseball was developed just before the middle of the 19th century but was interrupted during the Civil War. The National League of Professional Baseball was created in 1876, and it was another twenty-five years before the American League was formed. Basketball, which was developed by Dr. James Naismith in 1893, achieved quick success and was popular throughout the eastern part of the United States by 1900.

Consequently, the newly developed sports, football, basketball, and baseball, along with running became the primary means by which Indian athletes could achieve recognition in the non-Indian community. More traditional Indian sports such as double ball, shinny, hoop-and-pole or the court ball game were not widely adopted by the non-Indian population, and the game of lacrosse has never attained the popularity of baseball and basketball among non-Indians in the United States. Consequently, traditional sports did not provide for Indians a means for attaining widespread sports recognition within the non-Indian population.

Basis for Listing Individuals

The Indian athletes listed in this chapter are arbitrarily selected by the author. It is not an ''official'' list of superior athletes, and it does not have the sanction of any review body. They are not the same selections that might be made by another individual. I am confident that many worthy and distinguished athletes have been left out simply because of the lack of information available to me at the present time.

Still, the individuals discussed in this chapter achieved recognition that extended beyond their immediate community. Through participation at the highest level of competition, they achieved distinction as being among the very best in their sports during the period prior to 1930. Many received recognition as All-American college players, and others participated in the Olympic Games or achieved widespread recognition as amateurs in a variety of sports. Still others won acclaim in professional sports such as baseball, football, or ice hockey.

Many athletes included here have received recognition indicative of extraordinary national or international distinction, such as election to the American Indian Athletic Hall of Fame, the Baseball Hall of Fame, or the Football Hall of Fame. Much of the information on these individuals has been provided by the American Indian Athletic Hall of Fame, which is located at the Haskell Indian Junior College in Lawrence, Kansas. Participants are placed in alphabetical order.

Alexander Arcasa (1890-1962)

Alexander Arcasa was a member of the Colville tribe in Orient, Washington. He attended the Carlisle Indian School from 1909 to 1912 and excelled in football as a halfback and also in lacrosse. In football, he was named to Walter Camp's All-American team of 1912. In lacrosse, he was captain of the team that was designated as the best in the nation in 1912.

In 1972 Arcasa was one of the initial inductees into the American Indian Athletic Hall of Fame and has also been named to the Inland Empire Sports Hall of Fame.

Louis "Deerfoot" Bennett (1830-1896)

Louis Bennett was born on the Cattaraugus Indian Reservation, a member of the Seneca nation, near Buffalo, New York. His indigenous name, Hot-Tsa-So-Do-No, was translated to mean "He peeks in the Door." He became widely known as "Deerfoot" after outrunning a horse early in his career.

The professional racing career of Deerfoot is meticulously traced by Professor John Lucas (1983). He describes approximately two dozen of his races against other runners both in this country and in the British Isles. In fact, Deerfoot's most prominent running competition took place in Britain from 1861 to 1863. At that time in England professional racing, heavy wagering, and the awarding of prize money were commonplace. After defeating the best runners on this continent, including several visiting Englishmen, Deerfoot was lured to England where the competition was more highly organized and the prize money more lucrative.

The spectacular racing career of Deerfoot in England is described in great detail by Lucas, who cited approximately three dozen references, most of which are from the *Times* of London and other publications of the 1860s. Attention in this country was understandably devoted to the war between the states and thus gave little attention to promoting or even reporting sporting events.

Lucas describes many races ranging from four to twelve miles in which Deerfoot dominated. Crowds ranging from 4,000 to 15,000 attended these popular events. Whether the distances were relatively short (four miles), or longer (twelve miles), Deerfoot ran at close to a five-minute-mile pace. His recorded performances included a 4-mile race in 20 minutes 15½ seconds, 5 miles in 25 minutes 24 seconds; 6 miles in 31 minutes 16 seconds; 10 miles in 51 minutes 26 seconds; 11 miles in 56 minutes 56 seconds and 12 miles in 62 minutes 11 ½ seconds. These times, particularly the longer ones, would be the envy of all but a few runners today, a century and a quarter later.

After gaining considerable wealth in England, Deerfoot returned to this country in 1863 and after the war organized a traveling circus of runners. He continued to run until 1870 when, at the age of forty, he retired to the place of his birth. During his lifetime he had clearly dominated the best professional runners in this country and in England. He had set a standard of excellence that was to last well into the 20th century.

Charles A. "Chief" Bender (1883-1954)

Chief Bender was born into the Chippewa tribe in Brainerd, Minnesota. He played major league baseball as a pitcher with the Philadelphia Athletics in the American League from 1903 to 1917, appearing in five World Series. He was the top pitcher in the American League in 1911, winning eighteen games while losing only five. He also pitched a no-hitter that year. Connie Mack, long-time manager and owner of the Philadelphia Athletics, is quoted by S. Thompson (1983) as having said, "of all the pitchers I ever managed, the one I would select for a 'must win' situation would be Chief Bender" (p. 4). Overall, Bender won 204 games while losing 129. In addition, he coached with the Chicago White Sox and with the Philadelphia Athletics in the American League until 1953.

Much of Bender's early life was spent in boarding schools far away from his home. At the age of eight he was sent to the Episcopal Church-operated Educational Home in Philadelphia. Then at age thirteen, after a brief stay at home in Minnesota, he enrolled at the Carlisle School in Pennsylvania. In 1902, at the age of nineteen, Bender graduated from Carlisle and began playing professional baseball in Harrisburg, Pennsylvania. His successful career in the major league followed shortly thereafter. Bender was elected to the Baseball Hall of Fame in 1953 and to the American Indian Athletic Hall of Fame in 1972.

Big Hawk Chief (Early 1850s-?)

Big Hawk Chief (Koo-tah-we-coots-oo-lel-e-hoo-La-Shar) was a Pawnee in the plains of Nebraska. According to Bouc (1985) and *Ripley's Giant Book of Believe It or Not* (Ripley, 1976), Big Hawk Chief was the first-sub-four-minute-mile runner in recorded history. His feat was performed in 1876, seventy-seven years before Roger Bannister's first official four-minute-mile on May 6, 1954.

Big Hawk Chief enlisted in the Pawnee Scouts in 1876 to serve in the U.S. Army's campaign against the Sioux and Cheyenne in Nebraska and Wyoming. Commanding the Scouts was a cavalry officer, Luther North, of the "Fighting North" brothers. At the conclusion of the campaign along the Pine Ridge of Nebraska and the Powder River of Wyoming, the Scouts waited at Sidney Barracks to be released from service. It was during this time that his 4-minute-mile was recorded.

Big Hawk Chief was widely acclaimed as the greatest among the Pawnee runners, a nation of runners. Hearing of his running prowess, Luther North and Hughey Bean, a citizen of Sidney, set up a measured mile race to determine just how fast the Pawnee was. Some years later, writing in *The Fighting Norths and the Pawnee Scouts* (cited in Bouc, 1985) Robert Bruce quoted Luther North:

> Another man and I timed him, both with stop watches. He ran the first half in 2 minutes flat and the second in 1:58, or the mile in 3:58— so much faster than ever done before that we didn't believe the track was right, and had it remeasured with a steel tape.
>
> I had him run again. To this day no man has ever equalled it—my reason for believing that he was the fastest man on his feet, then or since. The army surgeon at Sidney . . . went carefully over him, stating afterward that Big Hawk Chief was the most perfect specimen of man he had ever seen. (p. 37)

This running feat will remain unofficial. However, the reputation of the Pawnee runners in general, and Big Hawk Chief in particular, and the attention to detail exhibited by Luther North make this a credible performance. The magnitude of this mile run is not fully appreciated until one compares it with other performances of that era. For example, in the U.S. Championships in New York in 1877, the mile was won by R. Morgan in a time of 4 minutes 49¾ seconds. According to Bouc (1985), the best official mile run anywhere in the world during the 19th century was run in 1886 by Walter George in London, England. Big Hawk Chief would have beaten him by 100 yards, and he would have beaten Roger Bannister by 10 yards.

Big Hawk Chief must rank among the greatest athletes of all time. His unofficial mile record was not to be surpassed for more than three-quarters of a century.

Elmer Busch (1890-?)

Elmer Busch was born into the Pomo tribe in California. He attended and played football at the Carlisle Indian School from 1910 to 1914. He was named as a second-team All-American tackle in 1913 and served as captain of the 1914 team. Busch began as a center but later switched to tackle. In three of his playing years at Carlisle (1911, 1912, and 1913) the team lost only one game per year. During these years Carlisle outscored their opponents by a total score of 1097 to 226 points. Busch was subsequently named to the All-Time Carlisle Football Team. In 1973 he was inducted into the American Indian Athletic Hall of Fame.

Wilson "Buster" Charles (b. 1908)

Buster Charles was born in Green Bay, Wisconsin, as a member of the Oneida tribe. He attended the Haskell Institute and the University of New Mexico, excelling in track and field (decathlon), football, and basketball. In football he was a "triple threat" performer, excelling in running, passing, and kicking. He starred as center on the basketball team. In track he was the National AAU Decathlon Champion in 1930, setting a record in the Kansas relays while winning five events and placing second in two others. In 1932 he was a member of the USA Olympic team, placing fourth in the decathlon. He was named to the American Indian Athletic Hall of Fame in 1972.

Albert A. Exendine (1884-?)

Albert Exendine was a member of the Delaware tribe in Bartlesville, Oklahoma. He enrolled at the Carlisle Indian School in 1899 at the age of fifteen. Exendine played varsity football for six years, from 1902 to 1907. As an excellent pass receiving end, he combined his talents with Peter Hauser to form the first prominent passing combination in 1907, just one year after the forward pass was legalized. He earned All-American recognition as an end in 1906 and 1907. In addition, he was captain of the football team and an outstanding student leader, serving as a positive role model for younger Indian students, especially Jim Thorpe. Exendine graduated from the Dickinson Law School in 1912 and returned to Oklahoma to practice law. He coached football at the Carlisle School (1908-1912), Georgetown University (1914-1922), Washington State University (1923-1925), and Oklahoma State University (1934-1935). Exendine was inducted into the American Indian Athletic Hall of Fame at the initial ceremonies in 1972.

Wallace L. Finger (b. 1902)

Wallace Finger (also called "Little Finger" and "Yellow Horse") was born on the Pine Ridge Reservation in South Dakota. He attended Haskell Institute during the mid-1920s where he distinguished himself in track. He was the premier runner on the 1926 two-mile relay team that was the best in the nation, winning and setting records in the Drake, Texas, and Kansas Relays. Finger was inducted into the American Indian Athletic Hall of Fame in 1973.

Joseph N. Guyon (1892-1971)

Joseph Guyon was a member of the White Earth Chippewa tribe in Minnesota. He attended and played football at the Carlisle School in 1911 and 1912, then attended and played at Georgia Tech in 1917 and 1918. He made the All-American team as a tackle in 1917 and as a running back the following year. Later he played professional football with the Canton Bulldogs, the Oorang Indians, the Kansas City Cowboys, and the New York Giants. Grantland Rice, dean of American sportswriters, placed Guyon on the all-time, all-Indian backfield along with Jim Thorpe, Pete Calac, and Frank Mt. Pleasant. Guyon was inducted into the National Professional Football Hall of Fame in 1966 and later into the American Indian Athletic Hall of Fame in 1972.

Albert M. Hawley (b. 1906)

Albert Hawley was born a member of the Gros Ventre-Assiniboin tribe in Hays, Montana. He attended Haskell Institute from 1925 to 1928 where he was a standout in football as a center. During the 1927 season he played the entire eleven-game schedule without missing a single minute. Coach R.E. Hanley selected Hawley for the All-Time, All-Haskell football team. Hawley transferred to Davis and Elkins College where he also played football, winning All-American Honorable Mention in 1928 and 1929. He was selected as an outstanding alumnus of both the Haskell Institute and Davis and Elkins College. After graduating from Davis and Elkins, Hawley served as teacher, coach, and principal at Indian schools in Idaho and Nevada. In addition, he served as reservation superintendent and held other positions, including that of AAU boxing commissioner in Nevada.

In Arizona, Hawley Lake was named in his honor. Hawley was inducted into the American Indian Athletic Hall of Fame in 1973.

Frank Hudson (1875-?)

Frank Hudson was a member of the Laguna Pueblo tribe in Paguate, New Mexico. He attended the Carlisle School from 1890–1900, excelling in football during the last 4 years of the century. He was one of the first players from Carlisle to achieve prominence, being selected on the Walter Camp All-American Second Team in 1897. He captained the Carlisle team in 1897 and played quarterback. Hudson was especially instrumental in bringing football prominence to Carlisle during its early years. As quarterback he led his team to victories over the universities of Illinois, Cincinnati, and Ohio State, all within one week. He was generally recognized as the best dropkicker in the country during his years at Carlisle. Hudson was inducted into the American Indian Athletic Hall of Fame in 1973.

Clyde "Chief" James (b. 1900)

Chief James was born into the Modoc tribe in Oklahoma Indian Territory. He played basketball at Missouri Southwest State College in 1924 and 1925, setting school and conference scoring records during those years. He later played AAU basketball from 1927 to 1947 with the Tulsa Eagles and the Tulsa Diamond Oilers. James was inducted into the American Indian Athletic Hall of Fame in 1977.

Jimmie Johnson (approximately 1882-?)

Jimmie Johnson was a member of the Stockbridge-Munsee tribe. He attended and played football at Carlisle from 1899 to 1903 and at Northwestern University in 1904–1905. As a quarterback he was selected on Walter Camp's All-American Team in 1903. Johnson made up for his small size with shrewdness and innovation. He is credited with calling and executing the "hidden ball" play against Harvard in 1903. He attended the Northwestern Dental School in Chicago where he completed his studies in 1907. He later established a very successful dental practice in San Juan,

Puerto Rico. Johnson was inducted into the American Indian Athletic Hall of Fame in 1972.

George Levi (b. 1899)

George "Little Skee" Levi was a member of the Arapaho tribe of Bridgeport, Oklahoma. He enrolled at Haskell Institute in 1922, following his more famous brother, John "Big Skee" Levi. At Haskell he played football and basketball and ran track from 1922–1926. Although not as accomplished as his brother, he did captain the 1925 football team and was a leader on the football team of 1926, which was undefeated and the highest scoring team in the nation. Levi received All-American honorable mention and was selected on the All-Time, All-Haskell second team. He was inducted into the American Indian Athletic Hall of Fame in 1982.

John Levi (1898-1946)

John "Big Skee" Levi was from the Arapaho tribe of Bridgeport, Oklahoma. Without question he was the most prominent of all athletes at the Haskell Institute and, in fact, was often referred to as "The Jim Thorpe of Haskell." As noted in chapter 9, Thorpe referred to Levi as "the greatest athlete I have ever seen," and thought him a better athlete than Thorpe himself. Levi won All-American honors in football at Haskell in 1923, beating out the great Ernie Nevers for the fullback position and sharing the backfield with Red Grange.

Like Thorpe, John Levi was a multitalented athlete, playing football, basketball, baseball, and track, the latter two while also taking part in spring football practice. McDonald (1972) reported that during a baseball game with Drake University, Levi also participated in a track meet against Baker University between innings, winning the shotput, discus, and high jump while in a baseball uniform. Plans to play professional baseball with the New York Yankees prevented him from trying out for the 1924 Olympic team. Levi did go to spring training with the New York Yankees in the spring of 1925 and was assigned to the minor league team in Harrisburg, Pennsylvania. Though hitting over .300, he returned to Haskell in August, telling McDonald (1972), "I got homesick. I had to come back to my people" (p. 20). Levi remained at Haskell for several years as a coach.

Levi was among the initial inductees into the American Indian Athletic Hall of Fame in 1972. (Additional information on John Levi's athletic achievements is included in chapter 8.)

Thomas Longboat (1886-?)

Tom Longboat was a member of the Onondaga tribe of the Six Nations Confederacy in New York state and Canada. He achieved prominence during the first decade of this century as a middle-distance runner in the eastern part of the United States and Canada. After several successes at shorter distances, Longboat entered and won the 1907 Boston Marathon in 2 hours 24 minutes 29 ⅘ seconds, nearly five minutes faster than the previous best time in the marathon. He became the most famous Indian runner since Deerfoot Bennett, also from the Six Nations, nearly a half century earlier. Longboat was acclaimed the first "World's Professional Marathon Champion" and his fame attracted crowds as large as 100,000 to his races. Still, widespread reports of his neglect of training and his heavy consumption of alcohol suggest that he could have been even greater than his record implies. Longboat has been inducted into the Canadian Indian Hall of Fame.

John T. "Chief" Meyers (1880-1971)

John Meyers was from the Cahuilla band of Riverside, California. He attended Dartmouth College where he excelled in baseball at the beginning of the 20th century. Subsequently, he was a catcher in the major leagues, playing with the New York Giants from 1908 to 1915 and with the Brooklyn Dodgers in 1916 and 1917. He batted .358 with the Giants in 1912, second in the league, and attained a lifetime average of .291. On the basis of catching in practically every game played by the Giants between 1908 and 1915, including almost all those pitched by the great Christy Mathewson, he earned the title of "Ironman." After one year at Dartmouth, he left to be with his mother who was very ill back in California. In his later years he stated that his greatest regret in life was that he never completed his college education. Meyers was inducted into the American Indian Athletic Hall of Fame in 1972.

Frank Mt. Pleasant (1884-?)

Frank Mt. Pleasant was born on the Tuscarora Indian Reservation in New York state. He attended the Carlisle School during the first decade of the 20th century and excelled in football as well as track-and-field events. As a quarterback on the football team, he won Second Team All-American honors in 1905. In addition, he was a member of the 1908 Olympic team, participating and finishing sixth in the long jump and the triple jump. After completing his work at Carlisle, Mt. Pleasant enrolled at Dickinson College where he became the first Indian to receive a degree from that institution. He later served as athletic director at Franklin and Marshall College in Lancaster, Pennsylvania. He was inducted into the American Indian Athletic Hall of Fame in 1973.

Phillip Osif (1906-1956)

Phillip Osif was a member of the Pima tribe on the Sacaton Indian Reservation in Arizona. During the mid-1920s he attended the Haskell Institute where he excelled in track and cross country. He captained the 1927 track team and was a member of the two-mile relay team that was undefeated in the Penn Relays, Kansas Relays, Texas Relays, Rice Relays, and the Knights of Columbus Games. In addition, he was National AAU Junior and Senior Six-Mile Champion. He excelled at all distances from 1,500 meters to 10,000 meters. In 1977 he was inducted into the American Indian Athletic Hall of Fame.

Bemus Pierce (1873-1957)

Bemus Pierce, from the Seneca Reservation in New York state, was one of the first Indians to achieve distinction in football at the Carlisle School. He attended Carlisle in 1894–1898 and was instrumental in the early development of football at that institution. Pierce was Second Team All-American guard in 1896 and served as captain of the teams in 1895, 1896, and 1897. He was a 6-foot, ½-inch, 225-pound lineman who regularly played sixty minutes of each game. After leaving Carlisle he played with the Akron Pros during the primitive years of professional football (1900–1903) and later with the Oorang Indians in the early 1920s. He coached for several years thereafter, most notably at the Sherman Indian School in California from which he retired in 1937. He was inducted into the American Indian Athletic Hall of Fame in 1973.

Theodore "Tiny" Roebuck (b. 1906)

Tiny Roebuck is from the Choctaw Nation in Lenton Indian territory. He attended the Haskell Institute where he excelled in football. In 1926 he was selected as an All-American tackle, among many other honors. His massive size (6 feet 6 inches tall and 270 pounds) served as an interesting contradiction to his nickname. Following his graduation from Haskell, he toured the country as a professional boxer and wrestler. In 1972 he was elected to the American Indian Athletic Hall of Fame.

Ed Rogers (1876-1971)

Ed Rogers was born into the White Earth Chippewa tribe in Libby, Minnesota. He attended both the Carlisle Indian School and the University of Minnesota, playing football at each institution. He served as captain of the University of Minnesota football team in 1901 and was selected on Walter Camp's Third Team All-American squad as an end in 1903. He returned to Carlisle to coach the team to a 9–2 record in 1904. Rogers went on to attain his law degree and practiced law in Minnesota for sixty-two years, earning recognition as the Outstanding Country Attorney in the United States in 1963. He retired in 1966 at the age of ninety. While practicing law in Mahnomen, Minnesota, he was appointed judge of the probate court. He was enshrined in the Football Hall of Fame for Pioneer College Players, and in 1973 was inducted into the American Indian Athletic Hall of Fame.

Reuben Sanders (1876-1957)

Reuben Sanders belonged to the Tututni–Rogue River tribe in Corvallis, Oregon. He attended the Chemawa Indian School and Wilmette College where he played football and baseball. In addition, he played with the Multnomah Amateur Athletic Club and the Salem (Oregon) Capital Athletic Club. At that time, prior to and shortly after the turn of the century, his football prowess was legendary. Sanders also excelled in baseball, track, and bike riding. He has been generally recognized as one of Oregon's greatest all-time athletes. In 1972 he was elected to the American Indian Athletic Hall of Fame.

Louis F. Sockalexis (1871-1913)

Louis Sockalexis was a Penobscot who was born and reared in Old Town, Maine. Prior to entering professional baseball in the late 19th century, he attended Holy Cross College where he excelled as a pitcher and out-fielder for two years. He pitched three no-hitters and batted .436 and .444 during his two years at college. Sockalexis broke into major league baseball in 1897 as an outfielder with the Cleveland Spiders where he batted .331 in sixty-six games. He played only three years, through 1899, and had a cumulative batting average of .313. According to writers and other observers, Sockalexis was among the most talented players of all time but his career was limited by his propensity for consuming alcohol.

The legend that developed around Sockalexis was based not on his statistical accomplishments in the game but on his great natural talent along with several astounding athletic feats. Hughie Jennings (1984), who managed Detroit during Ty Cobb's career, stated that Sockalexis "should have been the greatest player of all time—greater than Cobb, Wagner, Lajoie, Hornsby, and any of the other men who made history for the game of baseball" (p. 31).

Luke Salisbury (personal communication, 1985) of Chelsea, Massachusetts, a longtime researcher on Sockalexis, states that what impressed observers was Sockalexis' size, speed, and throwing arm. He apparently had a Willie Mays–type ability that had not been seen up to that time. For example, Jennings (1984) of Worcester, Massachusetts reported that while playing for Holy Cross in a game against Harvard, Sockalexis made a "lightning" throw to the catcher to prevent a runner from scoring. Two Harvard professors later measured the distance and announced that Sockalexis had established a "world's throwing record" of 138 yards (p. 31).

Part of the Sockalexis legacy in baseball was the name Indians for the Cleveland team. After being called the Spiders during Sockalexis' years (1897-1899), the team was later called the Bronchos, and Blues, and the Naps. In 1915 a Cleveland newspaper held a contest to select a new name and, according to Franklin Lewis's team history (cited in S. Thompson, 1983), the name Indians was selected as a tribute to the popularity of Louis Sockalexis.

Elijah "Eli" Smith (b. 1902)

From the Oneida tribe in Wisconsin, Elijah Smith attended the Haskell Institute from 1923 to 1926 and Davis and Elkins College from 1927 to 1929. He excelled in football, baseball, and track for four years at Haskell. He was a star on the 1926 football team, which was undefeated and the highest scoring team in the nation. In addition to being an outstanding halfback, Smith also established the Haskell record for kicking extra points after touchdowns. In 1925 he attained a batting average of .650 with

Haskell's baseball team. He went on to excel in both football and baseball at Davis and Elkins College, and he was voted the best ballcarrier and placekicker on their state championship team of 1929. In 1980 he was inducted into the American Indian Athletic Hall of Fame.

Louis Tewanima (1877-1969)

Louis Tewanima was a Hopi from the Second Mesa in Arizona. He attended the Carlisle School from 1907–1912 and achieved distinction as one of the greatest distance runners this country has ever produced. He was a member of the 1908 and 1912 U.S. Olympic teams. Tewanima won a silver medal for a second-place finish in the 10,000-meter run in 1912 and finished ninth in the marathon in the 1908 Olympic Games. In 1909 he established a world record in the indoor ten-mile run at Madison Square Garden. During this, and most other races, he exhibited the ability to change pace and sprint at regular intervals, a technique that discouraged other runners and usually left them far behind. Tewanima was selected as Helms Foundation member of the all-time U.S. Track and Field Team in 1954. In 1972 he was inducted into the American Indian Athletic Hall of Fame. (Additional references to Tewanima's running performances are included in chapters 8 and 9.)

Jim Thorpe (1888-1953)

James Francis Thorpe was from the Sac and Fox–Potawatomi tribes in Prague, Oklahoma. His achievements in football and track and field at Carlisle, his performance in the 1912 Olympic Games, and subsequent performance in professional football and major league baseball clearly make Jim Thorpe the greatest Indian athlete of modern times. He was, in fact, selected as the greatest of all American athletes of the first half of the 20th century by the Associated Press in 1950. (Chapter 10 is devoted exclusively to the athletic career of Jim Thorpe.)

Austin Ben Tincup (1892-1980)

Ben Tincup was a Cherokee from Rogers County in Oklahoma. He played major league baseball as a pitcher for the Philadelphia Phillies and Chicago

Cubs in the National League, beginning in 1914. He won greater recognition as a pitching coach and scout with the Yankees, Pirates, Browns, and Phillies. He was inducted into the Oklahoma Baseball Hall of Fame in 1971 and the American Indian Athletic Hall of Fame in 1981.

Egbert Bryan "Eg" Ward (b. 1900)

Eg Ward was from the Yakima tribe in Toppenish, Washington. He attended Haskell Institute and Washington State College. At both institutions he excelled in football, baseball, and basketball. During his years at Haskell (1923–1926), Ward served as captain of the Haskell baseball team and was named as quarterback on Haskell's All-Time team. In 1978 he was inducted into the American Indian Athletic Hall of Fame.

Gustavus "Gus" Welch (1892-1970)

Gus Welch, from the Chippewa tribe in Spooner, Wisconsin, attended Carlisle from 1911 to 1914 and served as quarterback on the last great football teams of that school. During his years as quarterback, Carlisle won thirty-three games while losing only three and tying two. Welch's exploits were somewhat overshadowed by the even greater attention given to his backfield mate, Jim Thorpe. Still, he captained the team in 1913 and made the second All-American team that year. Welch not only excelled in football but was an honor student and a leader among students. He was prominently mentioned as a helpful resource during the congressional investigation of 1914. He later played professional football with several teams, including the Canton Bulldogs. In addition, he served as head football coach of Washington State College from 1919 to 1923. Welch was inducted into the American Indian Athletic Hall of Fame in 1973.

Louis "Rabbit" Weller (1904-1979)

Rabbit Weller was from the Caddo tribe in Anadarko, Oklahoma. He attended Haskell Institute where he excelled in football from 1929 to 1931 and was recognized as All-American Second Team by the United Press. He later played professional football with the Boston Red Sox in the

National Football League and the Tulsa Oilers with the American Football League. Possessing great speed, Weller was noted for his long touchdown runs any time he got into the open. In a game against Oklahoma A & M, he returned a kickoff for a ninety-yard touchdown and later returned a punt for a ninety-five-yard score. Against Creighton he received a kickoff five yards behind his goal line and made a 105-yard run. In 1972 he was among the first group of inductees into the American Indian Athletic Hall of Fame.

Martin F. Wheelock (1874-1937)

Martin Wheelock was from the Oneida tribe in Oneida, Wisconsin. He was one of the first football players to bring distinction and recognition to the Carlisle program. He excelled on Carlisle's football teams from 1894 through 1902, establishing a longevity record during this period of relaxed eligibility standards. He served as team captain in 1899 and was selected All-American Second Team in 1901 and placed on the All-University team in 1902 by the *Philadelpia Inquirer*. Wheelock was inducted into the American Indian Athletic Hall of Fame in 1980.

Thomas "Wahoo" Yarr (1908-1941)

Thomas Yarr was born into the Snohomish tribe in Chimacum, Washington. He attended Notre Dame University and earned letters in football in 1929, 1930, and 1931 under Coach Knute Rockne. He played on the 1930 national championship team and was captain of the 1931 team. Yarr was named to the Associated Press All-American team in 1931 as a center. In 1982 he was inducted into the American Indian Athletic Hall of Fame.

Part III
Recent Developments

Chapter 12
Diminishing Visibility of Indians in Sports

During the first three decades of the 20th century, American Indians emerged in the forefront of modern sports. By any standard it is clear that Indian involvement and prominence at the upper levels of competition exceeded that which would have been expected based on their numbers in the population. (Chapters 9, 10, 11, and 13 of this book have illustrated the extraordinary success of teams and individuals from the Carlisle and Haskell schools, from Olympic competition, and from professional sports.) In fact, Indians were so prominent in sports that there was a widespread assumption that they were superior or natural athletes. As pointed out earlier in the text, the idea was often expressed that Indians should reduce their sport involvement and devote themselves to so-called more important endeavors.

It is apparent that Indians were in the forefront of sports visibility during the early part of the 20th century, and it became equally clear that their visibility in national sports diminished shortly thereafter. This phenomenon was noted by Steckbeck (1951): "For some twenty-odd years the Redmen raced across the stage of big-time football, leaving in their wake many a bewildered team...and then vanished from the American sporting scene forever" (p. vii). Although this comment may overstate the demise of the Indian athletes, it is true that after the first three decades of the century they were not heard from nearly so often.

Evidence of the Decline

There is substantial evidence of the decline of Indian sports prominence. An analysis of American Indian Athletic Hall of Fame records shows that the number of prominent Indian athletes peaked between 1910 and 1930 and has steadily declined since that time. Selection of Hall of Fame inductees has been made periodically since 1972 by a committee of Indian sports authorities. Table 12.1 provides an indication of the numbers of athletes selected between 1972 and 1982, grouped according to the decade of their primary sports prominence.

The peaking of selectees to the Hall of Fame during the 1910s and 1920s occurred despite the fact that no waiting period was imposed when the selection process was initiated in 1972. Some Hall of Fame guidelines mandate a minimal waiting period prior to selection (e.g., the Baseball Hall of Fame imposes a five-year minimum after retirement before one becomes eligible for selection). In fact, the only female selected to the Indian Athletic Hall of Fame, Angelita Rosal, was inducted during the second ceremony (in 1973) even though her prominence in the sport of table tennis occurred within the two years prior to that time.

In addition to the numerical reduction of Hall of Fame inductees in recent decades, the most prominent Indian athletes lived during the earlier years of this century. In fact, of the fourteen persons inducted during the first ceremonies held in 1972, all but one performed prior to 1932. The lone exception was baseball player Allie Reynolds, who was a prominent pitcher with the New York Yankees and Cleveland Indians in the 1940s and 1950s. Clearly, the majority of superior Indian athletes performed prior to 1930.

One could speculate that the reduction in Indian athletes is an appearance only and does not reflect an actual drop-off in Indian involvement

Table 12.1   Playing Era of the 47 Athletes Inducted Into the Indian Athletic Hall of Fame Between 1972 and 1982

	Decade of Athlete's Greatest Prominence								
	1890s	1900s	1910s	1920s	1930s	1940s	1950s	1960s	1970s
Number of inductees	2	6	9	11	6	5	4	2	2

Note.   Several persons have been inducted into the Hall of Fame for reasons other than athletic distinction (e.g., support for Indian sports programs, administration, Hall of Fame involvement, etc.). They are not included in this table.

in sports. There is some validity in that view; there may have been more Indians in sport during recent years than is generally known. Since around 1930 Indian identity has not been as firmly established as in earlier years because of increased off-reservation living, marriages between Indians and non-Indians, rights to privacy, and civil rights regulations. In addition, there have been distinct disadvantages to being identified as *Indian*. Some athletes were reluctant to volunteer information about their Indian heritage for social reasons, choosing instead to blend into the non-Indian community (i.e., to remain ethnically anonymous). In the early part of the 20th century and before, it was not easy to disguise one's racial background. Since around 1970, however, a rebirth in Indian pride and identity have increased tendencies to identify and project one's Indian heritage.

There may have been a degree of unidentified Indian athletic participation, and there may have been less interest in the press to highlight the exploits of Indian athletes. But these factors do not fully account for the reduced visibility of Indians in sport. The thesis of this chapter is that there has been a genuine reduction in nationally prominent Indian athletes that is not accounted for by visibility factors alone.

The causes for diminished Indian prominence in sports is open to much speculation. However, the most important factors appear to be (a) a reduction in opportunities for developing sports skills, (b) restricted opportunities for participation, and (c) a lessening of Indians' interest in competing with and against non-Indians. Fewer opportunities occurred when college athletics became virtually unavailable to Indians, and noncollegiate opportunities for Indians have never developed to the extent available for non-Indians. In addition, lowered aspirations and goals have led to self-imposed restrictions and isolation.

Reduced Opportunities: Participation in College Athletics

The great majority of prominent athletes, both Indian and non-Indian, gain national attention while participating in college athletics. These athletes often use college athletics as a springboard to a professional playing career. Football and basketball players almost always enter the professional ranks after first excelling at the college level. Though not so widespread, the same is often true in soccer, ice hockey, baseball, and track. In certain other sports, however, such as gymnastics, tennis, swimming, and ice skating, intense training begins at such an early age that the participants often reach their peak prior to college age. Still, practically all major sports and athletics, with the exception of boxing, are enhanced by college athletics.

College sports serve both as excellent training programs and as showcases in preparation for a career in sport. So it was with prominent Indian athletes in the early part of the 20th century. Most of them gained prominence at Indian colleges or training schools. Of the forty-seven athletes who were inducted into the Indian Athletic Hall of Fame between 1972 and 1982, forty-one of these are known to have taken part in college athletics (the great majority attended either Carlisle or Haskell). Most others attended Indian schools in the lower grades. Among Indians, therefore, college attendance and athletic prominence have been very closely connected.

Anything that interferes with college attendance concurrently interferes with sports participation. This is precisely what happened in the Indian community after around 1930. Before then the Carlisle School had served as the origin and center for Indian education and athletic achievement from the elementary school to the early college level. Prominence of the school in intercollegiate sports continued for about twenty years from 1895 until 1915. After 1915 strife surrounding a federal investigation of the school and other problems were so disruptive that both the athletic and educational programs were curtailed. The school was permanently closed in 1918.

Soon after the closing of the Carlisle School, the Haskell Institute, which had competed at a more modest level in athletics, upgraded the athletic program, seeking to become "the Carlisle of the West." During the 1920s Haskell served as the focus, or organizing center, for prominent Indian athletics. During this time Haskell fielded nationally prominent football and track teams, competing against Michigan State, Brown, Minnesota, and some of the other major universities of the nation. Several players were selected to All-American football teams, and some participated in the Olympic Games.

In the early 1930s federal authorities decided to de-emphasize sports at Haskell. All major college competition was terminated. *Indian Truth*, a publication of the Indian Rights Association in Philadelphia (1933) applauded this downgrading of sports.

It is gratifying to learn that athletics at the Haskell Institute are to be put on a sane basis. They have too long been tainted by commercialism and professionalism. A winning team at any price is not a good move for a Government Indian school. (pp. 3–4)

However, these practices were apparently acceptable for non-Indian universities, which have continued with major athletics up to the present day.

According to *Haskell Institute USA, 1884–1959* (Haskell Institute, 1959), the Indian commissioner's office in 1935 reaffirmed that "there must be no return to big time football (p. 41). In defending this course of action, the following observation was made: "The relation of football to physical culture is much the same as that of the bullfight to agriculture" (p. 16).

With the demise of the Carlisle School in 1918 and the reduction of athletic programs at Haskell around 1930, no Indian college competed in athletics against major colleges or universities. The Cherokee Indian Normal School, in Pembroke, North Carolina, subsequently called the Pembroke State College for Indians, and later Pembroke State University, achieved four-year college status in the late 1930s but did not compete in athletics against major colleges and universities. Neither did that institution recruit Indian students from outside the local (Lumbee Indian) community.

As a result of these developments, opportunities for Indian participation in college athletics at an elite level after 1930 were restricted to non-Indian colleges. During the 1930s, 1940s, and 1950s, this proved to be practically no opportunity at all.

As a general practice, Indians were essentially prevented from entering colleges involved in major athletic programs. Two types of barriers were presented. Many states, particularly those in the south, specifically prohibited non-white persons (including Indians) from attending white state colleges and universities. Where no such prohibitive laws existed, informal barriers often served the same purpose. Many qualified Indians were therefore either denied admission or discouraged from attending major colleges and universities.

A second major obstacle was equally effective in preventing the admission of Indians to major universities. The quality of education at Indian schools on or near reservations was such that graduates from these schools were ill-equipped to gain admission to major institutions. Some who were admitted were not adequately prepared to compete successfully in the academic program. Indian schools were clearly inferior to those in the non-Indian community, particularly in terms of preparing one for higher education. As a result, Indian youth with intellectual ability equal to that of their white counterparts performed poorly in admissions tests and in academic programs once admitted. The cultural shock was also difficult for many who moved from the reservation to the college campus.

Legislative restrictions (prior to civil rights laws of the 1960s), informal discrimination in the admission process, poor elementary and high school programs, and difficult cultural adjustments all served to restrict the number of Indians at major colleges after 1930. The proportion of Indians at major colleges was much smaller than the proportion in the population as a whole. In fact, the number of Indians involved in college athletics was no more than a fraction of what it had been during the Carlisle and Haskell years.

An analysis of the Indian Athletic Hall of Fame inductees confirms the notion that colleges diminished in their role as the dominant means for Indians to gain entrance into high-level amateur or professional sports. For example, during the forty-year period between 1895 and 1935, twenty-eight out of the twenty-nine inductees who were competitive during that period made their entrance into sports fame through college athletics (mostly at Carlisle and Haskell). However, for the following forty years, between 1935 and 1975, only eleven out of the eighteen inductees who were competitive during this period attended and participated in college athletics. In other words, college athletics accounted for 97 percent of the inductees before 1935 but only 61 percent of those since that time.

Non-Collegiate Athletic Opportunities

In addition to collegiate participation, another avenue to sports prominence has been amateur sports for youth at the community or club level. The phenomenon of intensive age-group athletic competition has developed rapidly over the past thirty years. Participants in these programs often go on to successful high school, college, and professional programs. Some participants go directly from youth sports clubs to competition at the Olympic Games or other elite national or international athletics. In fact, it is practically impossible for one to compete in gymnastics, ice skating, swimming, wrestling, tennis, golf, or other individual sports at the international level without having spent many years in a youth training program. Most champions and world class performers in these sports have begun serious training before the age of twelve. Unfortunately, this avenue for skill development has been largely unavailable to Indian youth.

The most highly publicized, and perhaps the most widely played, sport for pre–high school youth is Little League baseball. This program, which began spreading widely in the late 1940s and 1950s, is the route by which many young boys develop skills to compete later in other programs such as Babe Ruth leagues, the American Legion program, high school, college, and professional baseball. Similarly, local or national organizations promote skill development and competition in other sports such as football, basketball, soccer, field hockey, and volleyball for boys and girls.

Boxers from the inner city often begin their early training in a police athletic league or other community sponsored programs. Though usually not beginning at such a young age, track stars also have their start in formal community programs.

Opportunities to participate in formal pre–high school athletic training and competition provide a head start for many youth. As a general rule, however, Indian youth have not had equal opportunity to engage in such age-group competitions.

Sports experts have long assumed that most individuals require approximately eight to ten years of training to reach a peak performance level in complex activities such as gymnastics or swimming. The average age of those attaining national and international championships has dropped approximately eight years since 1900. Because most individuals need approximately the same amount of time to hone their skills, today's champions in gymnastics, swimming, and ice skating at the age of eighteen will have begun serious training around ten years of age. A half century ago athletes could begin training in high school and reach a peak in their early or mid-20s.

Indian youth on or near reservations do not have the opportunity to enter highly specialized sports clubs that have the best coaching and facilities. This is especially true for more exclusive sports such as golf, tennis, ice skating, or fencing. Sports camps with specialized coaching and training are becoming commonplace for youth who can afford them and who wish to advance rapidly. It is also true that well-organized programs in the more common sports such as baseball, football, and soccer are not readily available to the large majority of Indian youth. However, basketball programs for Indian youth are becoming more popular. Ice hockey clubs are frequently available in Canada. This has led to the entry of many Canadian Indians into the National Hockey League.

The lack of youth sports programs on or near reservations has resulted in Indian youth being less prepared to compete at the elite level, whether in college, in international amateur sports, or at the professional level. Until around the middle of this century, aspiring athletes, whether Indian or non-Indian, could begin their serious training during their teenage years and had ample opportunity to develop their skills to be competitive with others. Since around 1950, however, the advent of intensive youth sports programs has led to inequality of opportunity for development among various ethnic and socioeconomic groups. The black population is largely excluded from youth development programs in tennis, golf, swimming, ice skating, gymnastics, and skiing, and so are the Indians. Neither group has an adequate record of representation in these sports. Even in popular team sports such as basketball, baseball, and football, opportunities for Indians on reservations are sporadic. Opportunities are particularly limited where reservations are remote and the population is widely dispersed.

Limited Aspirations and Goals

In addition to reduced opportunities for participating in youth and college sports, a social climate has developed over the past several decades that depresses the sports aspiration of young Indians. Resistance to leaving one's family and friends and a desire to contribute to the family and community have resulted in self-imposed isolation of many Indian youth. When these factors are combined with a lack of confidence in competing within the non-Indian community, this isolation becomes very intense. No doubt these same factors serve as a deterrent to full development in non-sports areas also. One would be hard pressed to specifically itemize the origin and causes of this climate of exclusivity except to generalize that it has resulted from the stresses of Indian–non-Indian relations over the past 150 years.

The Dropout Phenomenon

The symptoms and effects of the Indian's depressed sports aspirations are widely recognized. The phenomenon is discussed by Gabriel (1979). In a *Sports Illustrated* article he observed that the Pueblo Indians of New Mexico are "natural born long distance runners" (p. 46) but rarely show any interest in competing after high school. In fact, he reports that a drop-off in enthusiasm is usually noted even before the student reaches the senior level in high school. Applebee (1982) has reported on the high drop-out rate among Indian athletes at several high schools in South Dakota. In discussions with Indian athletes at the Haskell Indian Junior College in 1984, I found that they exhibited less confidence in sports competition than their performance record would imply. Further, most showed no interest in continuing to participate in sports at a four-year college.

Reservation Indians are under great pressure to remain on the reservation, to assist with family necessities, and to remain within the social context of their peers. Of course, the desire to remain among one's friends is a natural human trait. However, among Indian youth, especially those on reservations, this tendency is particularly restrictive. Because of jealousy, fear of losing a friend, or perhaps for other reasons, young athletes experience pressure *not to succeed*. Some report a tendency to criticize or ridicule those who excel, especially if their success is likely to draw them away from the group or cause a change in life-style. One successful athlete at Haskell reported to me that his peers "cut you down a lot." He also stated that "they expect you to fail and laugh at you."

In his 1979 article "Running to Nowhere," Gabriel cites numerous cases of Laguna Pueblo youth who excelled in races before and during high school. To illustrate, he cites the case of Andy Martinez, who in the early 1970s ran the mile in an astounding 4 minutes 17 %0 seconds while a high school freshman. He was national AAU age-group cross-country champion and gave every indication that he would emerge as one of this country's best distance runners. After high school, however, he got a job in a local uranium mine and did not go to college. In fact, he never ran a race after high school. His case—a young athlete beginning with great promise but then dropping out—is cited as typical of young men in the community.

According to Gabriel (1979), the Laguna Pueblo High School cross-country team had won the New Mexico state cross-country championship for eleven consecutive years before 1979. As with other Indian groups throughout the continent, the Pueblo tradition is for the youth to run *distance* races as opposed to short ones. In track, few elect to take part in the sprints and most prefer the longer distances.

Despite the outstanding record of many high school runners, few elect to attend college. According to Jerry Tuckwin, the Haskell Indian Junior College track coach, a great many high school runners could win scholarships to practically any college in the country but most show no interest in continuing after high school.

The dropout phenomenon for Indian athletes has not only been observed by outsiders but by Indian youth themselves. In a visit to the Haskell campus in 1984, this writer talked with male and female athletes about their aspirations for future participation. Some of these athletes had well-established records, especially in track, that would lead one to expect that they could enroll in four-year institutions and attain considerable sports recognition. However, most conceded that they and most other Indian athletes would cease competition at the end of their Haskell experience.

An analysis of the Haskell athletes' plans for future participation revealed that those athletes who were reared on or near a reservation were most likely to drop out of sports and return to the reservation. In fact, none of the athletes who had grown up on a reservation planned to go on from Haskell to a four-year college. On the other hand, several athletes who had grown up off the reservation, in an integrated society, expressed plans to transfer to a four-year college and continue competition.

Several nonreservation Indian athletes expressed negative comments about peers from reservations because of their tendency to shy away from higher level competition. Comments such as "they are afraid they're not good enough" were voiced even thought the performance record would indicate otherwise. None of the female basketball or volleyball players believed that they were good enough to go on to a four-year college and compete successfully, and none planned to try. Sadly, several of the best female athletes stated that "our best friends hold us back."

Competing Pressures

Billy Mills, the 1964 Olympic champion in the 10,000-meter run, grew up on the Pine Ridge reservation in South Dakota. He has described the intense pressure exerted upon him while training for national and international competition. Friends urged him to ease up in his rigorous training regimen to join them in drinking and partying. Mills' refusal to do so was viewed as a rejection of their friendship and, indeed, the Indian way of life. He reported that a serious commitment to athletic training is incompatible with the social mores of the young men in the community.

Obviously this makes preparation for athletic competition especially difficult.

In a study of participation records and attitudes among athletes at three Indian high schools in South Dakota, Applebee (1982) found that aspirations to prepare for and perform at the next higher level were practically nonexistent. In fact, 82 percent of the students surveyed expressed the view that Indian athletes were more likely than other ethnic groups to drop out of athletic programs. Faculty in the schools also noted a higher dropout rate among Indian teenagers. Reasons given by the students were that they were tired of the sport. They also admitted to a fear of failing and a lack of confidence and drive. Equally important was their sense of a lack of support from family and friends.

The low aspiration level among Indian youth may be related to the absence of Indian role models. When asked to name a prominent female athlete, students at Haskell could not think of a single one. Male athletes could only offer the name of one prominent male athlete, who happened to be a fellow student at the same school. Of the 120 high school students in Applebee's study, only 4 percent could name a prominent athlete and identify the sport in which he or she participated. The view that there were few professional Indian athletes was expressed by 92 percent. Over half of the students said that there were few students (fewer than five) in the school who had the ability to become professional athletes.

Indian students at both the high school and college level believe that special problems are faced by Indian athletes. These include prejudice and discrimination by non-Indians, a tendency toward shyness and lack of confidence on the part of Indians, financial difficulties, and a high incidence of alcohol and drug problems. All evidence points to some truth in each of these claims.

Summary

In proportion to the rest of the population, the number of Indian athletes has declined since 1930, as has the image of the Indian as a superior athlete. This decline has coincided with restrictions placed on the Indian's sport participation. These restrictions have been both externally and internally imposed.

After 1930 Indian educational institutions were no longer available to promote major sports programs at the college level. The closing of the Carlisle School and the de-emphasis of sports at the Haskell Institute effectively closed off the traditional avenues of sports visibility. Thereafter, Indian athletes had to enroll in non-Indian colleges in order to participate in college sports. As a result of legislative restrictions, informal barriers, and the poor quality of education in Indian schools, entry into major non-Indian colleges was particularly difficult for several decades. Consequently, athletic participation by Indians at the college level was at a minimum during the 1930s, 1940s, and 1950s.

In addition, opportunities to take part in youth training programs and sports clubs have been much more limited for Indians than for non-Indians. Athletic programs such as age-group swimming, gymnastics, and tennis; special summer camps for golf, wrestling, and ice skating; and organized leagues for youth football, basketball, and Little League baseball are simply not as available for reservation Indians as for non-Indians in suburban or urban areas.

As a result of social developments over time, Indians have imposed restrictions and, in fact, a kind of sports isolation on themselves. There are internal pressures to keep Indians on the reservation and to limit serious sports participation to the high school level and even lower. Young men and women feel an obligation to remain with the family and contribute to its financial and social welfare. They also feel pressure from friends to remain and become a part of the traditional Indian community. These factors have served to diminish the Indian's involvement in sport since around 1930.

Chapter 13

Prominent Indian Athletes After 1930

After the early 1930s no Indian institution remained engaged in major college athletic competition. The system of education and support that had proven so successful at Carlisle and Haskell since late in the 19th century was no longer available for aspiring Indian athletes. Consequently, there was a significant reduction in the number of Indians being exposed to nationally prominent sports teams.

Indians competing in national-level sports after 1930 did so in the "open market," that is, without being surrounded by other Indians in similar competition. As a result, their traditional support system no longer existed. They did not compete as members of Indian teams but as minority members of non-Indian college or professional teams, or they competed in individual sports, such as boxing and running, in an essentially non-Indian climate.

Compared with the white and black population, the isolation in sport experienced by the Indian was in many respects unique. Of course, the white population was dominant in all amateur and professional sports until very recent years, and the black athlete often had a support system, such as the system of Negro baseball leagues that continued into the 1950s. In addition, black athletes have emerged as perhaps the most successful group in such individual sports as boxing and track during the past three decades. After 1950 their emergence in baseball, basketball, and football was so significant that the isolation previously felt by minorities in these special performance situations was largely removed. There were enough black players to provide a social support system when needed. However, the Indian never established sufficient numbers on any team or in any sport to experience this type of support.

The Indian's entrance into college sport after the early 1930s was an individual, lonely, effort—without the accompaniment of other Indian athletes and often without even the presence of other Indians at the institution. Young Indians continued to be involved in sports programs at Indian schools and in Indian communities but the level of competition was modest and usually did not include non-Indian communities.

This chapter reviews Indian athletes who achieved national distinction in sports after 1930 despite these conditions. Four of those included here (Ellis, Levering, Mills, and Walter Johnson) attended Haskell and achieved a level of prominence even though no national-caliber program existed at that institution. Two of these, Johnson and Mills, went on to other universities where they achieved considerable recognition. The other two, Ellis and Levering, went into amateur and professional boxing in which they became nationally prominent. Most of those included, however, attended other colleges or universities or excelled independent of any educational institution.

The standards of excellence for inclusion here are similar to those which were established for athletes named in chapter 11 (i.e., recognition indicative of extraordinary national or international distinction). Again, the selections are arbitrary and may not be consistent with judgments made by other individuals or groups.

George Armstrong (b. 1930)

George "Army" Armstrong was reared in Skeed, Ontario, son of an Ojibway mother and an Irish-Scot father. Although he did not have an opportunity to play organized ice hockey during his boyhood, Armstrong began playing road hockey. He later traveled to Sudbury where he played with an organized ice hockey team. In 1951 "Army" began playing with the Toronto Maple Leafs where he remained for a 21-year career. During this period he scored 292 goals and 476 assists and served as captain of the Maple Leafs for twelve of those twenty-one years.

In addition to Armstrong's distinction as a superb hockey player, he has earned recognition for his humanitarian endeavors. In 1969 he won the first Charlie Conacher Memorial trophy for his contributions as organizer of floor hockey for retarded children. He has also served as chairman of the Cerebral Palsy Association of Canada.

Ellison "Tarzan" Brown (1914-1982)

Tarzan Brown was reared as a member of the Narraganset tribe in Westerly, Rhode Island. He excelled in distance running, particularly the marathon. He won the Boston Marathon in 1936 at the age of twenty-two. During that year he won marathons on successive days in Port Chester, New York, and in Manchester, New Hampshire. He was a member of the U.S. Olympic marathon team in 1936 but failed to finish the race because of an injury resulting from his attempt to duplicate a British distance walker's style. In 1939 Brown again won the Boston Marathon, setting a record for the course. He won twenty of his twenty-two races during that year including not only the Boston Marathon but a major race at the New York World's Fair. Brown was elected to the American Indian Athletic Hall of Fame in 1973.

Rod Curl (b. approximately 1948)

Rod Curl is a Wintu Indian from Redding, California. Though standing only five feet five inches tall, he has been a successful golfer on the professional tour since the early 1970s. He joined the tour after spending several years as a construction worker and amateur golfer. In 1974 he won the Colonial National Open with a four-under-par 276, beating Jack Nicklaus by one stroke.

Chester L. "Chet" Ellis (b. 1913)

Chet Ellis was born into the Seneca nation at Red House, New York. He attended the Haskell Institute in the mid-1930s where he excelled as an amateur boxer. Ellis served as captain of the Haskell boxing team from 1935 to 1937. In addition to several state and regional honors, he became national Golden Gloves bantamweight champion in 1939. He later won the International Golden Glove Championship in the same weight class, thus becoming the first Indian to win boxing championships at the national and international levels. Ellis was inducted into the American Indian Athletic Hall of Fame in 1977.

Stacy Howell (b. 1928)

Stacy Howell is a member of the Pawnee tribe of Maryville, Missouri. He attended Murray A & M Junior College where he excelled in basketball. In 1947 he was selected as All-Conference and in 1948, Junior College All-American. Howell was placed on the Helm's Foundation and the National Association of Intercollegiate Athletes (NAIA) All-American team in 1950 while at East Central College. He was inducted into the American Indian Athletic Hall of Fame in 1977.

Jack Jacobs (1919-1974)

Jack Jacobs was a member of the Creek tribe in Holdenville, Oklahoma. He was a quarterback for the University of Oklahoma football team in 1939, 1940, and 1941. He established a punting record of 47.8 yards per kick in 1940 and was selected to play in both the Shrine game and the college All-Star game. He played professional football with the Washington Redskins, the Green Bay Packers, and the Winnipeg team in the Canadian league. As quarterback he led the Winnipeg Blue Bombers to the Grey Cup final in 1950 and 1953. Jacobs played twenty-two seasons in school, college, and professional football without missing a season. Following his playing days, he coached in the Canadian league. In 1973 he was enshrined into Canadian National League Hall of Fame. He entered the American Indian Athletic Hall of Fame in 1977.

Robert Lee Johnson (b. 1906)

Robert Johnson was born and reared in Pryor, Oklahoma. He played major league baseball with the Philadelphia Athletics from 1933 to 1942 and with Washington and Boston in the American League for the next three years. As a regular during all of these years he had a lifetime batting average of .296 and a total of 288 home runs. His brother, Roy Cleveland Johnson (b. 1904), played outfield for Detroit, Boston, and New York in the American League and Boston in the National League from 1929–1938, establishing an identical lifetime batting average of .296.

Walter Johnson (b. 1908)

Walter Johnson was born into the Walker River Paiute tribe in the White Mountains of California. He attended the Haskell Institute from 1929 to 1933 and later enrolled at the University of Redlands. He excelled as a fullback in football at both institutions, earning honorable mention All-American while at Haskell in 1931 and 1932 and was selected to play in the Shrine Game in 1932. He earned All-Conference honors while at the University of Redlands in 1934. Following his graduation in 1936, he began a thirty-three-year career as a teacher and athletic coach at the Sherman Indian School and later at the Stewart Indian School in California. Johnson was inducted into the American Indian Athletic Hall of Fame in 1973.

Nelson Levering (b. 1926)

Nelson Levering is a member of the Omaha-Bannock tribe of Macy, Nebraska. He attended Haskell Indian Junior College and earned widespread recognition as an amateur and professional boxer. He won the midwest Golden Glove championship in 1947 and the Kansas state welterweight championship in 1948. Levering fought on boxing cards with Joe Louis four times. As an amateur he won thirty-five of forty fights, and as a professional he won twenty-three out of twenty-eight, seventeen of those by knockout. He was inducted into the American Indian Athletic Hall of Fame in 1981.

Gene Locklear (b. 1949)

Gene Locklear is a Lumbee Indian who was reared on a tobacco farm near Pembroke, North Carolina. After excelling in high school baseball he was signed to a professional contract by the Cincinnati Reds. During four years in the minor leagues he won two league batting titles and was twice the league's most valuable player, once at the triple-A level and once in a double-A league. He spent five years in the major leagues, from 1973 through 1977, playing with the Cincinnati Reds, the San Diego Padres, and the New York Yankees. His best season was in 1975 when he played in 100 games and batted .321. Overall in his major league career he batted .274.

In addition to playing professional baseball, Locklear has been an accomplished artist since his high school days. During his playing years he was busy painting, putting on exhibitions, and achieving prominence as a painter in his home state. In addition, he received national exposure through television and newspapers, which depicted his Indian heritage along with his dual talents in baseball and painting. After retiring from baseball Locklear became a full-time artist, residing in California. (See additional references in chapter 14.)

Oren Lyons (b. 1930)

Oren Lyons grew up on the Onondaga reservation in New York state as a member of the Wolf Clan. He comes from a long line of superb lacrosse players. His grandfather, Ike Lyons, was a prominent player at Carlisle and also with the Onondaga reservation team around the turn of the century. Ike Lyons is pictured as a member of the 1904 Onondaga team shown in Figure 2.6. Subsequently, most males in his family have played lacrosse. Oren's son is currently a leading scorer with the Iroquois Nationals.

After dropping out of high school, Oren Lyons joined the U.S. Army and became a member of the boxing team of the 82nd Airborne Division. After getting out of the Army, he continued his amateur boxing career, fighting in the Golden Gloves and in the Sugar Bowl tournament in 1956. He then attended Syracuse University where he played on the lacrosse team and won All-American honors in both 1957 and 1958 as a goalkeeper. The 1957 team was undefeated.

After finishing college, Lyons spent several years as a commercial artist in New York City. He then returned to the reservation where he has been a community leader and traditional Faithkeeper. In addition, he has been an artist and a poet and a professor in American studies at the University of New York at Buffalo. Lyons has been a driving force over the past ten years in the revival of sports interest and cultural pride within the Iroquois community. He was the primary mover in establishing the Iroquois National Lacrosse team. In addition, he has served as spokesman for Native American traditions, including lacrosse, at the national and international levels.

William M. "Billy" Mills (b. 1938)

Billy Mills is an Oglala Sioux and grew up on the Pine Ridge reservation in South Dakota. During his early years Mills began running as a means of conditioning himself for boxing. Very quickly he became so adept at distance running that this took precedence over other athletic pursuits. He attended Haskell Institute and later the University of Kansas, excelling in track and cross-country at each. During his senior year at Haskell, he set seven high school records in the mile run, including exceeding one that had been established by Glenn Cunningham nearly thirty years earlier. He captained the cross-country team at the University of Kansas and won several conference titles in cross-country and in middle-distance events in track.

The highlight of Billy Mills' athletic career was winning the gold medal in the 10,000 meter run at the 1964 Olympic Games in Tokyo. He set an Olympic record in this performance and became the first American to win an Olympic race at so great a distance. In 1965 he set a world record in the six-mile run. Mills was enshrined into the National Track and Field Hall of Fame in 1976 and the American Indian Athletic Hall of Fame in 1978. A movie of his life entitled *Running Brave*, starring Robbie Benson in the title role, was released in 1983.

Rollie Thurman Munsell, Jr. (b. 1913)

Rollie Munsell, Jr., is from the Chickasaw tribe in Tuttle, Oklahoma. He attended the Chilocco Indian School and later excelled as an amateur and professional boxer. In the years 1932 through 1935 he won the Missouri Valley AAU championship in the 160-pound division. His more than 100 professional fights between 1938 and 1942 included a loss to heavyweight contender Max Bear. Munsell was inducted into the American Indian Athletic Hall of Fame in 1977.

Jessie B. Renick (b. 1917)

Jessie "Cab" Renick was born into the Choctaw tribe in Marietta, Oklahoma. He attended Oklahoma A & M during the late 1930s and won All-American honors as a forward on the basketball team in 1939 and 1940. He was later an AAU basketball All-American in 1947 and 1948 and was captain of the U.S. Olympic basketball team in 1948, which won a gold medal. In 1948 Renick became coach and player of the Phillips 66 Oilers and over the first three seasons led the team to a 153–9 record. He ended his playing career in 1952 and became a successful businessman in Bartlesville, Oklahoma. He was enshrined in the American Indian Athletic Hall of Fame in 1973.

Allie P. Reynolds (b. 1917)

Allie Reynolds, from the Creek tribe in Bethany, Oklahoma, played major league baseball as a pitcher with the Cleveland Indians from 1942–1946 and with the New York Yankees from 1947–1954. He led the American League in strikeouts in 1943 and 1952. He also led the league in earned run average in 1952 and 1954 and had the most shutouts in 1945 and 1952. He was voted the nation's professional athlete of the year in 1951. Reynolds won a total of 182 games while losing 107 with the Yankees and Indians.

Prior to going into professional baseball, Reynolds attended Oklahoma State University on a track scholarship. In addition to running the 100- and 200-yard dashes, he also played three years of varsity football. As one of the few college-educated players during his era, Reynolds was elected as the American League player representative from 1951 to 1953. In 1969, he became president of the American Association, a top minor league. Since retiring from baseball in 1954, Reynolds has been a successful businessman in his home state of Oklahoma. In 1972 he was inducted into the American Indian Athletic Hall of Fame.

Alex "Sonny" Sixkiller (b. 1951)

Sonny Sixkiller was born in Tahleguah, Oklahoma, a member of the Cherokee tribe. He was recruited to the University of Washington, where he excelled as quarterback during the early 1970s. Sixkiller was the leading collegiate passer during 1970, with an average of 18.6 completions and 227 yards per game. He played professional football in the National Football League for a short time but his career was cut short by injuries. Sixkiller was inducted into the American Indian Hall of Fame in 1987.

Joe Tindle Thornton (b. 1916)

Joe Thornton was born in Stilwell, Oklahoma as a member of the Cherokee tribe and attended the Chilocco Indian School. He excelled in archery and won many major titles after the age of forty. In 1961 he became world champion in archery in competition at Oslo, Norway, setting three world records. In 1963 and 1965 he finished second in world archery competition in Finland and Sweden respectively. In 1962 he won the British International Trials Championship. In 1967 and 1971 he was a member of the United States archery team that won the world team championship. Thornton won the national championship in 1970 at the age of fifty-four. He has served as a member of the board of governors of the National Archery Association, and president of the Oklahoma Archery Association. Thornton was elected to the American Indian Athletic Hall of Fame in 1978.

Jimmie Wolf, Jr. (b. 1934)

Jimmie Wolf was born in Mountain View, Oklahoma as a member of the Kiowa tribe. After completing the public schools of Hobart, Oklahoma, he enrolled at Panhandle State College and later at Oklahoma State College. At each level he excelled as a running back in football. He made the National Association of Intercollegiate Athletics All-American football team in 1958 when he led the National College Division as scoring champion. During that season he set a national record, scoring twenty-five touchdowns and eight in a single game. At Panhandle State he served as team captain in 1957 and 1958. After college Wolf worked with the Bureau of Indian Affairs in Anadarko, Oklahoma, and has been a prominent community leader. He was inducted into the American Indian Athletic Hall of Fame in 1973.

Chapter 14

Some Promising Signs for Indians in Sport

Despite the reduction of the visibility of Indian sports over the past several decades, as discussed in chapter 12, there are some encouraging signs today. Several developments over the past decade justify the expectation that the American Indians may soon be reestablished as prominent participants on the American sporting scene. This is not to suggest that they will assume the status of Indians in the first two decades of the 20th century—when they forged an image of being superior athletes, when their prominence in sports clearly exceeded their relative numbers in society. However, there are reasons to believe that they will assume a more visible place than they have during the past half century.

Some of the encouraging developments include (a) the establishment and growing impact of the American Indian Athletic Hall of Fame; (b) the development of national level Indian sports teams and organizations, particularly the Iroquois National Lacrosse Team and the National Indian Activities Association; and (c) some increase in individual sports accomplishments. Perhaps these grew out of increasing Indian sports interest and general Indian awareness. On the other hand, these developments may have contributed to the heightened Indian consciousness. Each development will be discussed briefly in this chapter.

American Indian Athletic Hall of Fame

The American Indian Athletic Hall of Fame was established in the early 1970s. Its purpose was to honor those persons who brought distinction through sports to themselves and to the Indian community at large. Starting with the first enshrinement ceremonies in 1972, selections have been made and induction ceremonies have been held approximately every two years.

The American Indian Athletic Hall of Fame is governed by a board of directors comprising one representative from each of the four geographical areas of the United States, plus three members at large—a total of seven members. Records, plaques, and memorabilia regarding each of the inductees are housed at the Haskell Indian Junior College in Lawrence, Kansas. According to Mr. Turner Cochran (personal communication, December 3, 1985), in order to be enshrined in the American Indian Athletic Hall of Fame, individuals must

1. be at least one-fourth degree American Indian or Native Alaskan blood, verified by the Board of Directors;
2. have made a national impact in a sport approved by the Board of Directors;
3. have merited recognition and distinction, and, who by their exploits, accomplishments, and activities in regard to sports and athletic events have brought fame and honor to himself or herself and Indian people.

Table 14.1 includes a list of the fifty-seven persons who have been inducted into the American Indian Athletic Hall of Fame in the eight ceremonies that have taken place between 1972 and 1985. As can be noted, inductees represent a great many tribes and come from a broad geographical area—from the Atlantic to the Pacific and from Canada to Mexico. Furthermore, their athletic specialties have included both traditional Indian activities (e.g., lacrosse, archery, running) and the full range of modern, popular sports (baseball, football, basketball, boxing, etc.) The time span of participation of the inductees ranges from the 1890s to the 1970s.

In addition to bringing appropriate recognition and prestige to the athletes themselves, these ceremonies and related publicity bring pride and honor to members of their tribe and community. This attention raises the likelihood that these persons can serve as role models for youthful aspirants in the community. The overall impact of the American Indian Athletic Hall of Fame will take some time to determine. However, this institution already serves a very positive role for the cause of Indian sports.

New Indian Sports Initiatives

Several new thrusts have been initiated to promote Indian sports during the past decade. These initiatives may have grown out of a general revival of ethnic pride throughout the nation, a resurgence of sports interests throughout society at large, the visibility of the American Indian Athletic Hall of Fame, or a combination of these and other factors. Some of this renewed sports interest has been reflected in Indian schools. However, it is presently not possible to say that school sports in Indian communities have shown any dramatic or sustained sports revival. Discussions with school officials, as reported by Applebee (1982) and Gabriel (1979), have revealed mixed reviews.

Nonschool activities seem to have led to more significant athletic developments within the Indian community than have schools themselves. Prominent among these developments has been the establishment of the Iroquois National Lacrosse Team and the National Indian Activities Association.

Iroquois National Lacrosse Team

Largely through the efforts of Oren Lyons (see biographical sketch in chapter 13), Wes Patterson (prominent Tuscarora lacrosse racketmaker), Sid Jamieson (university lacrosse coach), and other leaders of the Iroquois community, the Iroquois National Lacrosse Team was established in 1983. A gradual increase in visibility and team quality has taken place since that time.

Lacrosse has traditionally been the most important sport among the Iroquois. In fact, the Iroquois introduced this game to the international community. Teams from the Iroquois confederacy visited Britain and Scotland more than a century ago to exhibit and teach this game to the British. These teams visited Britain in 1869, 1876, 1883, and 1886 and played the game as guests of Queen Victoria. The British and Scottish subsequently distributed the game throughout the British Empire, including Australia.

The recently established Iroquois National Lacrosse Team includes representatives from each of the six nations of the confederacy (Mohawk, Oneida, Onondaga, Seneca, Cayuga, and Tuscarora). In 1983 the national team began rather informally by playing a limited number of games against college lacrosse teams, with only modest success. Then in 1984 the Iroquois National Team played a series of games leading up to the Olympic Games in Los Angeles (the Jim Thorpe Memorial Powwow games). This was in recognition of the return of Jim Thorpe's Olympic

Table 14.1 Inductees Into the American Indian Athletic Hall of Fame: 1972–19

Name	Tribe or nation	School(s) attended
Aitson, Amos	Kiowa	Riverside Indian School
Arcasa, Alexander	Colville	Carlisle
Bender, Charles	Chippewa	Carlisle
*Bennett, Robert	Oneida	Honorary Inductee: Former Bureau of Indian Affairs (BIA) commissioner, instrumental in founding American Indian Athletic Hall of Fame
Bray, David	Seneca	Cornell University
Brown, Ellison	Narraganset	
*Bruce, Louis R.	Mohawk-Sioux	Honorary Inductee: Former BIA commissioner, instrumental in founding American Indian Athletic Hall of Fame
Burd, Sampson	Blackfeet	Carlisle
Busch, Elmer	Pomo	Carlisle
*Carney, Sidney M.		Honorary Inductee: Instrumental in elevating Haskell Institute to Junior College status

(Cont.)

Teams, sports, years played, (selected) honors	Year inducted
Riverside Indian School football: 1944; boxing: 1944–1945; National AAU boxing champion (118 class): 1945	1982
Carlisle football and lacrosse: 1909–1912; All-American Football: 1912	1972
Philadelphia Athletics (baseball): 1903–1917; Top American League pitcher: 1911; Selected to Baseball Hall of Fame: 1953	1972
	1977
Cornell lacrosse, track, cross-country, basketball: 1976, 1977; All-American lacrosse: 1977; N. American Lacrosse Assoc. All-Star: 1975-1977	1981
U.S. Olympic marathon team: 1936; Boston Marathon winner: 1936, 1939	1973
	1973
Carlisle Football: 1909–1911, 1914–1915; All-American: 1911; Lacrosse, track & field: 1909–1911	1985
Carlisle football: 1910–1914; All-American: 1913	1973
	1985

Table 14.1 (Cont.)

Name	Tribe or nation	School(s) attended
Charles, Wilson	Oneida	Haskell University of New Mexico
*Cochran, Turner	Caddo-Chickasaw	Honorary Inductee: Instrumental in developing "Hall of Heroes" at Haskell Indian Junior College, Curator of American Indian Athletic Hall of Fame
Ellis, Chester	Seneca	Haskell
Exendine, Albert	Delaware	Carlisle
Finger, Wallace L.	Sioux	Haskell
Foster, Harold	Navajo	Central Arizona College
Franklin, Virgil	Arapaho-Kiowa	Chilocco Indian School Murray State College
Gawboy, Robert	Chippewa	Purdue University
Guyon, Joseph	White Earth Chippewa	Carlisle Georgia Tech University
Hawley, Albert	Gros Ventre-Assiniboin	Haskell Davis & Elkins College

(Cont.)

Teams, sports, years played, (selected) honors	Year inducted
Haskell track & field, football, and basketball: 1927–1931; U.S. Olympic (decathlon) team: 1932	1972
	1982
Haskell boxing: 1935–1939; International Golden Gloves champion (bantamweight): 1939	1977
Carlisle football: 1902–1907; All-American: 1906, 1907	1972
Haskell track: 1926; Established records in Drake, Texas, and Kansas Relays	1973
Central Arizona track & field; NJCAA All-American cross-country runner: 1972; Fastest cross-country time in nation for junior colleges: 1973	1978
Murray State boxing, football, baseball, and track: 1947–1948; National Golden Glove, and National AAU boxing champion (126 lb): 1945; All-Armed Forces featherweight title: 1946	1985
World swimming record in 200-yard breaststroke: 1955; Gold medal winner AAU Aquatic meet: 1955	1980
Carlisle football: 1911–1914; Georgia Tech: 1917–1918; All-American: 1917–1918; Professional football: 1920–1927 with Canton, Kansas City, NY Giants; Professional Football Hall of Fame: 1966	1972
Haskell Institute football: 1922–1928; Davis & Elkins football: 1928–1932; All-American: 1928, 1929	1973

Table 14.1   (Cont.)

Name	Tribe or nation	School(s) attended
Holmes, Robert T.	Ottawa	Haskell Riverside Junior College Texas Technological College
House, Gordon	Navajo-Oneida	Phoenix Indian School Fort Wingate Indian School Albuquerque Indian School
Howell, Stacy	Pawnee	Murray A&M Junior College East Central College
Hudson, Frank	Laguna Pueblo	Carlisle
Jacobs, Jack	Creek	Oklahoma University
James, Clyde	Modoc	Missouri Southwest State College
Johnson, Jimmie	Stockbridge-Munsee	Carlisle Northwestern University
Johnson, Walter	Paiute	Haskell University of Redland
*Lavatta, George P.	Shoshone-Bannock	Honorary Inductee: Continuous service to American Indian Athletic Hall of Fame
Levering, Nelson	Omaha–Bannock	Haskell

(Cont.)

Teams, sports, years played, (selected) honors	Year inducted
Haskell, Riverside, Texas Tech football, track & field: 1931–1938; Established Haskell records in 100-yard dash and javelin throw	1985
State lightweight boxing champion in Arizona, Nevada and Texas: 1948; All-Armed Forces lightweight boxing champion: 1945; Professional boxer: 1946–1949	1985
Murray A&M Junior College basketball: 1947–1948; Junior College All-American: 1948; NAIA All-American basketball: 1950	1977
Carlisle football: 1890–1900; All-American: 1899	1973
Oklahoma University football: 1939–1942; Professional football with Cleveland Rams, Washington Redskins, Greenbay Packers, Winnipeg Blue Bombers: 1942–1955	1973
Missouri Southwest State basketball: 1924–1925; Tulsa Eagles, and Tulsa Diamond Oilers (AAU basketball teams): 1927–1947	1977
Carlisle football: 1899–1903; All-American: 1903; Northwestern football: 1904, 1905	1972
Haskell football: 1929–1933; All-American: 1931, 1932; University of Redlands football: 1934–1935	1973
	1981
Midwest Golden Glove welterweight boxing champion: 1947, 1948; Won 23 of 28 professional fights, 17 by knockout	(1981)

Table 14.1 (Cont.)

Name	Tribe or nation	School(s) attended
Levi, George	Arapaho	Haskell
Levi, John	Arapaho	Haskell
*McDonald, Frank W.	Non-Indian	Honorary Inductee: Recognition for service to Indian youth and Indian people, coach and administrator at Haskell
Meyers, John	Cahuilla Band	Dartmouth College
Mills, William	Oglala Sioux	Haskell University of Kansas
Mt. Pleasant, Frank	Tuscarora	Carlisle
Munsell, Rollie	Chickasaw	Chilocco Indian School
Osif, Phillip	Pima	Haskell
Pierce, Bemus	Seneca	Carlisle
Renick, Jessie	Choctaw	Oklahoma A & M

(Cont.)

Teams, sports, years played, (selected) honors	Year inducted
Haskell football, track, and basketball: 1923–1926; All-American (honorable mention) football: 1926	1982
Haskell football: 1921–1924; All-American fullback: 1923; New York Yankees baseball: 1925	1972
	1978
New York Giants baseball: 1908–1912; Brooklyn Dodgers: 1916–1917; Batted .358 in 1912	1972
Track and cross-country at Haskell and University of Kansas: 1955–1962; Gold medal (10,000 meters) at Olympics (establishing record): 1964	1973
Carlisle football and track & field; All-American quarterback: 1905; U.S. Olympic team (long jump and triple jump): 1908	1973
Missouri Valley AAU boxing champion: 1935; More than 100 professional fights: 1938–1942	1977
Haskell track & cross-country: 1924–1927; Captain of two-mile relay team that was undefeated in Penn, Kansas, and Texas Relays; National AAU junior and senior six-mile champion	1977
Carlisle football: 1894–1898; First American Indian All-American: 1896; Professional football: 1900–1901; Homestead Athletic Club, Akron Pros, and Oorang Indians: 1922	1973
Oklahoma A & M basketball: 1937–1940; All-American: 1939, 1940; Captain of U.S. basketball team in Olympic Games (gold medal): 1948; Coach-player with the Phillips Oilers: 1948–1952	1973

Table 14.1 (Cont.)

Name	Tribe or nation	School(s) attended
Reynolds, Allie P.	Creek	Oklahoma State
Roebuck, Theodore	Choctaw	Haskell
Rogers, Ed	White Earth Chippewa	Carlisle University of Minnesota
Rosal, Angelita	Sioux	
Sahmaunt, Joseph	Kiowa	Cameron State Junior College Oklahoma City University
Sanders, Reuben	Tututni–Rogue River Tribe	Chemawa Indian School Wilmette College
Smith, Elijah	Oneida	Haskell Davis & Elkins College
Tewanima, Louis	Hopi	Carlisle
Thorpe, Jim	Sac & Fox Potawatomi	Carlisle

(Cont.)

Teams, sports, years played, (selected) honors	Year inducted
Baseball pitcher with Cleveland Indians: 1942–1946, and NY Yankees: 1947–1954; Best earned run average in American League: 1952, 1954; Led league in strikeouts and shutouts for 2 years; America's Professional Athlete of the year: 1951	1972
Haskell football and track: 1923–1927; All-American track: 1926; Professional boxer and wrestler	1972
Carlisle football: 1896–1897; University of Minnesota football: 1901–1903; All-American: 1903.	1973
Member of U.S. Women's Table Tennis Team (at the age of 17): 1972–1973	1973
Cameron State Junior College basketball: 1957; Oklahoma City Univ.: 1958–1960; All-American (honorable mention): 1959–1960	1978
Chemawa Indian School football: 1890s; Wilmette College football: 1890s; Legendary distinction as participant in football, baseball, track, and bike racing in Athletic Clubs in the state of Oregon	1972
Haskell football, baseball, track: 1923–1926; Established national record for extra points kicked; Davis & Elkins College football, baseball: 1927–1929.	1980
Haskell track team: 1907–1912; U.S. Olympic team: 1908, 1912; Won silver medals in 5,000- and 10,000-meter runs: 1912; Held world record (10 miles): 1909	1972
Carlisle football and track: 1907–1912; Canton Bulldogs, New York Giants football: 1920–1929; New York Giants baseball: 1913–1919; Olympic Games (winner of pentathlon and decathlon): 1912; Greatest Athlete: 1st half 20th century (Associated Press)	1972

Table 14.1   (Cont.)

Name	Tribe or nation	School(s) attended
Thornton, Joe Tindle	Cherokee	Chilocco Indian School
Tincup, Austin Ben	Cherokee	Haskell
Ward, Egbert B.	Yakima	Haskell Washington State College
Weller, Louis	Caddo	Haskell
Welsh, Gustavus	Chippewa	Carlisle
Wheelock, Martin	Oneida	Carlisle
Wolf, Jimmie	Kiowa	Panhandle State Oklahoma State
Yarr, Thomas C.	Snohomish	Notre Dame University

*Honorary Inductees were enshrined into the Hall of Fame for services related to the promotion of sports programs for Indians, or to the Hall of Fame itself. However, most of these persons were distinguished athletes in their own right.

gold medals, which were taken from him following the 1912 Olympic Games (see chapter 10). The Iroquois National Team played a series of five games in a tournament involving several international teams.

Nearly 100 years after their last visit to England (in 1886), the Iroquois Nationals were invited by Team England to return for a series of games. The Nationals accepted the invitation and visited the British Islands in 1985, where they won three games, tied one, and then lost to Team

Teams, sports, years played, (selected) honors	Year inducted
World archery champion: 1961; Member of world champion U.S. Archery Teams: 1967, 1971; National Archery Champion (at age 54): 1970	1978
Major league baseball player with the Philadelphia Phillies and Chicago Cubs: 1914–1915; Coach and scout with Yankees, Browns, Phillies	1981
Haskell football, basketball, baseball: 1923–1926; Selected as quarterback on Haskell's All-Time team; Washington State College football, basketball, baseball: 1927–1928	1978
Haskell football: 1929–1931; Professional football with Boston Red Sox (NFL) and Tulsa Oilers (AFL)	1972
Carlisle football team quarterback and captain: 1911–1914; All-American: 1912; Canton Ohio bulldogs: 1915–1917	1973
Carlisle football: 1894–1902; All-American: 1901; "All-University" (Philadelphia *Inquirer*): 1902	1980
Panhandle State football: 1955–1956; Oklahoma State football: 1957–1958; NAIA All-American: 1958; National scoring champion: 1958	1973
Notre Dame football: 1929–1933; All-American center: 1931; Captain of national championship team: 1931	1982

Note. Appreciation is expressed to Mr. Turner Cochran, Curator of the American Indian Athletic Hall of Fame, for reviewing a draft of this table and providing valuable suggestions.

England by a 16–14 score in the finals. The symbolism of that trip is exhibited in the 1985 photograph taken in front of the 100-year-old Urmston Lacrosse Club (see Figure 14.1).

In July 1986 the Iroquois team hosted three other national teams in a tournament held at the University of Buffalo. These exibition games involving world-class teams were preliminary to the World Lacrosse Championships, which were held in Toronto, Canada, during the following

Figure 14.1. Two members of the Iroquois National Team pose in front of the Urmston (England) Lacrosse Club. This club was established 100 years ago as a result of the Iroquois visit to England. Photo by Rick Hill, Iroquois National Lacrosse Team.

week. The Australian National Team, the British National Team, and the United States National Team all competed against the Iroquois team. During these games the Iroquois team showed that it was definitely capable of being competitive in international level competition. In 1985 and 1986 the team was coached by Sid Jamieson, a Mohawk, who is also the coach of the Bucknell University team. The 1986 series of games was sponsored by the Iroquois Nationals, the State University of New York, and the Native American Peoples Alliance. Figures 14.2 and 14.3 provide photographs of some of the action in the 1986 competition.

Already the Iroquois National Lacrosse Team has initiated plans for traveling to Australia and the British Islands during the next two years for international lacrosse competition. The excitement of the community in support of this national team is obvious when one observes the spectators and talks with community members. In addition, the interest of young males, particularly family members of players and officials, is clearly evident.

Among the Iroquois lacrosse has primarily been a men's game. Nevertheless, there has been continuing interest among women and some now play on teams. This interest was stimulated in 1984 when the Iroquois were invited to play in the Canadian Invitational Women's Lacrosse

Figure 14.2. Action during the Iroquois-Australian games in Buffalo, New York, July 1986. Photo by Steward/Gazit.

Figure 14.3. Coach Jamieson meets with members of the Iroquois Nationals during a break in the 1986 competition in Buffalo, New York. Photo by Rick Hill, Iroquois National Lacrosse Team.

Figure 14.4. Iroquois National Women's Team in 1986. Photo by Rick Hill, Iroquois National Lacrosse Team.

Championships scheduled for Montreal. An Iroquois Women's team was quickly organized and participated successfully in the tournament. Because lacrosse is so widely played by women, both nationally and internationally, and because of the long-standing interest in the sport throughout the Iroquois community, the girls and women have made plans for continuing play. Figure 14.4 shows the 1986 Iroquois National Women's Team.

The elders among the Iroquois Nations see this revival of lacrosse as a means of providing hope and encouragement for young people and for the community at large. It is considered a means of unifying the total Indian community. In a *New York Times Magazine* article Lipsyte (1986) quoted Oren Lyons:

> Lacrosse is one of the ways we can pull it all together again. You know Indian kids aren't fishing so much anymore. They're doing drugs, no jobs, crime's up, we got to give them hope. The National Lacrosse Team can do that. (p. 65)

This international play, involving *field*, or traditional, lacrosse, represents a return to a game that has been somewhat neglected by the Iroquois for more than a decade. A more popular game during recent years has been *box* lacrosse, which is played in a more restricted area, usually indoors, and with fewer players. The return to field lacrosse requires some adjustment in strategy and team play. Nonetheless, basic skills are similar, so the adjustment has not been a major obstacle.

National Indian Activities Association

The National Indian Activities Association (NIAA) was founded in 1974 for the purpose of conducting national championships in basketball for Indian teams. This venture, which has included both men's and women's teams, has proven so successful that it has continued each year since that time. In addition, several other sports have been added for national competition. The national Indian basketball championships are held each year during the third week of April at a site that varies from year to year. In 1987 the tournament was held in Oklahoma City and will be shifted to a West Coast site in 1988.

Fast-pitch softball championships are conducted by the NIAA each year for both men's and women's teams. These have proven very popular over the past several years and are strongly supported by Indian teams on the national level. Consequently, plans are under way to hold slow-pitch softball tournaments for both men and women next year.

The NIAA has conducted a national Indian golf championship since 1975. However, the attraction for this tournament has been mostly at the regional level. Plans are being made to hold a national bowling tournament within the next year. In view of the strong interest of many Indians in bowling, it is believed that this will become one of the more popular events.

Satch Miller of Warm Springs, Oregon, was one of the founders of the NIAA and currently serves as its president. Mr. Miller reports that plans are in progress to establish a network for the NIAA within each state. This would increase awareness of athletic opportunities among Indians and also provide a means for local competitions prior to the national championships.

The NIAA appears to offer practically unlimited possibilities for promoting athletic competition at the local and national level. A related benefit of this would be an increase in sports consciousness for all Indian youth and adults.

The Lumbee Indians: An Example of Continuing Sports Tradition

Outside the structure of a formal American Indian school, such as Carlisle or Haskell, or a formal Indian support program, such as the Iroquois

National Team or the National Indian Activities Association, isolated examples of Indians excelling in popular sports continue today. Many of those individuals who attained distinction were featured in chapter 13. In addition, certain Indian communities have a established tradition of developing athletes who have excelled at national and regional levels. One such group is the Lumbee Indian community of southeastern North Carolina. Three individual success stories of Lumbee Indians follow.

During the 1970s *Gene Locklear*, a Lumbee Indian, played baseball with the Cincinnati Reds, the San Diego Padres, and the New York Yankees. Immediately after finishing high school, Locklear signed a professional contract and played four years in the minor leagues. Twice he won league batting titles, as well as most valuable player awards, once at the triple-A level and once in a double-A league. Locklear spent five years in the major leagues, from 1973 through 1977. His best season was in 1975 when he played in 100 games and led the San Diego Padres in batting with a .321 average.

In addition to playing professional baseball, Locklear has won acclaim as an artist. He began painting during his high school years after taking a correspondence course in art. He continued painting during his baseball-playing years. In 1976, as a member of the New York Yankees World Series team, his artistic work was featured on national television with TV host Joe Garagiola. In addition, his paintings, which often reflect his rural Indian upbringing or sports background, have been exhibited in numerous places around the country. One of these, ''The Tobacco Farm,'' was chosen to be hung in the White House in Washington, DC. Since retiring from baseball, Locklear has devoted full time to his work as a painter. Figure 14.5 shows a photograph of Locklear as a player with the San Diego Padres. Figure 14.6 shows him posing in front of one of his paintings at a recent exhibition of his works.

Another Lumbee Indian, *Dwight Lowry*, after playing baseball at the University of North Carolina and spending three years in the minor leagues, was called up to the Detroit Tigers in 1984. He served as backup to all-star catcher Lance Parish on the team that won the world series. After spending the 1985 season in the minors, he was called up again in 1986 to assume regular catching duties when Parish was injured. For much of the season he led the team in batting average and at the season's end was hitting above .300. See figure 14.7 for a photograph of Lowry as a member of the Detroit Tigers in 1986.

Lumbee Indians have often excelled in track-and-field activities at Pembroke State University, located in Pembroke, North Carolina. One such person was *Victor Elk* who established several university and state records in distance running during the 1970s. Elk won the state collegiate championship in a six-mile run at Duke University during his junior year. In addition, he made the National Association of Intercollegiate Athletics All-American team in cross-country. He won most of his races in college

Figure 14.5. Gene Locklear as a member of the San Diego Padres. Photo courtesy of Gene Locklear.

Figure 14.6. Gene Locklear with one of his paintings (1986). Photo courtesy of Gene Locklear.

Figure 14.7. Dwight Lowry as a member of the Detroit Tigers in 1986. Photo courtesy of Dwight Lowry.

Figure 14.8. Victor Elk as a member of the Pembroke State University cross-country team during the 1970s. Photo by Elmer Hunt, Pembroke State University. Used by permission.

at distances between two miles and six miles. Figure 14.8 shows Elk as a member of the Pembroke State University team in the 1970s.

After the Haskell Institute was downgraded to high school status in the early 1930s, no four-year Indian college existed until Pembroke State College for Indians was established in the late 1930s. This institution remained as an all-Indian college until desegregation was initiated in the mid-1950s. Today, Pembroke State University is one of the constituent universities of the University of North Carolina system. Indians now make up only about 20 percent of the enrollment, or a total of about 400 students. Nevertheless, for the past half century this institution has served as a focus of community support for those local Indian students interested in participating in athletics, and the institution has had a host of outstanding Indian athletes, especially during the past two decades. Many have won All-American honors in baseball, basketball, track, and wrestling. Several graduates have gone on to play professional baseball.

Some Continuing Contributions

In addition to providing a multitude of games, equipment, and traditions, the American Indian has helped shape today's sporting scene in many indirect ways. For example, American Indian names have added to the color and perhaps the character of today's sports, both at professional and amateur levels. Names such as Indians, Redskins, Braves, and Chiefs are widely used by teams from major league football and baseball, universities, high schools, and even teams from Little League or Pee Wee levels. Though often dismaying to some Indians, these names, along with elaborately attired mascots, are no doubt selected to reflect the courage, skill, and cunning traits assumed to be characteristic of the traditional Indian. Selection of particular tribal names such as the Seminoles, Mohawks, and Apaches indicate admiration for the image of a particular Indian group.

There are also indirect Indian influences in less visible ways. For example, peanuts, popcorn, crackerjack, chocolate, and chewing gum were developed and used by Indians long before non-Indians came to this continent. One can easily understand how spectator behavior, especially for children, would be far different without these items. Their availability is often more important to youngsters than the outcome of the game. Without the influence of the American Indians, the concept and enjoyment of modern sports could be far different than they are today.

References

Adair, J. (1968). *The history of the American Indians.* New York: Johnson Reprint. (Original work published 1775)

Adams, E.C. (1946). *American Indian education.* Morningside Heights, NY: Kings Crown Press.

Applebee, A. (1982). *The relationship of values, attitudes, and interests to participation in interscholastic athletics among selected American Indian youth.* Unpublished doctoral dissertation, Temple University, Philadelphia.

Baldwin, G.C. (1969). *Games of the American Indian.* New York: Norton.

Beatty, W.W. (1941). Education of the American Indians, *Encyclopedia Americana,* **15**(61).

Beauchamp, W.M. (1896). Iroquois games. *Journal of American Folklore,* **9**, 269–277.

Bennett, W.C., & Zingg, R.M. (1935). *The Tarahumara: An Indian tribe of northern Mexico.* Chicago: University of Chicago Press.

Bernstein, R. (1972). Jim Thorpe: Son of triumph and tragedy. In W. Grimsley (Ed.), *The sports immortals* (pp. 28–33). Englewood Cliffs, NJ: Prentice-Hall.

Blanchard, K. (1974). Basketball and the culture-change process: The Rimrock Navajo case. *Council on Anthropology and Education Quarterly,* **5**(4), 8–13.

Blanchard, K. (1981). *The Mississippi Choctaws at play: The serious side of leisure.* Urbana, IL: University of Illinois Press.

Blanchard, K. (1984). Play and adaptation: Sport and games in native America. In *Oklahoma University papers in anthropology,* Norman: University of Oklahoma Press.

Blasiz, R. (1933–1934, December–January). The practice of sports among the Indians of America. *Mind and Body, 40*, 416–417.

Bouc, K. (1985). A nation of runners. In L. Johnson (Ed.), *Nebraskaland* (pp. 36, 37, 47, 48). Lincoln: Nebraska Games and Parks Commission.

Brackenridge, H.M., (1814). *Views of Louisiana, together with a journal of a voyage up the Missouri River.* Published in Pittsburgh.

Brown, J.E. (1953). *The sacred pipe: Black Elk's account of the seven rites of the Oglala Sioux.* Norman: University of Oklahoma Press.

Bureau of Indian Affairs. (1970). *Answers to your questions about American Indians.* Washington, DC: U.S. Department of the Interior.

Carlisle honors her Olympic victors on the return from Stockholm. (1912, September 13). *The Carlisle Arrow.* (From the Carlisle Indian School, Carlisle, PA)

Cartwright, G. (1792). *A journal of transactions and events during a residency of nearly sixteen years on the coast of Labrador* (Vol. 1). Published in Newark.

Carver, J. (1956). *Travels through the interior parts of North America.* Minneapolis: Ross and Haines, Inc. (Original work published 1796)

Catlin, G. (1944). *North American Indians* (Vol. II). Edinburgh, England: John Grant. (Original work published 1841)

Catlin, G. (1965). *North American Indians* (Vol. I). Minneapolis: Ross and Haines, Inc. (Original work published 1841)

Cheska, A. (1982). Ball game participation of North American Indian women. In R. Howell (Ed.), *Her story in sport.* West Point, NY: Leisure Press.

Clapin, S. (1894). *Dictionnair Canadien-Francais.* Published in Boston.

Colombi, D.J. (1983, June 21). Lists. *The Philadelphia Inquirer*, p. D2.

Copway, G. (1972). *The traditional history and characteristic sketching of the Ojibway Nation.* Toronto, Ontario: Coles. (Original work published 1851)

Costo, R. (1982, November–December). Jim Thorpe: His medals restored, justice done at last. *Wassaja.* San Francisco: Indian Historian Press.

Culin, S. (1907). Games of the North American Indians. In *Twenty-fourth annual report of the Bureau of American Ethnology to the Smithsonian Institution, 1902-1903.* Washington, DC: Government Printing Office.

Daniel, Z.T. (1892). Kansu: A Sioux game. *The American Anthropologist, 5*(3).

Deloria, V., Jr. (1969). *Custer died for your sins.* New York: MacMillan.

Dewey, E.H. (1930). Memoranda and documents. Football and the American Indians. *New England Quarterly, 3*, 736–740.

Dorsey, G.A. (1903). *The Arapaho sun dance.* Published in Chicago.

Dorsey, G.A. (1904). *Traditions of the Arikara.* Published in Washington, DC.

Dorsey, J.O. (1888). Omaha Sociology. In *Third annual report of the Bureau of American Ethnology to the Smithsonian*. Washington, DC: Government Printing Office.

Dorsey, J.O. (1891). Games of Teton Dakota children. *The American Anthropologist*, **4**.

Ducatel, I.I. (1846, January and February). A fortnight among the Chippewas of Lake Superior. *United States Catholic Magazine*.

Dunbar, J. (1882). The Pawnee Indians. *Magazine of American History*. **8**.

Eells, M., (1877). *Bulletin of the United States Geological Survey*, **3**(1).

Eskenazi, G. (1982, October 14). Jim Thorpe's Olympic medals are restored. *The New York Times*, pp. A1, B18.

Eubank, L. (1945). Legends of three Navaho games. *El Palacico*, **52**(7).

Ewers, J.C. (1944). *The story of the Blackfeet*. Lawrence, KS: Haskell Press.

Flannery, R., & Cooper, J.M. (1946). Social mechanism in Gros Ventre gambling. *Southwestern Journal of Anthropology*, **2**(4).

Flaskerd, G.A. (1961). The Chippewa or Ojibway moccasin game. *Minnesota Archaeologist*, **23**(4).

Fontana, B. (1979, May). Runners of the West: Tarahumara. *Arizona Highways*, pp. 38–52.

Friedl, E. (1975). *Women and men: An anthropologist's view*. New York: Holt, Rinehart and Winston.

Fuchs, E. (1970, January 24). Time to redeem an old promise. *Saturday Review*, pp. 54-57, 74-75.

Gabriel, B. (1979, November 26). Running to nowhere. *Sports Illustrated*, pp. 46–60.

Gobrecht, W.J. (1969). *Jim Thorpe–Carlisle Indian*. Carlisle, PA: Cumberland County Historical Society and Hamliton Library Association.

Goellner, W.A. (1953). The court ball game of the aboriginal Mayas. *Research Quarterly*, **24**, 147–168.

Gridley, M. (1974). *American Indian women*. New York: Hawthorne Books.

Guttmann, A. (1978). *From ritual to record: The nature of modern sports*. New York: Columbia University Press.

Haddon, A.C. (1903). A few American string figures and tricks. *The American Anthropologist*, **5**(2), 213-223.

Haines, E. (1888). *The American Indian*. Chicago: Mas-Sin-Magan.

Hallett, L.F. (1955). Indian games. *Massachusetts Archaeological Society Bulletin*, **16**(2).

Hamilton, C.E. (Ed.). (1972). *Cry of the thunderbird, the American Indian's own story*. Norman: University of Oklahoma Press.

Haskell Indian Junior College. (1983). *Student handbook*. Lawrence, KS: Author.

Haskell Institute. (1959). *Haskell Institute USA 1884–1959*. Lawrence, KS: Author.

Hayden, F.W. (1862). *Contributions to the Ethnography and philosophy of the Indian tribes of the Missouri Valley*. Published in Philadelphia.

Hodge, F.W. (1890). A Zuni foot-race. *The American Anthropologist. 3*, 227–231.

Hoffman, W. (1890). Remarks on Ojibway ball play. *The American Anthropologist, 3*, 131–137.

Hoffman, W.J. (1896). The Menomini Indians. In *Fourteenth annual report of the Bureau of American Ethnology to the Smithsonian Instituion, 1892–1893*. Washington, DC: Government Printing Office.

Hoffsinde, R. (1957). *Indian games and crafts*. New York: Morrow.

Hough, W. (1888). Games of Seneca Indians. *The American Anthropologist, 1*, 132–141.

Howell, R.A., & Howell, M. (1978). The myth of 'Pop Warner': Carlisle revisited. *Quest, 30*, 19–27.

Indian Rights Association. (1933, January). *Indian Truth, 10*(1), 5.

Jackson, C.E. (1965). *Identification of unique features in education at American Indian schools*. Unpublished doctoral dissertation, University of Utah.

Jennings, H. (1984, November 27). HC's Louis Sockalexis is honored in Maine. *Evening Gazette* (Worcester, MA), p. 31.

Jette, M. (1975). Primitive Indian lacrosse: Skill or slaughter? *Anthropological Journal of Canada, 13*(1), 14–19.

Jones, P. (1861). *History of the Ojibway Indians*. Published in London.

Kane, P. (1859). *Wanderings of an artist among the Indians of North America*. Published in London.

Laubin, R. & Laubin, G. (1980). *American Indian archery*. Norman: University of Oklahoma Press.

Lesser, A. (1933). *The Pawnee ghost dance hand game: A study of cultural change*. New York: Columbia University Press.

Lipsyte, R. (1986, June 15). Lacrosse: All American game. *New York Times Magazine*, pp. 28–33, 65–66.

Long, J. (1790). *Voyages and travels of an Indian interpreter*. Published in London.

Lucas, J. (1983, Fall). Deerfront in Britian: An amazing American long distance runner. 1861–1863. *Journal of American Culture*, 13–19.

Lumholtz, C. (1895). Tarahumari life and customs. *Scribner's Magazine, 16*, 296–311.

MacFarlan, A.A. (1958). *Book of American Indian games*. New York: Associated Press.

McCaskill, J.C. (1936). Indian sports. *Indians at work, 3*(22).

McDonald, F.W. (1972). *John Levi of Haskell*. Lawrence, KS: Haskell Institute.

Meeker, L.L. (1901). Oglala games. *Bulletin of the Free Museum of Science and Art*. Published in Philadelphia.

Michelson, T., (1927). Notes on the ceremonial runners of the Fox Indians. *Bulletin 85*. Washington, DC: Bureau of American Ethnology.

Michener, J. (1976). *Sports in America.* New York: Random House.

Mooney, J. (1890). The Cherokee ball play. *The American Anthropologist,* **3**, 105–132.

Mooney, J. (1896). The ghost dance religion. In *Fourteenth annual report of the Bureau of American Ethnology to the Smithsonian Institution, 1892–1983.* Washington, DC: Government Printing Office.

Myers, W.E. (1928). Indian trails of the Southeast. In *Forty-second annual report of the Bureau of American Ethnology to the Smithsonian Institution, 1924–1925.* Washington, DC: Government Printing Office.

Nabokov, P. (1981). *Indian running.* Santa Barbara, CA: Capra Press.

Neihardt, J.G. (1951). *When the tree flowered: The fictional autobiography of Eagle Voice, a Sioux Indian.* Lincoln: University of Nebraska Press.

Nelson, E.W. (1899). The Eskimo about Bering Strait. In *Eighteenth annual report of the Bureau of American Ethnology to the Smithsonian Institution, 1896–1897* (pt. 1). Washington, DC: Government Printing Office.

Newcombe, J. (1975). *The best of the athletic boys: The white man's impact on Jim Thorpe.* Garden City, NY: Doubleday.

Owens, J.G. (1891). Some games of the Zuni. *Popular Science Monthly,* **39**, 39–50.

Powers, F.J. (1969). *The life story of Glenn S. (Pop) Warner: Gridiron's greatest strategist.* Chicago, IL: Athletic Institute.

Rader, B.G. (1983). *American sports: From the age of folk games to the age of spectators.* Englewood Cliffs, NJ: Prentice-Hall.

Ripley, R.L. (1976). *Ripley's giant book of believe it or not.* New York: Warner.

Ritter, L.S. (1966). *The glory of their times: The story of the early days of baseball told by the men who played it.* New York: Macmillan.

Romans, B. (1921). *A concise natural history of east and west Florida* (Vol. 1). New Orleans: Pelican. (Original work published 1775)

Ryberg, R.F. & Belok, M.V. (1973). *Exploration in the history and sociology of American Indian education.* Meerut, India: Sadhna Prakashan.

Salter, M.A. (1971). *Games in ritual: A study of selected North American Indian tribes.* Unpublished doctoral dissertation, University of Alberta, Canada.

Seton, E.T. (1979). Gospel of the red man. *The Indian Historian,* **12**(4), 24.

Skinner, A.B., & Satterlee, J.V. (1915). Folklore of the Menomini Indians. *Anthropological Papers of the American Museum of Natural History,* **13**(part 3), 217–546.

Steckbeck, J. (1951). *The fabulous redmen.* Harrisburg, PA: J. Horace McFarland.

Stevenson, M.C. (1903). Zuni games. *The American Anthropologist,* **5**, 691–702.

Stevenson, M.C. (1904). The Zuni Indians. In *Twenty-third annual report of the Bureau of American Ethnology to the Smithsonian Institution, 1901–1902.* Washington, DC: Government Printing Office.

Teit, J. (1900). The Thompson Indians of British Columbia. In *Memoirs of the American Museum of Natural History* (Vol. 2). Published in New York.

Thompson, J.E.S. (1941, April). Yokes or ball game bets. *American Antiquity,* 6(4), 320–326.

Thompson, S.I. (1983). The American Indian in the major leagues. *Baseball Research Journal,* 13, 1–7.

Thwaites, R.G. (1892). The Wisconsin Winnebagoes. *Collections of the State Historical Society of Wisconsin,* 12, 425.

Turkin, H. & Thompson, S.C. (1951). *The official encyclopedia of baseball* (Jubilee Edition). New York: A.S. Barnes.

Vanderwerth, W.C. (1971). *Indian Oratory.* New York: Ballantine.

Von Kotzebue, O. (1821). *A voyage of discovery* (1815–1818). Published in London.

Walker, J.R. (1905). Sioux games. *Journal of American Folk Lore,* 18, 71.

Wheeler, R.W. (1979). *Jim Thorpe: Worlds' greatest athlete.* Norman: University of Oklahoma Press.

Whitney, A. (1977). *Sports and games the Indians gave us.* New York: David McKay.

Whitney, C. (1907, January). Ranking of 1906 football teams. *Outing Magazine,* p. 537.

Willett, M. (1831). *A narrative of the military actions of Colonel Marinus Willitt.* Published in New York.

Williams, R. (1643). *Key into the language of America.* Published in London.

Wissler, C. (1922). *The American Indian* (2nd ed.). New York: Oxford University Press.

Wolfe, B. (1978). Jim Thorpe. In *World Book Encyclopedia* (Vol. 19, p. 205). Chicago: World Book–Childcraft International.

Wood, W. (1634). *New England's prospect.* Published in London.

Wulff, R.L. (1977). Lacrosse among the Seneca. *Indian Historian,* 10(7), 16–22.

Author Index

Subject Index